Yoga Sadhana Panorama

Volume One

YOGA SADHANA PANORAMA

VOLUME ONE

*Compiled from lectures and satsangs given during the
Poorna Sannyasa Week, Karma Sannyasa Week,
Yoga Festival Week and Yoga & Meditation Weekend
at Satyananda Ashram, Mangrove Mountain, Australia,
May 1994.*

Swami Niranjanananda Saraswati

of

BIHAR SCHOOL OF YOGA, MUNGER (BIHAR), INDIA

Published by
   Bihar School of Yoga,
   Munger, Bihar 811201, India

First Bihar School of Yoga edition 1995
Reprinted 1999

ISBN
   81-86336-00-1

Edited by
   Sannyasi Atmatattwananda
   Swami Satyadharma Saraswati

Printed by
   Bhargava Bhushan Press,
   Trilochan,
   Varanasi, UP, India

PART ONE

Discourses during the
Poorna Sannyasa Week

A New Direction

MAY 1, 1994

Greetings from Paramahamsaji, from Bihar School of Yoga, India, and from myself, to all of you. Paramahamsaji is now leading a different kind of lifestyle which, according to the tradition, is one step or stage further in sannyasa life. Paramahamsaji has said many times that, "When I took sannyasa, the purpose was not to open ashrams, to have disciples or to become a guru. At that time my aim was to know myself, to realise or to have a glimpse of the higher nature. In order to overcome my karma, desire, ambition and ego, I had to play the role of teaching and propagating yoga. Now, since I have fulfilled my commitments and duties, exhausted my karmas and ambitions, I am leaving the things which represent my desires and aspirations in order to progress further on the sannyasa path." This was the thought which initially prompted him to leave the ashram and all contact with everyone he had known, and to discover what was beyond the normal level of understanding in relation to yoga, spiritual life and sannyasa.

Aspirations and weaknesses

We tend to think of yoga and sannyasa as something which will immediately and drastically transform or change our lifestyle. We think that within a very short period of yoga practice, we will attain experiences in meditation which will

3

bring us closer to our higher nature. We often tend to forget that, along with our aspirations and spiritual ambitions, there are our physical needs and weaknesses as well. Generally, this is where we fail. Many times we tend to become too centred in our own aspirations and forget or ignore the intricacies of the many weak components within our personality.

A good example of this behaviour within ourselves is our own expression and communication. Seventy five per cent of the time, we are more aware and concerned with what other people are doing. Very rarely are we aware of ourselves internally. The remaining twenty five percent of the time, we are aware of our 'I' identity—I want this, I want that, I think this, I do that. In both of these states of mind, either looking at another person critically or trying to fulfil our own desires, the spiritual aspirations or ambitions get mixed up with our weaknesses and then there is stagnation in sannyasa life.

It has been correctly stated in much of the literature that out of thousands of seekers there are few who find the path. Out of those who have found the path, there are very few who eventually walk the path. Out of those who actually walk the path, there are even fewer who attain their goal. We all come into the first category and I do not think that we have the ability to reach the second or the third stage, that is to walk and to attain, because in order to do that, one has to change internally. Changing externally is just feeding the intellect. Changing internally is the real essence of yoga.

There are many people who meditate with hopes of seeing or experiencing something different. Possibly no one meditates with the intention of becoming aware of the short-comings and weaknesses, the karmas and samskaras, and of overcoming them. Initially, if one meditates to realise the karmas and samskaras and to confront oneself rather than escape from oneself, then any kind of attainment or achievement becomes simple and spontaneous. It is only after the first realisation of one's weaknesses that a change begins to take place. The human mind and personality are like a blackboard which we are writing on constantly. Towards the end of our life, we find that nothing definite or concrete has

4

been achieved, because we have written too many things which have superimposed themselves upon one another, and nothing can be read on our blackboard.

Purification from within

So, it becomes necessary to first clean the personality and the mind of the samskaras and karmas. That happens when there is the attitude of seva. The word *seva* cannot be translated as selfless service; that is only a general expression. The word seva means an effort to purify oneself from within by being aware of the normal daily interactions, duties and obligations. In this context, when we are performing seva with the body, mind and spirit, first there is awareness, then discrimination, then performance, and the direction of that performance is creative.

Normally, every thought we think, every action we perform, is influenced by the gunas, tendencies or qualities of our nature, just as the same knife can be used to murder somebody, to chop vegetables, or to save a life. The way in which we use the knife represents a quality, a guna. When the knife is used for a destructive purpose, it is tamasic. When used to chop up vegetables, it is rajasic, and when used to save somebody's life, it is sattwic.

So, by first becoming aware of the karma and samskara, we are able to channel or give a new direction to all the different expressions of our behaviour and personality. This is a very important aspect of spiritual life. Yoga is not important; it is simply a tool or vehicle which is used. Before using a tool, the desire to use it must be there. That is the beginning of yoga, the desire to develop self-awareness or to discipline the self.

What is Yoga?

The Patanjali *Yoga Sutras* have stated in the second sutra that yoga is controlling the patterns of the mind, *chitta vritti*. However, that statement does not represent the fullness of yoga. The definition of yoga is given in the first sutra, *Atha yoga anushasanam*, which has been translated as: 'Now begins the instructions on yoga'. However, the word *anushasan*

5

means 'discipline': *anu* meaning 'the subtle' and *shasan* meaning 'to rule', 'to govern'. *Atha* means 'therefore'; *yoga* means 'Yoga'; *anushasan* means the way to control the subtle expressions of one's personality. So, *Atha yoga anushasanam* means, 'Therefore, Yoga is the way to control the subtle expressions of one's personality'. That is the actual definition of yoga according to Patanjali. When he is asked again what happens after attainment of this control over the subtle expressions of the personality, he answers, *Yogaschitta vritti nirodhah*; then one attains the ability to block or to channel the currents of consciousness, the vrittis.

The currents of consciousness are either tamasic or rajasic. None of us are sattwic and we have never experienced the sattwic nature. We talk about it and we impose certain rules upon ourselves, but following that trend, that system, is not becoming sattwic. All of our actions and thoughts, all the different expressions of our behaviour and nature are tamasic and rajasic, in different intensities and degrees. The sattwic nature does not manifest in our life at all. We may say that love and compassion can be sattwic, but they cannot, because of the conditioning behind our expression of these qualities. Sattwa is unconditioned and uncoloured. To attain the sattwic state, which is an expansive state, one practises yoga.

Practical understanding and acceptance
There is a process of understanding which is not an intellectual one, but rather is on a more personal and practical level. Intellectual concepts or understanding have not really helped the evolution of consciousness in its totality. We speak about *manas, buddhi, chitta* and *ahamkara*, as the four aspects of the mind. Each one comprises twenty five percent of mind. The intellectual concepts belong to the realm of buddhi. With this twenty five percent of awareness, you cannot change the remaining seventy five percent of the mind. By developing the intellect to the maximum, by reading hundreds of books and being an incredible analytical person, you still cannot change the remaining seventy five percent unless you are a jnana yogi.

6

We have been stuck in the intellectual understanding, linear thinking: B must follow A, C must follow B. Therefore, sometimes we block ourselves from reality. Reality says one thing, but our beliefs and ideas tell us something else. In the distance we see smoke and there is an immediate thought of fire. Being a physical phenomenon, the majority of the time, it may be possible that where there is smoke there is fire. A time comes, however, when the thoughts change and we decide to check what kind of fire it is. In the course of time, ideas and thoughts change again, and according to these changes we act and behave differently. It is a process of gradual realisation, like walking up the steps; one cannot be in the middle and think, 'I am at the top'. One cannot be on the second or third step and consider that to be the final achievement. In order to come to this realisation, the samskaras and karmas have to be seen, observed, directed and channelled.

This is what can be imbibed by us when we see the lifestyle of Paramahamsaji. How he was before, how we all reacted in our own way at the news of his departure and how we are now, seeing that there is something more beyond the normal training and teaching to which we have been exposed. A university professor teaches nuclear science through formulas and books. A student obtains a degree in nuclear science by studying in the university. Then comes the period of experimentation and creation of something. Learning, experimentation, creativity and fulfilment; these are the four stages.

In Paramahamsaji's present lifestyle, we see both creativity and fulfilment in the first stage of learning. Some of us are in the stage of experimentation and implementation. We do not have to change our position, condition or state in life, but a change has to occur internally, in our attitude, ideas and thoughts. Only then can we say that we are actually moving forward. So, acceptance with greater commitment to life, with the idea of reaching the end and achieving the goal, has to be the main thrust. We have to make an effort to find a solid direction in our life that can help us grow internally.

7

Attainment and
Transformation

MAY 2, 1994

Once someone asked Paramahamsaji whether it was possible
to attain self-realisation in one lifetime. Paramahamsaji said,
"No, it is not possible." The person then asked whether or not
all the effort which we make in life, and all the practices that
we do are useless, if the end result is not realisation. Paramahamsaji said, "No, the effort that we make is not useless." That
reality, which we are trying to realise or to get a glimpse of, is
not bound by the concepts of time and space. It is a transcendental reality. Our mind, nature, personality, motivations and
drives are bound by the experiences of time, space and object.

Therefore, we have a limited mind and it is not possible
to experience the transcendental nature with a limited brain
and mind. All the practices and systems, that have slowly
evolved in the course of time, aim at altering and expanding
our nature and mind, and raising the awareness. Once we are
able to transform the mind then that unconditioned, transcendental reality will be experienced. This answer has always
guided me in terms of observing, analysing and experiencing
what I am doing in life. This is exactly what I have seen in
Paramahamsaji's life; a continuous striving to attain new
dimensions of experience in ways that are incomprehensible
and unknown to us. We are all so caught up in our own rational
mind, that it becomes difficult to experience what is beyond
the intellect, the buddhi.

8

Linear thinking verses experience

The human consciousness has a very wide spectrum of which the mind, personality, and gunas are only a small fragment. However, because we are constantly caught up in an intellectual analysis of situations and conditions, we tend to miss the subtle realities. When we do become aware of these subtle realities through our intellect, we either tend to accept them as good or reject them as bad in relation to ourselves, our beliefs and our personality. In this way, we are continuously following a linear path.

The aim of yoga is not to attain self-realisation. The different states of attainment are an indication of transformation within the personality. Attainment always goes side by side with transformation. If there is no transformation within, there cannot be any attainment. There are two types of knowledge. One is book knowledge and the other is experiential knowledge. In book knowledge, whatever is written follows a sequence. If we study any literature, we will come across that sequential process.

Since we are practitioners of yoga and familiar with the *Yoga Sutras*, we can see the progression there. From discipline, we come to mind control. From mind control, we come to realisation of the inner nature. With the realisation of the inner nature, we come to the experience of *prajna*, 'wisdom'. With the experience of prajna, we come to the state of meditation, and that meditative state evolves into samadhi. That is the process of yoga as mentioned in different books. Our intellect automatically follows that linear direction.

Experience is different to the sequential progression that is described in literature. When talking about experience, we have to consider the different aspects of the human personality, such as strength, weakness, ambition and need. This is what I call the SWAN theory. S-W-A-N represents strength, weakness, ambition and need. With any yoga practice or other system which is adopted, our experiences are subject to our strength, weakness, ambition and need. These are very real, predominant factors in our life and we cannot ignore them. So, experiences can never be labelled uniformly with a rubber

9

stamp. They vary from individual to individual. It is the management of our own nature which is important in our life and in any form of yoga practice.

Therefore, yoga is not a system for attaining realisation, but a system of self-management. In this context, yoga becomes a technique which makes us aware of ourselves. The change through yoga occurs at a deeper level and not at the surface. When things begin happening at a deeper level, then transformation takes place. When things happen at a superficial level, then we are feeding ourselves with new ideas without wiping out the old concepts. That way there is more and more accumulation of ideas and concepts in our life. Before sleep at night, we should ask ourselves objectively, "What have I gained in my life?" We may feel that we have gained something on the surface, but deep inside transformation has not taken place.

People talk about opening the mind, heart or mooladhara chakra. A long time ago, somebody made the statement, "All difficulties emanate from the human mind." This theory carried on for a couple of hundred years, then someone else stated, "No, it is not the head. All problems come from the heart." This theory also carried on for some time until Freud appeared on the scene and said, "All problems arise from the mooladhara area: suppression of the sexual drive." Then Einstein came along and he said, "Everything is relative." In the same way, yoga says that transformation takes place on all levels simultaneously; we cannot pinpoint any one area. Because we are focused on one area and not aware of the other areas, there is no balance.

Four tendencies of the personality

How can we attain this balance which results from a homogeneous view of what is happening at the different levels of our personality? Yoga says that there are four instinctive tendencies which constantly alter the expressions of the human personality and behaviour. They are as follows: (i) *ahara*, craving; (ii) *bhaya*, fear or insecurity; (iii) *nidra*, sleep, and (iv) *maithuna*, sexual urge. These four tendencies

10

constantly affect and alter our thought, behaviour and interaction. If we observe these four tendencies in ourselves, we will find that they are constantly interacting with, altering and changing the different areas and levels of our personality.

Maithuna represents the awakening of mooladhara and swadhisthana chakras, or the unconscious mind, the deeper mind, the instinctive samskaras and karmas. Ahara represents the awakening of manipura and anahata chakras: craving fulfilment, whether for food or emotion. Bhaya represents insecurity or fear, related with the upper region, vishuddhi and ajna chakras. Why? Because the real transformation in the human personality takes place when vishuddhi and ajna are activated. At that time the fear of losing one's identity becomes very strong, losing the concepts and perceptions to which we are accustomed, fear of the unknown. Nidra is blocking out all these aspects and going into a state of total blankness.

These are the areas of our psychic blocks, which are represented in the practice of bandhas. For example, in moolabandha there is a block of the perineal muscles; in uddiyana bandha, a block of the diaphragm; in jalandhara bandha, a block of the neck. These are the three main areas with which we have to work. When we are unable to work with these areas or when fear or insecurity come up, then there is total oblivion, blankness, a state similar to that of sleep.

Process of attainment

Through the practices of yoga, we have to work with these four aspects of our personality: ahara, nidra, bhaya, maithuna. When we are in control of these, then the mind changes. *Dhyana* (meditation) cannot change or transform the mind. It is definitely a process, but we have to work with these four levels, and that happens in *pratyahara* (sensory withdrawal) and in *dharana* (concentration). Pratyahara is the most important technique in yoga. It is more important than dhyana. Dharana is also more important than dhyana. It is very difficult to master pratyahara and dharana. One should not confuse the process and the experience that comes from the process, with the attainment and the aim.

11

In yoga and in spiritual life there is no leaving any-thing. Things automatically drop away as we progress and evolve. Due to our insecurities in life, we become very agi-tated if someone tells us that we have to drop this or leave that. We feel insecure if we have to change our lifestyle and habits, if we have to alter anything which we are accus-tomed to. That happens because we are not yogis. Yoga is a process of attainment. When you are climbing the stairs, do you worry about your foot leaving the lower step or do you concentrate on putting your foot on the upper step? When you put your foot on the upper step, then naturally, the lower step is left behind.

When you feel insecure about having to change or leave something, yoga says, "No, that is not the point at all. Concentrate on where you are going to put your next step and be firm in it. When you are able to do that, the previous step will be left behind naturally, without any fear." So, attainment always comes before any kind of change in the normal progression. You are always climbing. Things drop away only after you have attained a certain state, just as when you moved from one class to the next in school, you were looking forward to being in the next class, not feeling inse-cure about leaving the last.

Acceptance

So, why not apply the same principle in yoga? I used to become insecure and fearful, thinking about what was going to happen in the future. People used to say, "Learn to accept." I used to think, "That is an old answer. Everyone says accept, but accept what?" Suddenly, in a flash it came to me that people do not know the real meaning of acceptance. It is very easy for me to tell you to accept. But, depending on your situation, you will think, "What does he mean by accept, when I'm going through difficulties in life?" One day there came a point when I said, "Okay Mind, you rest for some time. Don't guide me, let me guide you." Then the process of acceptance became effortless, because when there is attain-ment first, transformation happens naturally. That was the

12

meaning of acceptance which I learned: effortless evolution, effortless growth.

In Paramahamsaji's life we have seen this happen. When he changed from the ashram lifestyle to a wandering lifestyle, we all felt very deeply in our hearts that he was leaving us. That was our insecurity and attachment through which we lost the vision of the teaching he had given us for all those years. We used to say that he was a fantastic guru, yet we never imbibed his teachings. That was our shortcoming, yours and mine. Some people went through heavy head trips. There were many people who returned their *dhotis* and *malas* and said, "Well, if he's no longer a Guru, then I'm no longer a disciple."

These kind of reactions show that we have not been able to imbibe the essence of the teaching, and until we make an effort to alter the vritti of our own mind, we will not be able to do so. The vritti of our mind is always tamasic or rajasic; it is never sattwic. If the vritti is tamasic, we are so self-centred that we block out other aspects. If it is rajasic, we are so self-centred that we put ourselves above other people. Sattwa remains an intellectual concept.

Inspiration

Paramahamsaji did not allow this to happen in his life; he moved from one stage to the next. When he was in Rishikesh with Swami Sivananda, discipleship was as important to him as establishing an ashram, a system or a movement. After establishing the Bihar School of Yoga, being the preceptor was as important to him as eventually leaving it and saying, "Now, I am free to follow the path of sannyasa." That is why I always feel that he is neither a guru nor a disciple, neither a person nor a god, but just an inspiration. His form, his image is that of inspiration. I have never looked upon him as a guru, an administrator or a yoga teacher. I have always seen him as an inspiration that has guided me and reminded me again and again not to be static, to keep on moving. "The woods are lovely, dark and deep, but I have promises to keep and miles to go before I sleep." We fear the

13

walk of many miles and we get stuck in the woods, thinking they are so lovely and wishing to remain there.

Clarity of vision and direction

Unfortunately, despite having been involved with yoga for many years, there are very few who have maintained that clarity of vision and direction. For us, yoga is simply a practice which we do. Every morning we get up and practise asana and pranayama. At night we sit down and practise mantra and meditation. We think that just by doing this we are practising yoga and that we are going to eventually see the light. If it were that easy, then I would be in India today and not here, and you would all have a radiant aura around your heads. Everyone who practises yoga would have that radiant aura. The system of yoga does not fail. It is the human understanding of yoga which falls short.

In the galaxies of saints, you can count on your fingers the number who have attained a high stage, those whom we call masters, such as Ramakrishna, Vivekananda, Aurobindo, Ramana Maharishi, Sivananda. If we recognise them as masters, we have to also see the kind of lifestyle which they led, the mentality which they had and the ideas which they conveyed. If we go deep into their life and teachings, we will see that they all have gone through a process of internal change and transformation. Those who can reach that level are bound to transcend the limited nature of mind, to overcome and change the samskaras and karmas, and ultimately experience the transcendental, unconditioned reality.

Yoga has two big brothers, one is Tantra and one is Vedanta. Yoga is a practical system. Tantra is a system which emphasises acceptance of one's natural lifestyle and mentality, and alteration of the natural vrittis. Once that is attained, then Vedanta emphasises the experience of oneness, unity. If we are able to combine Yoga with Tantra and Vedanta, then the process becomes complete. In our programme here we shall look at the different approaches of Yoga, Tantra and Vedanta, as means and systems of transcendence. We shall also look at the different lifestyles which are prevalent in the

14

world, and at the lifestyle of karma sannyasa or poorna sannyasa which we have adopted, and see how the direction of these sannyasa lifestyles can help us take a few steps further in our quest for a different experience.

Bhagavad Gita

Introduction

MAY 2, 1994

I will start with a simple understanding of one yogic text which is known as the Bhagavad Gita. In the yogic tradition there have been many texts which have delineated the different aspects of yoga. The *Yoga Sutras* of Patanjali, for example, define the psychological process of yoga. They begin with a description of the eightfold path of yoga: *yama, niyama, asana, pranayama, pratyahara, dharana, dhyana* and *samadhi*, with the purpose of harmonising the physical, mental, spiritual and interactive aspects of an individual.

If we study the *Gheranda Samhita* of Sage Gheranda, the *Hatha Yoga Pradipika* of Swatmarama, the *Goraksha Samhita* of Gorakhnath, the *Shiva Samhita* of Shankara and other traditional yogic literature, we can see a sequence in them. They describe various processes by which one can eventually come to terms with the different expressions of the human personality. They begin from an awareness of the body and mind, and they aim towards the attainment of inner experience.

However, this kind of theory or understanding does not bring us any closer to spiritual life. In spiritual life there has to be an integration and a proper understanding of the extreme involvement of an individual in relation to the *gunas*, or attributes, to the manifest nature and to the experience of spirit which is transcendental. The study and the practical

16

experience of the *Srimad Bhagavad Gita* can help in this process of experiencing and harmonising the external and internal manifestations of nature and the self.

Action and meditation

There are two areas of life which have to be looked into. One area is that of action and the other is that of meditation. We can relate to action quite easily, because it is an external process. Meditation becomes difficult to relate to because it is an internal process. We tend to identify a meditative process as something we do for some time after which we again fall back into the normal pattern of living. This is where a discrepancy and imbalance is seen in our own effort to experience the spiritual nature.

In our life, we are also unable to link the aspect of karma, or action, with dhyana, meditation. This leads to a misunderstanding of our inner, spiritual life and there is no growth or evolution. Karma and meditation have to be understood. The best way to understand the interaction of these two aspects is through the teachings of the Bhagavad Gita. Although this has been taken as a traditional text or as the sayings of an avatar, the ideas conveyed are relevant in our present day situations, in order to understand and develop a broad vision of life. It is with this in mind that I would like to begin our study and in-depth discussion on the Bhagavad Gita.

Story of the Bhagavad Gita

In ancient times, there was a war between two factions of the same family, the Pandavas and the Kauravas. During that period, a special man was involved whose name was Krishna. Why was he special? Not because he was considered to be an avatar, but because he had an understanding of the human nature and personality, and was able to provide a clear vision and direction to his close followers and friends. He was a spiritually awakened person who lived according to the laws of dharma. His vision was not restricted to himself or to his near and dear ones, but encompassed all. His actions had a purpose, to establish the knowledge and awareness of personal

17

commitment in relation to society and the world. For this reason, he was special.

Krishna took the side of the Pandavas as a non-aligned person, and due to circumstances, he became the charioteer of Arjuna, who was a commander of the Pandava army. Before the beginning of the war, when the two armies met on the battlefield, Arjuna underwent a state of depression, dejection, conflict and anxiety, because he saw his friends, relatives, childhood companions, and gurus in the arts of warfare and governance, ready to fight against him. In that state of depression, he lost his view, or his inner, mental clarity, and was unable to decide on his actions. He was confused about what he should do. His dharma of a warrior, of protecting and living in harmony with the people, came into conflict with the situation with which he was faced.

Arjuna thus begins to question his entire philosophy of life. What is the aim of being born in this world? Is it simply to take birth, grow up, perform your role in life and then die, or does life have a greater purpose? Krishna explains to Arjuna all the interactions in life which are related to the self, to the senses, to the near and dear ones and to total strangers. The Gita begins in this way. Arjuna says, "I am totally dumbfounded, I do not know what to do. My mind is clouded; I cannot think clearly or properly. I have absolutely no desire to fight and to attain glory."

Krishna describes a simple process of realising the different faculties of the mind and personality. He instructs Arjuna in the process of understanding karma and dharma, and experiencing the higher nature while performing karma and dharma. This is the beauty of the Bhagavad Gita. It should not be taken as a philosophical book. Rather it should be understood as a guideline to help us evolve, to attain maturity in our life.

Dharma

This is not the only Gita. There are eighteen different Gitas, but this one, expounded by Krishna, is considered to be the most important, because of the process that it has

18

followed. It is divided into eighteen chapters which represent the evolutionary process of a human being, trying to evolve from the mundane, manifest level to a higher, transcendental level where the vision of dharma is clearly seen.

Despite our intellectual understanding and philosophy, we are easily influenced by people, by circumstances and by events. Our entire life is constantly being conditioned and changed by these three aspects. Our mind is constantly being coloured or influenced by the events, circumstances and the people with whom we come into contact. In this process, the concept of reality is lost. To keep sight of the reality has been the aim of the Bhagavad Gita. In expounding the philosophy of the Gita to Arjuna, Krishna says that it is necessary to go through the ups and downs in life, but one should not lose the vision of dharma.

Before going further into the study of the Gita, I would like to explain this term dharma, because it is a very misunderstood concept and a misused word. *Dharma* is often translated as 'religion', 'philosophy' or 'a principle in life'. Sometimes it is translated as 'duty', 'obligation' or 'commitment'. In reality, dharma means something else. In Sanskrit texts dharma has been defined as: *Dharayete iti dharmah*. *Dharayete* means something which is retained, imbibed, expressed, and which helps one transcend or evolve. This something which is held, retained, used and expressed, is known as dharma. What is it that we hold, retain, use and express? Qualities of life which are not restricted by the human nature.

These qualities of life are not restricted to the expressions of mind, feelings or behaviour alone, but simultaneously influence all levels: physical, subtle and psychic. These qualities are inherent and they are sattwic by nature, but our expression or concept of them is not sattwic. If we want to express a quality in our life, we will observe that it is mainly rajasic. The initial identification with that quality is restricted and limited to self, I, me. As long as this 'I' is involved in the experience of a quality, a guna or an attribute, we experience it in the rajasic form. Rajas represents the surfacing of the 'I'

19

nature. Initially, when we begin the process of yoga, we are starting at the rajasic, not the sattwic level.

Dharma is like a thread which holds the different beads of a mala together. One bead represents the physical dimension, one the mental dimension, one the psychic dimension. Each bead represents a different dimension, experience and expression, but there is only one thread which links all of these beads together, and that is the thread of dharma. So, the states of experience in the totality of life are based on the principle of dharma. Dharma is based on the principle of karma.

Three types of karma

Every form of interaction is known as *karma*. There are three main types of karma. The first is karma, interaction or activity performed by the mind. We are talking of mind here in terms of the yogic terminology as the totality of *manas, buddhi, chitta* and *ahamkara*, that is *mahat tattwa*. Karmas are performed by the mahat tattwa. The second form of karma is known as *vacha* which means interaction in the manifest world with family, friends, society, nation and world. This external interaction of an individual with others, in which we express our feelings, thoughts and behaviour, is the externalised karma.

The third karma is performed by buddhi (buddhya). *Buddhya* means the rational understanding of what is happening externally and internally, the aspects of knowledge, wisdom, recognition and understanding. The process of knowing and understanding is not necessarily an intellectual process, rather it is the non-rational feeling of 'I realise'. This non-rational feeling of 'I realise' is the karma of buddhya. So, dharma is based on these karmas: dharma representing the qualities which are ultimately sattwic or pure by nature and karma representing the manifest aspect of dharma.

Harmonising desire, philosophy and action

A problem tends to arise at a certain stage of life. We are unable to harmonise our deep, innermost thoughts or our philosophy with our actions and our external thoughts.

20

Our individual philosophy is based on some kind of spiritual or creative aspiration. Our thoughts are based on the external influences and our actions are based on the need and the drive of the physical and mental senses. Most of the time we are unable to harmonise these three: action, desire and philosophy. Our philosophy leads us in one direction where there is some experience of harmony. Our desires move us in another direction, and our actions limit our performance in the manifest dimension. This incompatibility between the three is the cause of confusion. Yoga aims at providing this harmony.

Paramahamsaji used to say that yoga is a means to integrate the faculties of head, heart and hand, meaning intellect, emotion and action. For many of us, yoga is a physical process, and for others, yoga is a spiritual process. Whatever our concept of yoga may be, and whatever other teachers and masters may say about it, in order to be efficient and proficient in life, there must be an integration and harmonisation of the actions which are performed by, the desires which motivate and the personal philosophy which guides an individual through life. When harmonised, these three aspects give the realisation of dharma. After that, the karmas are altered and changed. This has been the main thrust of the Bhagavad Gita.

Sannyasa as a Lifestyle

MAY 3, 1994

I would like to make it very clear from the beginning that our concepts and ideas of sannyasa or yoga are dependent on our moods, beliefs and attitudes. I am saying this as an Acharya of the tradition of sannyasa. For two thousand years in the history of sannyasa, there have been seven traditions. These seven traditions had seven Acharyas who were not public figures. They used to live in the background, working, teaching, doing their sadhana and guiding people, isolated from society and even from the sannyasis. Some years ago a new tradition was established. Now, I am not speaking to you as a sannyasin of the Saraswati order initiated by Paramahamsaji, but as the Acharya of the order of this tradition.

We have to remember that yoga is a system distinct from and different to sannyasa. In the past many of us were influenced by the teachings of Paramahamsaji, many of us were initiated into sannyasa and adopted the robes of a sannyasin, but the aim and the direction in our life was never clear to us. We considered that by taking sannyasa we could become overnight prophets which would be profitable in the course of our lives. While we are here, I would like all of you to forget the concepts that you have had or still have about sannyasa. With an open mind and an open heart, try to pick up the ideas which will be conveyed to you during this week, beginning with sannyasa as a lifestyle.

Although there are many components of sannyasa, we are going to limit our discussion to a few components or ideas.

Sannyasa is a lifestyle and nothing more than that. In the past, Paramahamsaji has made it very clear that it is a lifestyle in which you dedicate yourself to a particular course of inner, spiritual evolution and upliftment. No doubt you can pursue this goal by either living in an ashram environment or as a householder in society or living like a recluse in isolation. Whatever the lifestyle may be, the basic principles of sannyasa do not change, and that is awareness of the lifestyle of a sannyasin.

Time and thought management

How does the lifestyle of a sannyasin reflect in the external world, in our external life? In two ways. They are known as *kaal sanyam*, 'time management', and *vichar sanyam*, 'thought management'. This may seem irrelevant, but it is important in terms of attaining practicality in life. The concept of time management is very simple: be on time to fulfil your duties and commitments. This also reflects clarity of mind, alertness and awareness, rather than a dissipated state.

The second concept is thought management, which is one of the most important aspects of sannyasa. Time management is external; thought management is internal. We can deal with time management, but thought management is difficult to deal with because of the intricate nature of our personality. Clarity of mind, vision, direction, commitment, performance and behaviour, all reflect inner thought management. As human beings, despite our intellectual attainment and knowledge, we are not able to control or direct our inner behaviour, expression or thought. It is here that we need the help of yoga in order to manage the thought process and to attain inner clarity.

The beginning of yoga

The beginning of yoga is a simple process. We have read that yoga is controlling the vrittis, the modifications, of the mind, and we have been intrigued by this idea. How can one control the vrittis? While studying the *Yoga Sutras* and other related literatures, we come across different concepts of the vrittis, different concepts of pain and pleasure, different concepts which can help us evolve. Unfortunately, however, we have missed a very basic point, which is the first sutra: *Atha yoga anushasanam*. Nobody has given a proper definition of this sutra. I will give it, so that you can understand the beginning of yoga.

Atha means 'therefore'. *Yoga* means 'yoga'. *Anushasan* means 'inner discipline'. *Anu* is a root word which means 'subtle aspect', 'inner nature' and *shasan* means 'to rule', 'to govern'. So, according to this sutra, governing the inner expressions of the personality, knowing the expressions of the mind and personality, is yoga. Once we are able to understand this principle, transformation takes place in our nature and mental clarity is obtained. This is an inner achievement and this is how sannyasa reflects or manifests on the physical dimension in relation to our society, body, behaviour and attitudes.

The beginning of spiritual life

So, what is the purpose of time and thought management? The yoga tradition states that there are four areas of life which have to be balanced. They are known as the four *purusharthas*: (i) *artha*, social, financial and personal security; (ii) *kama*, fulfilment of desires, aspirations and ambitions; (iii) *dharma*, awareness of one's commitments and obligations in life, and (iv) *moksha*, inner freedom. Balancing these four aspects: artha, kama, dharma and moksha, is the aim of yoga and the beginning of one's spiritual life.

A car has four wheels and our life also has four wheels. At present, two tyres are punctured and our car is moving along on the two unpunctured tyres. There is a general feeling that artha and kama, attainment of security and fulfilment of desires, are the areas of householders. Dharma and moksha, awareness of one's duties and the drive to transcend the limited nature of the human personality, are the areas of renunciates. There is an imbalance in this concept.

24

In spiritual life, these four aspects all have to be strengthened together, so that there is proper balance or harmony in the totality of life. Even as a sannyasin or a recluse, there is a need for security and for fulfilment of desires, aspirations and ambitions. As a householder, there is a need to realise one's inner dharma and to come closer to moksha. Even for a person who is actively involved in the world, there is a need to transcend the limiting qualities of life. So, these four aspects have to be combined and the combination of the four in yoga is known as spiritual life.

Yoga, Tantra, Vedanta and Sannyasa do not view spiritual life as an isolated lifestyle. There are many people who think, "If I meditate, I will evolve spiritually." There are many people who believe that, "If I see heavenly, divine visions, it means that I am changing." As human beings, we tend to emphasise the aspect of logic, especially with the concepts that have evolved in the western cultures. We have emphasised logic to such an extent that we can pretend to be what we are not, and not only pretend, we can also believe what is not. This kind of pretending and believing in that pretence is not a homogeneous or harmonious growth of the inner nature.

There has to be a combination of the four aspects of life in order to experience real spirituality. Sannyasa is a lifestyle which aims to harmonise these four aspects, and it makes no difference whether you live in the society or in the mountains. There is a beautiful saying of Paramahamsaji: "There is no noise in the market place and no silence on the mountain top." The environment may be different, but it is our attitude and mental conditioning that reflect the state of either dissipation or of quietness. It is this aspect that sannyasa tries to develop within with the different practices of Yoga, Tantra and Vedanta.

Four barriers
Just as yoga defines and deals with the five vrittis: *pramana, viparyaya, vikalpa, nidra* and *smriti*, in the same way, sannyasa also tries to control and direct the four vrittis which are known as: *maithuna, ahara, bhaya* and *nidra*.

25

Maithuna represents not only the sexual urge or desire, but the instinctive urges that are inherent in the deeper layers of our personality. Ahara means physical, mental and emotional satisfaction and fulfilment. All these are different aharas. There is ahara of the body, the different foods which sustain the body: vegetarian, non-vegetarian, etc. In the same way, there is the diet which sustains the emotions. The craving for fulfilment and achievement is there. When a craving is fulfilled, there is satisfaction and contentment.

Bhaya means fear or insecurity, which can be social, external, personal, internal, emotional or spiritual. When it relates to the spiritual dimension, it is fear of the unknown. When it relates to the physical dimension, it is fear of the manifest world, the body, social fear. Nidra means sleep, but in this context, it means blocking out. Creating a wall and being unaware of what is happening on the other side of the wall, being happy in the confinement which we have created for ourselves, that is nidra. These are the four vrittis or expressions of the human personality, the four barriers which the sannyasa lifestyle tries to overcome by following certain other principles.

Five components of sannyasa

In Tantra, you might have heard of the five 'M's: *mansa*, meat; *madhya*, wine; *maithuna*, sexual activity; *mudra*, grain, and *matsya*, fish. Sannyasa does not deal with the five 'M's; it deals with the five 'S's which are: *seva, swadhyaya, santulan, santosha* and *samarpan*. These are the five components of the sannyasa lifestyle. If you have integrated these five into your life, then you can call yourself a sannyasin. In brief, seva means service; swadhyaya, self-study, self-knowledge, self-awareness; santosha, contentment; santulan, balanced action, and samarpan, balanced dedication.

These are the five components or limbs of sannyasa. When we think of sannyasa and the vrittis that sannyasa tries to overcome, which are defined as: ahara, nidra, bhaya and maithuna, then in order to reduce these and to awaken the five 'S's within, a system has to be adopted. This system is

26

not purely yoga, but a combination of the yogic, tantric and vedantic systems. It is in this context that we will be looking at the various principles of Yoga, Tantra, Vedanta and Sannyasa in the following days.

Bhagavad Gita

Brief Outline of Chapters I-IV

MAY 3, 1994

The first chapter of the Gita is about depression and anxiety; the second chapter is about Samkhya; the third chapter is about karma; the fourth chapter is about jnana-karma; the fifth chapter is about karma sannyasa, and the sixth chapter is about dhyana. Before going further, let us look at the first four chapters independently, in brief.

YOGA OF DESPONDENCY—Chapter I

The first chapter is about the yoga of depression and anxiety. A strange thing has happened here. Krishna has named all these different chapters 'Yoga', and yet the beginning is about a very real conflict. Why do people generally come to a system like yoga? In order to learn how to manage the mental processes, to make themselves quiet internally, and to be more balanced. Some come for therapy and others come to release their stress. There are many reasons but they all show that there is some form of imbalance which is not accepted by the individual. That imbalance is taken as a shortcoming in life. It shows loss of vision of the dharma of the body, the dharma of the mind, the dharma of the family, the dharma of the society, the dharma of desire, the dharma of karma. There is some loss or imbalance due to which certain internal conflicts arise.

These conflicts and problems are like the heads of the serpent Hydra. We chop off one and another appears. We chop off that one and yet another appears. Due to our linear vision, we only see the head which is in front and not that which is behind. When we see the first head, we think that is the main cause of the problem. When we chop that head off, when we overcome that problem, we see the next one. This is the result of a linear or grounded vision. At ground level we see everything from that perspective, and are unable to see beyond it.

Once a mentally disturbed person came to the ashram and said, "Swamiji, I'm really confused. I do not like nature. Nothing is uniform in it. The grass is too small, the trees are too big, the shrubs are tiny. I have this intense desire to go around the world with a chain saw and make everything the same height." His logic was so incredible that he almost convinced me that he was right. Eventually, however, due to the grace of Guru, my logic won. I suggested to him that he should look down while flying on a plane, then he would see everything the same size. Later on, I came to know that this man had become a pilot. He was living in the cockpit all the time. This is also similar to the yogic vision.

In the yogic vision, there are seven layers of consciousness. Each layer is a more evolved state of mind, perception and experience, beginning from mooladhara and going up to swadhisthana, manipura, anahata, vishuddhi, ajna and sahasrara. In this way, evolution takes place in human life. Depression or anxiety is the result of blocked evolutionary experience. If we were able to experience the evolutionary process within ourselves, then there would not be any conflict. But no, we hold on to things and get caught in that circle or wheel, and that becomes our life.

SAMKHYA YOGA—Chapter II

So, in order to come out of this state of despondency, Krishna begins with the description of the Samkhya system. Here the human personality is seen in different stages from the unmanifest to the manifest, in the form of energy, tattwas,

29

nature, gunas, mental senses (jnanendriyas) and physical senses (karmendriyas). Krishna tells about the Samkhya system with a view to impressing upon Arjuna—the seeker or the sadhaka, and let us consider that we are all sadhakas, practitioners—that there are many dimensions of human experience which must be perceived stage by stage.

What we feel in this dimension, in the form of pain or pleasure, creates a change in our subtle dimensions too. When we feel depressed, it is evident that this state affects the pranas, the physical system, the mental system, the feelings, thoughts and rationality. So, one thing which is happening affects all these various dimensions, right from the most gross to the most subtle. If we consider something to be purely external, that is our misconception. It is only the manifest mind which says, this is external, but the effect and influence of this affects the entire personality.

In this chapter, Krishna describes how to find a balance between the actions, the desires and the real aspirations in one's life. If there is disharmony between the actions, the desires and the inner aspirations of life, then one has a fall. That is quite evident; it is real. One cannot take this as a simple idea. Our aspiration may be to evolve, to experience the unknown. Our actions may be as per the needs of the body, the senses and the mind. How can I evolve if I am bankrupt, if I have nothing to eat and I am starving? So, actions and desires are different. Desires are limited to the mental structure. Desires are influenced by our weaknesses and ambitions which are related with the manifest world. Krishna has emphasised that a fall is possible if one is not able to harmonise these three aspects: aspiration, desire and action.

So, the Gita continues in a peculiar way. Do not consider yourself to be just a body which you see. Do not consider yourself as just a mind which you can experience in parts. Every action in life, every thought in life, every interaction in life, influences the entire human structure. In the following chapters of the Gita, Krishna has described what can be done in order to balance the human structure, the totality of the human dimension.

KARMA YOGA—Chapter III

The third chapter of the Gita deals with a very important aspect of our life and that is karma. Here karma has been linked with the word yoga. In order to understand this chapter in depth, we will have to look at these two ideas separately. What is karma? It has been understood that karma belongs to the realm of Prakriti, the manifest nature, and not to the dimension of Purusha, the unmanifest consciousness. Every form of karma, every form of action that is performed by an individual belongs to this realm of Prakriti, the manifest dimension. It is in this respect that we have to understand how an individual performs karma and how karma actually influences human behaviour.

Understanding karma

There is a very clear concept that karma arises due to the attractions and desires in life, and the experience of that karma continues for an extended period until it reduces in intensity. The events which give birth to a karma are actually static in nature. Experiences or circumstances which we encountered in our childhood are remembered by us now because of this karmic link, the link of action. Experiences that may have happened thirty years ago are remembered by us due to the karmic link. The event which gave birth to a karma, to a karmic link, took place a long time back, but the influence of that event has carried on. So, the events and the situations that create a karma are considered to be static, not dynamic forces. The static forces create ripples in the realm of Prakriti, the manifest personality, mind, emotions, behaviour, and the experience continues.

Take the example of a flower, which is static on the shrub, tree or small plant. It remains there; it does not move with you as you move around the garden. That flower, which is fixed in one place, has a smell emanating from it. Smell has the ability to move with the breeze. Depending on the direction of the wind, if you happen to be in the right place at the right time, or the wrong place at the wrong time, you can get the

31

whiff without even seeing the flower. So, there is the recognition that there must be a flower somewhere. The same thing occurs with a piece of putrid flesh. It is lying in a corner and when the breeze blows, you get that smell. How far the smell carries depends on the intensity of the breeze. Many times the smell is carried for long distances, but if there is no breeze, the smell remains confined to its source.

In the same way, the karmas, events, situations or objects are always static. It is the flow of the mind which carries the smell of that static object for long periods of time. That smell can carry on for a month or for years together, depending on how hard the wind is blowing in our own heads. This movement of the nature of mind and personality is known as karma. Due to the dissipation of human nature and behaviour, because we are unable to attune our faculties with one another and focus them at one point, karmas play a very vital role in understanding ourselves.

Attraction and repulsion

In the *Yoga Sutras*, it has been stated that pleasures arise when there is attraction, and pain arises when there is repulsion. These are the two sutras:

Sukhanushayi ragah. Duhkhanushayi dveshah.

So, when there is attraction to an object or event, there is identification with it, and then the feeling of pleasure arises. If there is repulsion for an object, event or idea, then pain and suffering arise. So, attraction and repulsion in the manifest dimension, in the realm of Prakriti, are the two forms of karma. These karmas, which are actually creations of our own nature, of our own mind, are so powerful that our entire life is affected by them. The karmas in the manifest dimension belong to the realm of the senses, mind and psyche. These three combined can become a very solid force, influencing the basic structure of life. When the dissipation of the human personality is very powerful, when the wind blows in forceful gusts, then we are swept off our feet. Every one of us experiences being swept off our feet in times of pain and pleasure. That is karma.

32

The reason why the word yoga has been included here is because yoga provides an awareness of the karmas, of the point where they are born, of the point where they take place and where they are experienced by a human being. It is like the recognition that a beautiful smell is emanating from this rose flower, or a putrid smell is emanating from this piece of flesh, causing the attraction and repulsion. It is not just the acceptance of that attraction or repulsion, but acknowledging it as an experience only, which makes yoga relevant in terms of karma. This is the aspect of karma yoga which Krishna tries to emphasise to Arjuna in the third chapter of the Bhagavad Gita. As long as you are in the realm of Prakriti, in the manifest dimension, with the senses, the nature, the gunas, the attributes and qualities, and the mind, you cannot escape from these karmas.

These karmas are like seeds planted in our own consciousness which, in the course of time, grow into trees. The seed which you plant today will become a tree, bearing fruits and flowers in the future. If the tree which grows from that seed is sick and weak with bugs eating away at it from inside, then what does the gardener do? He chops it down and plants a new one. Are we able to chop our own tree which is sick, infirm and rotten from inside? No, we carry the dead tree with us and that is the effect of karma which is carried on from generation to generation, from life to life.

Detachment and discrimination

In karma yoga, one needs to acquire the ability to recognise the solidity and the strength of the tree. If the tree is hale and hearty, then you can leave it, but still it needs pruning. Once I asked a disciple to prune the trees of the ashram. It took him six months to prune three trees, and I thought this was quite symbolic. I used to watch him go to the garden with his shears and secateurs. He would stand in front of the tree and look at it from all angles possible—top, branches, base. He would scratch and shake his head, pick one branch and snip it. After that he would stand back and look at the tree again from all directions. The day he left I went with a saw!

33

Whether he enjoyed pruning the trees or not I do not know. However, watching him definitely gave me the insight that, no matter how long it takes, this is how one has to trim and prune the tree. Look at it from all angles, find out where the sickness lies, which branch is affected, which is dead, and chop it off. Do not allow the sickness to spread all over. In fact, thousands of years ago it was said that, in order to disconnect the karmas, it is necessary to have a sharp instrument which is comprised of detachment and discrimination. Detachment is the sharp edge and discrimination is the handle. So, you hold the handle of discrimination and use the sharp edge of the instrument, which is detachment, to chop the karma. That way, the seed planted today will become fruitful in years to come.

This is the theory and the practice of karma yoga. Karma yoga is not just hard work; rather it is recognition of the mental states which you are experiencing at the time of the practice and learning how to deal with them. Recognition of attraction, the pleasure that is derived from a situation, and repulsion, the suffering which is derived from another situation, and the need to remain healthy and hearty, is karma yoga. This is the basic theory of the third chapter of Gita.

JNANA-KARMA YOGA—Chapter IV

In the fourth chapter, the same concept is further expanded by incorporating the aspect of *jnana*, 'wisdom' or 'knowledge'. The fourth chapter of the Gita is about karma yoga with knowledge. This is a very important aspect, meaning that karma is not an unconscious involvement; it has conscious recognition. We humans are very instinctive beings. Instincts belong to the realm of the unconscious. We react, but we have never learned how to act. We react to many things, and in that reaction, different aspects of our personality come into play. These reactions take place due to the ambitions, aspirations, weaknesses, desires or thoughts, which are limited to self and which are rajasic in nature.

Reactions are always rajasic; that is their basic nature. If there is a very hard reaction, then it can be tamasic, a very limiting, confining situation which submerges the vision inside the water and does not allow a clear view of the surroundings. The eyes have clear vision out of the water, but if you dive into the water, open your eyes and look around, the vision will be blurred. The same clarity will not be there. The sense organs are similar. There is no loss of vision, but in different situations and circumstances, whether out of the water or in the water, recognition of that faculty changes, depending on the environment.

It is that awareness which is the aspect of wisdom or knowledge, having recognition of the karma, the source of the karma, and knowing whether it is influenced by the ego, by a deep, unconscious desire, by some form of motivation or ambition, or by a desire for status, power or control. An idea, which is initially rajasic, becomes tamasic. Power and ambition, which start off as rajasic motivations, become tamasic later on. So, wisdom is an important aspect. Knowledge of the self is necessary in order to convert karma yoga into a form of sadhana.

Sadhana is not a short term practice. The *Yoga Sutras* state clearly that sadhana must be practised for a long time with faith and regularity. Only then can a firm foundation be achieved. Three things are mentioned here: perseverance, regularity and faith. Regularity is continued awareness of that sadhana. There are people around the world who have practised yoga for many years and feel that this exposure is enough. After that, they move on in different directions, still considering themselves to be master, and if not master, at least ace. This is only an intellectual trip. They may call themselves yogi, ace or master, but I am a sadhaka, and I will never stop being a sadhaka. I know that I will never be a master. I know that I will never be an ace. I will be what I am, according to my limitations, mentality, samskara and karma, which I have been exposed to and which I have not yet cut down. It is as simple as that. So, sadhana is comprised of three aspects: regularity, faith and long term practice, until perfection is obtained.

Therefore, in the life of a yogi, sadhana is considered to be most important. A *yogi* is a person who is aware of the direction in which he has to move. A *bhogi* is a person who is lost and does not have a clear direction. A bhogi is caught in the trips of pain and pleasure, and has a heavy heart and a clouded mind. A yogi has a clear direction and is able to keep that direction even in the most difficult situations and dissipated environments. Krishna has many times said to Arjuna, "Be thou a yogi." It is a good idea to adopt this philosophy in our life too. Let us all be yogis and have that ability to find direction no matter how gloomy the day, no matter how cloudy the sky. If gloominess creates cloud formations in the mind, then one is a bhogi. If, despite all the gloom, one's mind shines with the light of the sun, then one is a yogi. This is jnana-karma yoga as described in the fourth chapter of the Gita; karma yoga with knowledge, recognition and acceptance of the situation combined with the necessary effort to go beyond that.

Current BSY Projects and Paramahamsaji's New Life

MAY 3, 1994

Since January 1994, we have undertaken various projects in Bihar. Each project is important because it entails taking yoga to the professional levels of society. The first project is the teaching of yoga in all the medical colleges in the state of Bihar. This has been approved by the state authorities. A team of doctors and swamis are visiting medical colleges and conducting specific yoga therapy training programmes for the medical students and doctors. We have recently received approval and sanction to teach yoga therapy to the sixteen thousand registered medicos in Bihar.

After a month of basic yoga therapy training, each medico is given a certificate which is recognised by the Indian Medical Council, and then instructed to use yoga therapy along with the regular medical practice. So far, we have covered two medical colleges and two districts. The practitioners of these two districts have sent their recommendation to the head office of the Indian Medical Council to incorporate yoga into the MBBS syllabus. We are preparing a one year syllabus which will be incorporated into all the medical training courses throughout India. This is a big achievement on the medical front. The Indian medical professionals are as sceptical as the medicos all over the world, so their acceptance is a landmark in the field of yoga.

Yoga in prisons

The second project undertaken with the approval of the state authorities is the teaching of yoga to the convicts in prisons. There are thousands of convicts in Bihar. So far we have only dealt with two prisons, but in the course of time we hope to cover the entire state. The reports that we have received from the convicts are very encouraging. Many are feeling the benefits and effects of the practices which they do in a positive manner. I have called this project 'Operation Valmiki'. Valmiki was a dacoit who eventually reformed and became the first poet in history. He wrote the story of Rama, the *Ramayana*. So, since we are dealing with convicts and trying to make them saints with halos, this operation represents the thrust and direction of the teachings.

Yoga in local villages

The third project which we have undertaken is yoga activity in the villages. I send two swamis out with a team of volunteers from the villages to live together for ten days and do every type of work from cleaning the drains, clearing the roads, to teaching yoga, conducting satsang, listening to the villagers' problems, trying to help them, and also introducing a very simple understanding of the yogic literature. We have had fantastic results in this area. In two villages, approximately three hundred people have taken a sankalpa to leave firearms. We have selected the most crime infested areas, so to see that they are able to surrender their arms and leave the lifestyle of crime is very heartening for us.

Formation of a Yoga University

The fourth project is converting Ganga Darshan into the first yoga university in the world. We have applied to the federal government to grant us the status of Yoga University which will have three faculties: (i) Faculty of Yoga Philosophy, (ii) Faculty of Yoga Psychology, and (iii) Faculty of Applied Yogic Sciences. This last faculty will be subdivided into three groups: (i) fundamental yoga research, (ii) therapy research and (iii) practical application with outside field work.

We have raised a team of seven hundred medical professionals, professors and teachers within India, who will be contributing their time and knowledge to this university project. There are many professional people here also, and I request all of them to contribute their suggestions and ideas. It does not matter whether they are able to come to India or not; their support will go a long way. This is one of the major activities of Bihar School of Yoga which will eventually change the entire structure of yoga in relation to the society and the environment in which we live.

Another project which is currently under way is the establishment of a yoga faculty in the universities which are run by the federal and state governments. We have already established a yoga centre in one university, providing the syllabus for it, and the appointment of teachers who have taken their test at the ashram.

Shifting of BSY

The next project which I am contemplating now is the shifting of Bihar School of Yoga from Munger to another place. With the formation of a yoga university, BSY will have little or no role to play. The infrastructure of BSY will pass on to the university and Bihar School of Yoga will become an ashram, offering basic yoga and sannyasa training, where aspirants can lead a natural lifestyle. When I return to India, I will be visiting different places in order to find a suitable location for the new ashram. We would like it to be in the mountains, much like Mangrove, with forests, creeks and natural water supply. We are planning to use mud construction for the buildings. There will be the traditional gurukul system or the concept of ashrama that we read about in books, a very simple lifestyle.

Yoga for the army

The Indian Army has introduced yoga into their training programmes, not for physical fitness, but for the management of the mind and mental problems, especially in high altitude and desert areas. Courses are currently being conducted for the soldiers and officers at twenty two thousand feet on top of Siachen Glacier which is supposed to be the highest battlefield in the world, bordering India, China and Pakistan. In that locality, the soldiers undergo a lot of hardships: lack of oxygen, hallucinations, isolation from their families and the rest of the world. The Chief of Army Staff for the land forces came to Munger, during the Tyag Golden Jubilee World Yoga Convention, in order to discuss the application of yoga for the management of mental states in the armed forces, and different future projects.

We have already conducted a camp for the desert deployments who undergo the same problems minus the high altitude. So far, it has given very good results. The Indian army is contemplating setting up an academy of yoga on the same lines as a military academy, which will be run by the army. After discussions with their medicos and psychologists, we are to set it up and provide a balanced programme of yoga which can be used for the mind management of the soldiers. This is a very important aspect of experimentation in yoga. The Indian land forces number over one million. These people are pulled from different localities and villages. After their retirement or the completion of their term, they will go home. If the results are good and they feel they have derived some benefit from yoga, there will be a further expansion of the yogic systems.

These are some of the activities which are taking place in relation to yoga in Bihar. Personally, I feel a great sense of pride, achievement and satisfaction that these changes are taking place. From a bunch of rag-tag swamis, we are going professional. Whatever we are doing now has always been the aim or the fulfilment of the vision which Paramahamsaji had for the yoga movement.

Paramahamsaji leaving BSY

So, that is what is happening in relation to yoga. In order to tell you what is happening in relation to sannyasa and to our social involvement, I will have to go back to the beginning. Paramahamsaji left the Bihar School of Yoga finally in

1988. Prior to that, he handed over the charge of the institution to one person who did not know anything about it, and that person was myself. I had lived abroad most of my life, so I did not know what was happening with the yoga movement, what was in Paramahamsaji's mind or what direction he wanted the yoga movement to take in the future. I came during an interesting period, the period of crisis with which some of you are familiar.

The news of Paramahamsaji leaving everything and not wanting any interaction with the people whom he had known since the start of the yogic mission was creating a lot of conflict and crisis, even amongst the swamis in Munger. Everyone was feeling uncertain and I was feeling more unsettled than anyone else. One week after Paramahamsaji handed me the charge, he decided to have a six month holiday in Australia. I was stuck in Munger with people whom I did not know and who did not know me, so from the beginning there was an uncertainty.

When Paramahamsaji left the ashram, very few people knew that he was going. The celebration of Guru Poornima finished around 30th July, and it was only then that he gave us a hint of what he was going to go. During that Guru Poornima, Paramahamsaji gave his heart to all present. Then, on 8/8/88, he left the ashram, taking only a few dhotis and one hundred and eight rupees with him, and declining every kind of help and assistance from us.

Earthquake

On 20th August, twelve days after Paramahamsaji had left, there was an incredible earthquake in Munger. I thought to myself, "Is he playing like Krishna?" When Krishna knew that his time had come, he directed the events in such a way that his entire clan died fighting with one another and no one survived. Krishna knew that after his death these people would become unruly, so he played with the events and finished them all off before he departed. So, after Paramahamsaji's departure, when the earthquake came, I thought: "Paramahamsaji has left the

41

ashram, and now he is bringing down this seven storey building." Strangely enough, although the whole of Munger was affected by the earthquake, which registered 6.5 on the Richter scale, there was not even a hairline crack within the ashram premises. Symbolically, that gave me a lot of encouragement. The ashram is solid, yoga is solid, and we are solid in our direction and aim.

After this, Paramahamsaji wandered around India, practically incognito. Even his closest disciples were unable to recognise him when they passed him on the way. Swami Chidananda did not know that Paramahamsaji had been staying in Rishikesh for three days until after he had left. Towards the end of his wanderings, Paramahamsaji was trying to decide what to do next, waiting for some guidance, for his whole life has been guided, either by the Guru or by God.

Twenty Year Cycles

Reflecting back on Paramahamsaji's life, we can see certain turning points. When he was in Maharashtra, he went to the place of his ishta devata. This is the other side of Paramahamsaji, not the scientist swami that you have come to know, but the sannyasin swami that Paramahamsaji is. In India, there are special places called *siddha teerthas*, awakened shrines. Each of these is a place of power, the place of *ishta devata*. The place of Paramahamsaji's ishta is Trayambakeshwar, one of the twelve *jyotir lingams* of Shiva, where the image is of a three-faced Shiva lingam.

There, in early 1963, Paramahamsaji received a mandate, guidance or inspiration, in which the message was, "Go and spread the message of yoga, and yoga will become the culture of tomorrow." That became the slogan for his movement. Paramahamsaji tells that, upon receiving this message, he made another enquiry as to how he should carry it out, because it was a very tall order. Teaching yoga, pawanmuktasana and yoga nidra, to a rag-tag bunch of swamis is a different matter to taking yoga into the professional field and establishing it as a scientific system which can help to develop the personality, mind and nature.

42

Paramahamsaji prayed to his ishta devata to give him the strength to fulfil this mandate. He then received that divine energy which made him move continuously and work for the propagation of yoga. The time period set for this work was twenty years. In his lectures and discussions, Paramahamsaji has said that his life is divided into twenty year cycles. He left home and joined his Guru when he was about twenty. He established Bihar School of Yoga when he was around forty, and he left the yoga mission, adopting a different lifestyle, when he was around sixty. So, it was a twenty year cycle in his life that finished in January 1983.

In August 1982, when Paramahamsaji came to America, he was in a different frame of mind—introverted, thoughtful and isolated within himself. It was then that he said to me, "You have to come back to India." That was a rude shock for me and I asked him, "Why?" He asked, "Do you want to come to India?" I said, "No, I don't want to come to India." He asked, "Why?" I said, "What will I do there? If I am away from you, then I can work for you. When I am with you in the ashram, then I am not utilising my abilities. But, if you want me to come and you call me, then there is no power on this earth that will stop me from coming." Soon after that he called me at very short notice. Swami Vivekananda and I had come back from a trip and there was a telegram waiting for me at the ashram: "Return to India by 16th positively." I boarded the plane on the 14th and reached Munger just before midnight on the 16th.

Deoghar
In Trayambakeshwar on the day of Guru Poornima in 1989, one year after his departure from Munger, Paramahamsaji received a second message which became the future direction and guidance for his life. This message was: "Go to my cremation ground." The region of Deoghar where Paramahamsaji lives now has been recognised traditionally and mythologically as the cremation ground of Lord Shiva. On that day, Swami Satsangi had come to see Paramahamsaji. He was living in a cowshed on a hill, doing his

43

sadhana there in total isolation. He said to Swami Satsangi, "This is the message I have received and this is the land that I have been shown in my vision. Go to Deoghar and you will find it there."

That same day Swami Satsangi left for Deoghar to find the land. Deoghar is another siddha teertha where an ancient temple of Shiva, one of the jyotir lingams, stands today. Upon reaching Deoghar, Swami Satsangi went into the temple and asked the deity, "Help me find the land and fulfil the instruction of my Guru." When she came out of the temple, one of the priests or pandits asked her, "Why have you come here?" She said, "I am looking for some land." He said, "I know of one place. Do you want to come and see it?" She went with the man and to her amazement, the place which he showed her was the land which Paramahamsaji had seen in his vision. So she said, "Alright, we'll take it." I went with her to the owner who said, "How did you know about this land which I decided to sell only this morning?" We told him how our Guru had instructed us and he said, "Your Guru must be a great mahatma. Take the land. It is all yours." So, for a very small price, we acquired it.

We built a hut on the property and informed Paramahamsaji. Then, Swami Gyanprakash, who is now the President of Bihar School of Yoga, went to Tryambakeshwar with the news that: "The land of your vision is ready." On that day, the 8th of September, Swami Sivananda's birthday, Paramahamsaji again went to the temple of his ishta devata. There he removed his malas, watch and dhoti for the last time. Placing them in a bundle near the shivalingam, he said, "You gave me the command, the instruction and the robes. Now, I am returning everything to you. I have fulfilled your order." Then he left Tryambakeshwar and came to Deoghar where he started his sadhana in the area of Rikhia.

Sadhana

Paramahamsaji's sadhana changes from time to time. Our sadhana involves asana, pranayama and meditation, but the sadhana of a Paramahamsa sannyasin is different,

44

involving a lot of hard austerity, *tapasya*. One day, he received another message: "Provide your neighbours with the facilities that I have given you." He was thinking about this and what to do, when I happened to go there for a visit. He said, "Niranjan, I have received this instruction, but I do not have any financial assets. I have left everything which was mine and now it is up to you to fulfil this command."

The previous night all the swamis of the Alakh Bara had a dream in which the message that they also received was to do something for the villagers in the vicinity. In the sannyasa tradition, when you perform higher sadhana, you have to give daan after the culmination of each phase. *Daan* means giving what you have earned to others. Although one may see it as social work, traditionally it is not. Whenever Paramahamsaji completes a cycle of his sadhana, Sivananda Math, the institution which has been given the job of helping society by any means available, goes out and performs this daan work, or gifting. We began with the project of simple housing.

Siddha

Paramahamsaji remains confined to his sadhana area. He never comes out or goes around the villages. One day, after his sadhana, he called Swami Satsangi and said, "In one village there is a widow. She cannot use her hands due to arthritis. She has six children; the eldest is twenty. Their house has burned down and they are living under a tree. Locate them and construct a house for them." He did not name the village. It took Swami Satsangi three days to locate the village, to find the widow and to get all the details.

It was exactly as Paramahamsaji had described. The woman had arthritis in her hands and could not move them. The eldest son was a rickshaw driver earning an average of twenty rupees a day with which he used to support the mother, five brothers and himself. So, there are times when Paramahamsaji suddenly gets up from his sadhana and says, "Go there and do this." When we go, we find that the need is there. If we do not receive specific instructions from him, then we simply continue our work in the locality.

45

When I experience these kind of events, I feel strongly that Paramahamsaji has become a *siddha*, one who can see what is happening. Many cases like this have occurred. For example, a very sick woman came with intestinal tuberculosis. Dr. Aparna, the resident physician, said, "I can't help you." When Paramahamsaji came to know of this, he was furious. He said, "How could you say that you cannot help that woman? Find her and give her some medicine." Dr. Aparna replied, "We don't have any medicine for that type of disease." Paramahamsaji said, "Then give her aspirin, but give her something." The woman was called and Dr. Aparna gave her three tablets of aspirin. One week later the woman returned hale and hearty. All kinds of tests were performed and there was absolutely no trace of the disease.

When Dr. Aparna tried to tell Paramahamsaji what had happened, he gave the instruction, "Dr. Aparna will not enter the gates. I do not want to see her or hear the story that she has to tell." Whenever I see a situation like this, it makes me aware that I am in the presence of a siddha, a person who is able to control the elements and nature. Paramahamsaji hides that ability of his quite well, but it is increasing day by day. It is quite incredible; I cannot express it in words. You have to see him, to be in his presence, to feel that energy. In fact, many people have experienced that they cannot sit in front of him for more than a few minutes. His eyes are like laser beams: bright, sharp, clear and piercing. They go right through a person and one feels fidgety and very uncomfortable.

Establishment of the Alakh Bara

Paramahamsaji has also established another tradition. In the sannyasa system, apart from the ashramas and peethas, we also have the tradition of Akhara and Alakh Bara. An ashram is a place where everyone is welcome. Peetha is the place where the Shankaracharyas, or the heads of the sannyasa tradition, stay. There are four peethas in India where the four main Shankaracharyas of the Dashnami sannyasa tradition, to which we belong, stay. Then, there are seven Akharas where the

46

Acharyas of the sannyasa tradition stay. There are seven different groups and each one has a particular Acharya.

Beyond that is the tradition of *Alakh Bara*, invisible boundary or invisible locality, which is restricted to the Paramahamsa sannyasins. The Alakh Bara gradually developed around Paramahamsaji. This happened because of the lifestyle that Paramahamsaji adopted for himself. Since 1991, whoever takes poorna sannyasa, karma sannyasa or jignasu sannyasa is given a code of conduct on behalf of the Alakh Bara. The Alakh Bara is the supreme authority for the sannyasins of our tradition. This is the tradition which has evolved around Paramahamsaji or through his inspiration.

There was a process of selection for the Acharya of the Alakh Bara. Those of you who went to India in 1990 will remember that I was totally isolated for a period of time. I did not see or speak to anyone. I had to complete a thesis on the tantric, vedic, upanishadic and yogic traditions, which was then presented to the Acharyas. There was a period of approbation, and then the Acharyaship ceremony took place. It is for that reason that you see me with three stripes on my forehead. This is the story of what has happened since Paramahamsaji left Munger, the direction that the ashram has taken, and some of the different activities that are taking place.

Bhagavad Gita

Dhyana Yoga (Part I)

MAY 4, 1994

The sixth chapter of the *Bhagavad Gita* is about karmic meditation. In the first sloka, Krishna begins to tell Arjuna about the relationship between the meditative state of consciousness and the karma or action that is performed by the senses, body and mind. There is a difference between the process of meditation in other systems of yoga and that which is explained in the Bhagavad Gita. In the yogic literature, meditation has been described as a technique, a process of becoming. In the Gita, meditation has been explained as a process of experiencing, of knowing the state of being. So, in our study we will look at meditation, or *dhyana*, from both the yogic angle and from the angle that the Gita is trying to emphasise.

A short meditation practice

Close your eyes for a few moments. Become aware of the body and the stillness in the body. Become aware of the silence within the body. In the state of silence, recognise and observe your feelings. Recognise and observe your thoughts. Recognise and observe what the senses are experiencing. Observe what you are feeling. Identify your feelings. Observe your thoughts. Identify your thoughts. Observe the sensory inputs. Recognise them, be aware of them. Observe your expectations and sankalpas.

48

Recognise them; be aware of them: expectations of yourself, expectations of being here, expectations of your life.

Become aware, and recognise your ambitions and desires. Be aware of ambitions in relation to your external, social life; in relation to your internal, spiritual life. Be aware of desires in relation to your external, social life; in relation to your internal, spiritual life. Become aware of your needs in relation to your body, mind, ego and inner life. Become aware of your sankalpas and aspirations which are actually the focusing of your will-power for the attainment of a desire, goal or aim for satisfaction and fulfilment in life. The sankalpa is both external and internal. Now be aware of the state of serenity within. Open your eyes. Hari Om Tat Sat.

Dimension of karma

In this short meditation practice, we were trying to look at ourselves in totality. We can even say that we were trying to look at the ocean with all the waves, currents, flows and movements. That ocean is our personality, the manifestation and experience of ego, aspiration, ambition, desire, sankalpa, sensory input and mental input. That is the yogic process of observing what is happening in the inner, mental personality. In the latter half of the practice, we try to see the ocean absolutely still and motionless without any movement, mirror-still. The aspect of serenity inside and projecting that serenity outside is the culmination of yoga.

When we were observing ourselves and everything that was happening inside, watching the feelings, emotions, thoughts, desires and expressions of mind, we were not watching the so-called mental states, but the karma, the action, that is continuously taking place inside. Karma is movement which is created, experienced and performed by and through the senses, the mind, the ego, Prakriti, the gunas or attributes of life. We live in the dimension of karma all the time, karma which is external, which is subtle and which is psychic by nature.

When a seed is planted in the ground and given the proper conditions, it undergoes a change, a transformation, a process of growth. In the same way, all our karmas, from the causal to the manifest level, are in a process of continuous growth and change. There is always an expectation of the karmas; that is known as expectation of the result. When we become aware of karma, we also become aware of the necessities in life: the things we need and want or do not want, our likes and dislikes. Our entire interaction with life is based on what 'I' desire and do not desire.

Three aspects are considered important: (i) identification with 'I' as an individual, me; (ii) attraction to the world of objects for satisfaction and fulfilment; (iii) repulsion, rejection of that which is not desirable. These three aspects continuously change and alter the perceptions of our personality. 'I' identification changes the expression of our personality. Attraction and rejection change the expression of our personality. Linked with the concept and identity of 'I', and with attraction and repulsion, is the desire for a result which eventually culminates in satisfaction and fulfilment. If the result does not culminate in satisfaction and fulfilment, then another form of craving arises to take the place of the first desire, another way to attain satisfaction and fulfilment in life. This is the realm or dimension of karma.

Bhogi, karma yogi and karma sannyasin

A karma yogi is an individual who is able to remove the attraction to the results of karma from his life. He does not crave for the result or fruit of action, whether good or bad, positive or negative. Rather, performance of karma as a spontaneous expression of his nature and personality is his aim. The main aim of a karma sannyasin is to reach a meditative, contemplative process in the performance of karma, where the effect or influence of karma is seen in the psychic personality.

The karma yogi tries to overcome the desire to obtain a good result from the action, while the karma sannyasin tries to reach a contemplative state in life which helps him to understand the entire interaction of karma from the manifest to the unmanifest dimension. In other words, a karma yogi does not need to simplify the necessities of life. One can continue increasing these necessities to any extent desired, as long as there is no identification with the result, with the fruit of the karma, whereas a karma sannyasin makes a continual effort to reduce or to simplify the necessities in life. This is the basic difference between a karma yogi and karma sannyasin.

Both the karma yogi and the karma sannyasin are aware of the karmic interaction taking place externally and internally, from the realm of the senses, ego and emotions to the realm of the elements or *tattwas*. Up to this point, we are all aspirants, walking the same path. When there is identification with the result and an expectation of something good happening, then we get labelled as bhogis. *Bhogi* here means craving for satisfaction and fulfilment which is temporary in nature, because after one level of satisfaction and fulfilment has been attained, another level or desire is going to come up. We are caught in that process from which there is no escape. Identification with the world of name, form and idea is bhoga.

The karma yogi goes through the same process, but has no expectation. Life without expectation may sound very boring, but it is this kind of life which makes us aware of the inner expressions, in terms of energy, vitality, prana, psychic abilities and attainments. Then there is the karma sannyasin who has all this realisation and understanding and makes a continuous effort to simplify the necessities of life. This is how a start is made to understand the karma and develop a meditative awareness of the karmic interactions in the first verse of the sixth chapter of the Bhagavad Gita. The statement of the first verse is simple and straightforward: 'Discharge of action without support of, or attachment to attainment or result is karma yoga or involvement in action by a sannyasin and by a yogi.' I have already discussed the theory of karma. However, one point which needs to be understood is the usage of the words 'sannyasin' and 'yogi'.

51

Sannyasin

A sannyasin is a person who is aware of himself perfor.n-
ing the karma, the action, and is able to renounce identification with the action and overcome the idea of doership: I am
the performer. Human beings have the peculiar tendency of
making themselves the centre of all activity. We feel that we
are indispensable, and if we did not exist, then the world
would fall apart at the seams. We tend to project that deep
involvement with the world of the senses, with the manifest
dimension, with the mind within ourselves.

That is the idea of doership: I am doing, I am performing,
I am acting, I am indispensable. When this 'I am' grows
within, it feeds the ego, which leads to a further generation of
desires and ambitions related with the manifest dimension,
the manifest world. The ego is totally under the influence of
the three gunas, the attributes of nature, which are classified
as tamasic, rajasic and sattwic. As long as that identification of
the ego with the gunas is present, one cannot let go of the
identity or the idea of doership.

A sannyasin, whether poorna, karma, jignasu, makes a
conscious effort to firstly, observe the karma that is performed
by the self. Meditation in action, observation of the performance of karma, begins from this point onwards. The second
stage is channelling the karma, which means harmonising the
gunas, the tamasic, rajasic and sattwic tendencies. The karma
which is influenced by these tendencies is to be harmonised
and channelled, so that it becomes an elevating, rather then
a limiting force and experience. The third stage in the life of
a sannyasin is understanding the attachment and involvement of the ego, the 'I', to the karma that is being performed
externally by the senses in the physical dimension, and internally by the mind in the mental dimension.

The fourth stage involves letting go of the concept of
doership. The karmas continue to be performed, but without
that deep identification and involvement. When your blad-
der is full and you go to release the pressure, is there a deep
involvement or identification with the process of sitting on
the toilet? No, it is a natural process. All the karmas, the

interactions, are eventually viewed as natural processes, belonging to the dimension or realm of body and mind. Even the thoughts and desires cease to be magnetic forces constantly attracting us to situations and events, and simply become a natural process of expression. As long as we have a body and mind, we will continue to be influenced and affected by the nature and needs of the body and mind. However, that in-depth involvement and the superimposition of 'I' on the performance of the actions will not be there. So, that is the concept of sannyasa, letting go of the idea and the concept of doership.

Yogi

A yogi is a person who has attained harmony which is multi-dimensional. It is not just harmony in the realm of behaviour, interaction, emotion, thought or desire, but harmony in a deeper sense, involving all the attributes of the body, mind and spirit. Although body, mind and spirit are seen as three different units, they are one. Can one separate the mind from the body? Can one identify where the mind is located in the body? Can one isolate the spirit from the body and the mind? Can one identify where the spirit is located in the body or mind? No. If we try to do that, it will only be a form of speculation. We cannot separate the three, but we have given them three names in order to understand the karma, the method in which they interact with each other.

The mind interacts with the body in a particular way. The spirit interacts with the mind and body in a particular way, but they are one unit. In fact, we can say that the mind is an extension of the spirit, a useable form of the spirit in the manifest nature. The body is a further extension of the spirit, a useable form of that energy in the manifest world of senses and objects. So, the mind and spirit are all pervading. A practitioner of yoga, who practises one hour of asanas every morning, is not a yogi. One who is able to harmonise the experience of body, mind and spirit through a process of sadhana and understanding is termed a yogi.

So, the process of becoming a sannyasin or a yogi is not something external which can be adopted as a form of lifestyle, behaviour or discipline. Once a person is able to renounce identification with action and karma and harmonise the experience of body, mind and spirit, then there is a natural acceptance of the forces which motivate the body and mind to act according to their nature. Once there is acceptance of the dharmic karmas, which are performed according to one's nature, one attains realisation. This is the aim, the goal, the state of dhyana or samadhi, that we are trying to move towards. The final acceptance of me, as I am. When we say to ourself, not intellectually but in the depth of our being, "I am that I am", then we are what we are.

Sankalpa

The second verse of chapter six says:

*Without renouncing sankalpa
no one can become a yogi.*

What is sankalpa? Sankalpa is the focusing of the will, the energies of the mind and spirit, in order to attain a desire, aim or goal, for the purpose of satisfaction and fulfilment. This sankalpa can be seen in two different ways. All our motivations which guide us in life to attain something, to experience satisfaction and fulfilment, are desires. These are the external sankalpas. The same desire, the same force which takes us inwards to experience that inner harmony is another form of sankalpa. Again, our motivations and desires are influenced and their course is altered by the gunas: tamas, rajas and sattwa.

In the ancient literature, we find passages which state that God had the desire to create, to become many from one. Even God was not free from desire, so how can we become free from our desires? If desire is a force that can motivate God, the supreme being, to become many from the state of one, then where do we stand? Paramahamsaji used to say, "As long as the mind is buffeted by the strong gale of desire, one cannot have that inner realisation of the higher Self." This statement

54

of Paramahamsaji's indicates that we, as people who are involved in the manifest dimension, experience a form of desire which is rajasic and tamasic by nature. However, there is another form of desire which is sattwic.

Gunas

What is the meaning of sattwa, rajas and tamas? Sattwa is the state of luminosity, where one becomes the light, where one knows that 'I am the light', where one experiences the self-effulgent nature. Rajas is the state which is linked with the sustenance of and identification with ego, the 'I' principle in the world, and the recognition of me as an individual, an independent unit in the world. The superimposition of that 'I' over everything else is the nature of rajas. 'I' becomes the most predominant factor in our behaviour and interactions.

Tamas is a condition of life, mind, behaviour and thought, which becomes very powerful and restrictive. It does not allow the human being to alter, change or rise above that state. Tamas is becoming established in one specific condition and being unable to find the way out, or stagnating in one particular state. We can sit in this room day in and day out, mentally conceptualising that outside there are the sun, trees, buildings, flowers, plants and beautiful scenery. Having that mental concept is one thing and not making the effort to get out of the room is another. When we feel bound or confined, that is tamas.

So, rajas and tamas are the two attributes, or gunas, which influence every individual. Sattwa is not powerful at all, rather it is just a momentary glimpse of that pure nature with which we cannot identify. Insecurity, fear and inhibition are created when we try to change the nature of tamas. In order to counteract that insecurity, fear and inhibition, rajas becomes more powerful. When one is weak, sensitive, uncertain, fearful and insecure, then the tamasic state is experienced in its full potential. In order to avoid that self-image, one tries to project oneself as a strong, dominant figure, thus becoming a big bully. Therefore, in

55

every big bully there is a small, crying child, the state of tamas and rajas. The attainment of harmony within the self leads to the experience of sattwa, the true nature of the Self, the nature of light and self-effulgence. We tend to look for light outside and not inside.

Recognition of sankalpa

In sankalpa, all the desires and motivations which guide our life are always geared to the attainment of something external. Buddha used to say that in the path of realisation, one finally has to give up the desire to be realised. In the desire that 'I want to be realised', there are three aspects: 'I want' is one, 'to be' is another, and 'realised' is the third. These represent our aspirations related to the self, the manifest person or individual. Even in the higher states of meditation, one has to gradually give up the desires, ultimately including the last desire, 'I want'. When the last desire or sankalpa is given up, then the mind becomes free from the fetters of Prakriti, the nature, the manifest energy, and one attains the state of realisation.

We have to begin with the process of recognising the sankalpa. Our ambition is part of our sankalpa. The sankalpa which is made in yoga nidra is also a desire, but it is aimed at improving the self and not further binding the self. So, through this sankalpa, we are changing the nature of tamas into rajas, and directing the nature of rajas into sattwa. One must be aware of the sankalpa which is made during the practice of yoga nidra. It is the focusing of the will to attain something. If people smoke, then they can make the sankalpa, 'The need to smoke cigarettes is leaving me.' Not that they will leave the cigarettes. That desire to leave is a sankalpa. Sankalpa is seen in two ways: attraction and repulsion. When there is attraction or repulsion in a desire or an ambition, then that has to be managed properly.

Pratyahara and dharana

Management of attraction and repulsion can be simplified through the practices of meditation, self-observation, self-analysis and self-understanding. In order to overcome the fixed patterns of mind and thought, one needs to go through the practices of pratyahara and dharana. The normal karmas are to be combined with practices of pratyahara and dharana. I always say that meditation is very simple but pratyahara is the most difficult practice to do. How can we think it is easy to withdraw the dissipated nature of the mind and focus it on one point? If we find this easy to do, then we are only looking at the superficial nature and not at the deeper nature of mind.

It is easy to become aware of the thoughts, but difficult to become aware of the samskaras, the karmas, and even more difficult to become aware of the transcendental, pure, inner nature, which is not influenced by Prakriti. In order to come to this level, we have to go through the entire process of self-observation in pratyahara and perfect it. Having gone through this process, starting with practices such as antar mouna, yoga nidra and ajapa japa, a realisation of certain areas of our mind and nature takes place.

This realisation has to be further developed and expanded until eventually we are able to see the entire mind— the gross, the subtle and the causal, in one thought, in one glimpse, in one vision. This is the state of pratyahara. When we are able to see the entire mind in one thought, then concentration takes place and we begin to experience one-pointed awareness. That is dharana. Dhyana is very far from our reach. Neither you nor I have ever experienced what dhyana or meditation is.

A Celebration of Sannyasa

MAY 4, 1994

Coming back to Paramahamsaji's establishment in Deoghar and the formation of the Alakh Bara, in the course of this undertaking, I had to go and meet the different Acharyas and Shankaracharyas of the sannyasa tradition. After discussions with them, a code of conduct for sannyasins was formulated. In sannyasa, the impressions or samskaras of different cultures play a vital role. Sannyasa represents a tradition which, although it may have an international connection, was originally evolved by the rishis or seers who gave a lot of thought to the aim and direction of human life.

Five components of sannyasa
There are five components of sannyasa which have to be considered. The first aspect is *seva* which means 'service'. Why seva? After all, everybody performs some form of service in their own way. The concept of seva which evolved in the tradition of sannyasa gave a different dimension to the concept of service. What kind of dimension? Normally, whenever a service or an action is performed there is an expectation behind it, not necessarily of the result, but of an inner satisfaction or gain. There is also the aspect of recognition that 'I' am performing this seva, this service. This desire for some form of recognition or attainment has to be transformed into a sattwic achievement.

58

There is a definite lack of sattwa in our own approach to life. We are not sattwic. We are rajasic and we are tamasic. Sometimes, like a gust of fresh, crisp, cold wind, sattwa brushes against our life as a momentary experience. Then, there is the feeling or the experience of inner creativity, harmony, joy, transcendence and freedom. After that experience has passed, we again experience our rajasic and tamasic nature, where the 'I' becomes more important. So, seva aims to provide the awareness of sattwa.

The second aspect of sannyasa is *swadhyaya* which means 'self-study', 'self-awareness' or 'self-knowledge'. Swadhyaya is not an intellectual process, rather, it is a process of realisation of what 'I' am at present. If you analyse carefully, it becomes quite obvious that human beings constantly live in the past, fantasize about the future, and ignore the present. It is here that swadhyaya, self-awareness or self-knowledge, plays a vital role. The aim of swadhyaya is learning to live in the present. In order to live in the present, one needs to have a strong mind, a strong sankalpa or determination, and knowledge of the intricacies of human nature. Therefore, swadhyaya is experienced knowledge related to the human personality.

Santosha, which means 'contentment', is the third component of sannyasa life. Contentment is not that simple a quality to realise in life. In order to be fully content in life, one has to know the SWAN theory. SWAN is an acronym which represents: Strengths, Weaknesses, Ambitions and Needs. Every individual has his own strengths which can manifest in the intellect, emotions, willpower, clarity of mind, and performance of action. These are the strengths which help us to move forward in life, which provide us with the stamina to continue. At the same time, we are subject to weaknesses which can be experienced or felt in many areas: fear, insecurity, lack of self-confidence, lack of willpower and lack of mental clarity.

Ambition is the third aspect of the SWAN theory. Ambition can also take many forms, such as fantasies which are beyond our strength and means to attain. Ambition is a motivating force. Some people desire the moon and others

59

desire something which is simple to attain. Ambition is not something physical or mental. The Sanskrit word for ambition is *mahatwakanksha*, which means a desire that manifests in the realm of *mahat*, of *buddhi*, *manas*, *chitta* and *ahamkara*. By the time it filters down to the surface of the mind, to our rationality, it has been changed, shaped and altered by many other attributes, circumstances and situations.

Finally, the fourth aspect of the SWAN theory is need. The body, the emotions and the mind all have certain needs. These needs are vital for their maintenance and sustenance. So, in order to have santosha, contentment, it is necessary for us to develop an awareness, a recognition of these four different aspects in the SWAN theory. When these four aspects of our personality are harmonised and balanced, then santosha or contentment is achieved.

The fourth component of sannyasa is *santulan* which means, 'harmony', 'balance' or 'equilibrium'. Balance must be developed in all the aspects of life: balance in action, in desire and aspiration; balance in the faculties of head, heart and hand; balance of the external and the internal environment. This balance is attained after going through and perfecting the first three components of sannyasa.

The fifth component is *samarpan* which means 'dedication'. Samarpan is a very beautiful word, sama plus arpan. *Sama* means 'equipoised', 'harmonised'; and *arpan* means 'to offer'. Samarpan is the offering or dedication of the balanced nature of an individual. This dedication, or samarpan, is an experience which is felt internally. When these five components are perfected, only then is sannyasa fulfilled. These are the five qualities which every sannyasin must cultivate in his life.

After discussions with the different Acharyas and the Shankaracharyas, who represent the tradition of sannyasa, keeping these five components in mind, a code of conduct was devised, which was accepted by the authorities of the sannyasa order. This code of conduct is being implemented in our tradition, and also in those traditions which are connected with the seven Akharas, the places of the seven Acharyas of the sannyasa tradition.

Yoga cycles

After the completion of this undertaking, on the 14th February 1992, an idea came. Since we are taking yoga into the professional field, why not launch it with a bang? This idea evolved into the celebration of yoga, the Golden Jubilee, conducted in November 1993. After the preparations began, it dawned on me that even for such functions there is a cycle. Swami Sivananda conducted the first World Religion Conference in Rishikesh, in 1953, which launched his movement of the Divine Life Society and gave it a solid footing. In 1973, twenty years later, Paramahamsaji celebrated the Golden Jubilee of Swami Sivananda's fifty years of renunciation. The theme of that convention was 'World Yoga Conference'. From 1973 onwards, Paramahamsaji began his mission of propagating yoga on a large scale.

Twenty years later, in 1993, we, the disciples of Paramahamsaji, conducted another convention to celebrate the fifty years of renunciation of our Guru. It is like history repeating itself. The theme of this convention was 'Integration of Yoga and Science'. Another peculiar thing happened. Paramahamsaji established the Bihar School of Yoga in 1963. The convention was conducted in 1973. I took over from him in 1983 and the World Tyag Convention was conducted in 1993. So, there is another ten year cycle in between. What will happen in 2003? I do not know. It is not our plan; something is happening naturally and spontaneously, without any prior thought.

Tyag Golden Jubilee

The Tyag Golden Jubilee was held from 1st to 4th November 1993. Many professional people came from all parts of the world. Munger is a totally isolated place with absolutely no facilities or accommodation whatsoever, so everything had to be organised right from scratch. There were six hundred and sixty delegates from thirty two countries, six thousand delegates from twenty states of India, and another six thousand local delegates from Bihar and Munger. So, it was a gathering of about twelve thousand.

61

The Governor of Bihar, who represents the President of India, inaugurated the convention. Swami Chidananda was the chief guest. Some of the top cardiologists, doctors and scientists in India came to this convention. Two Acharyas of the sannyasa tradition also came, along with many other eminent, non-aligned sannyasins. It was like the yoga olympics. England took away the trophy, with the discourse of Swami Pragyamurti, Director of the London Satyananda Yoga Centre, on the treatment of AIDS through yoga. One case which had been confirmed as being HIV positive has become HIV negative after nine months of yoga practice. Of course, in this process many people departed from their bodies, but definitely hope came for those people who are in the early stages of this disease, that through the practices of yoga they could help themselves.

During this convention, the day after the inauguration, there was a freak thunderstorm. The roof of the marquee collapsed, but the spirit and the determination was so high that we all continued as if nothing had happened. There were about four hundred volunteers working round the clock. The swamis, many of whom had come from outside the ashram during that period to help us out, and the other volunteers, did not sleep for five days continuously. It was impossible to sleep during the day, because of the activities, responsibilities and duties, and it was impossible to sleep at night due to putting new hay and carpets on the ground for the next day's programme, because everything was wet. Trucks used to run back and forth all day and all night bringing hay from the local farms. There was not a single carpet shop in Bihar which had not contributed carpets to this convention. These only lasted for one hour, because as they became wet, we removed them, brought more from another place, put them down, and that was how it continued.

New President of BSY

The convention was the launching pad for all the activities and projects which I have told you about. Having started

62

these projects, it is now time to turn the gaze to distant shores. With the help of other sannyasins, it has taken me eleven years to give a new direction to the yoga movement. It is not an overnight job, but things are moving now, and I feel a sense of pride, happiness and contentment, about the contribution that we have been able to make.

During the convention, it was announced that Swami Gyanprakash would take charge of Bihar School of Yoga. She officially replaced me as the President on 15th February this year. She was born in Colombia, South America, and has lived with Paramahamsaji since the age of fifteen. She received all her education and yoga training in Munger. Now she is looking after the management of the day to day affairs of the Bihar School of Yoga, thus enabling me to travel and follow up these projects, and to create new projects in different parts of the world.

Let us see what kind of projects come up for Mangrove Mountain and how far we are able to implement them with the co-operation and help of the swamis who are living here. I feel that spiritual life has to be seen from different angles. Institutional involvement is one thing, yogic involvement is another, sannyasa commitment is something different, and personal life is different again. These are aspects of life which we must look into before deciding the direction of future activities.

Developing sattwa

Many of you may think that I have come here to change things, but I have not come here to change anything. Rather, I come here to support what you are doing. We all have our aim and direction, and it is impossible for anyone to impose his aim and direction on another, because this goes against the principles of nature, the human *prakriti*. There has to be a recognition of the human nature. Therefore, I have not come here to change anything, but to support you in what you are doing, and to give you a push if you are not doing anything. Human beings have their limitations. I have my limitations; you have your limitations. One cannot expect

63

anything more than that. We all live and function within our limitations, within the structure of our SWAN theory, and it is the recognition and management of these aspects which can eventually ignite the light within.

If we are unable to recognise what we are, then no matter what we do we will always be a failure. Human nature expresses itself in many different ways. There are strengths which can be used to raise our level of consciousness and to harmonise our thoughts, behaviour and actions. In order to do this, we must learn how to be sattwic, not rajasic or tamasic. We must try to be sattwic. Sattwa is the quality of light. Sattwa does not mean simplicity. Sattwa does not mean spontaneity. These are the qualities which manifest after attaining sattwa.

Warning bell

Hypertension is present when there is stress. Disease arises when there is imbalance. Disease cannot be the cause of disease; imbalance is the cause of disease. Hypertension is not the cause of hypertension; stress is the cause which is creating hypertension. Headache is not the cause of a headache; tension is the cause of headache. Headache is only a symptom, a warning bell of what is happening inside the personality.

I will tell you a true story to illustrate this point. When I was living in America, we had a fridge with a red warning light. It was an old fridge which we picked up from the corner of the road where it had been thrown out. We set up our ashram by picking up useful items that were thrown in the rubbish. The red warning light used to flash on and off without any apparent reason. I looked at the fridge, but could not work out what was wrong with the red light. I could not fix it up, because it was too old, and no mechanic was going to come and fix it. That red light always made me feel that something was wrong, so eventually, I took a hammer and bashed it, and that was the end of the problem.

This is what we do to ourselves. Something is wrong, the red light flashes and we try to deal with the warning signal, rather than finding out what is causing the red light to flash. We get a headache, so we pop a pill and eventually the headache goes away. The red light is bashed, but the fault which is within remains there. That is how we treat ourselves. So, we must emphasise again and again, that sattwa is the answer.

Yoga or any other practice or system can be the means to know the circuits of the body and mind, but the real instrument to correct the malfunction of this equipment, which we know as personality, is sattwa, the light, the nature of light, the quality of light. An effort has to be made to achieve sattwa in life, and it is this message which I want to impart this time. In order to convey this message, we are looking at some of the literature which is related to the growth of the human personality and the aim of yoga. However, the direction remains the same: sattwa.

Samkhya

MAY 4, 1994

There are many who believe the Samkhya system to be a part of the Indian philosophy, and from the philosophical viewpoint, they may be right. From my own studies of the subject, I feel that Samkhya is not a philosophy. It is a description of the many layers or dimensions which are relevant to the growth of the individual, from the unmanifest to the manifest. Samkhya is a darshana. The word *darshana* means 'to have the realisation of', 'to have the vision of' or 'to have the experience of'. The experience of what? Of Samkhya. The literal meaning of the word *samkhya* is 'numbers'.

It is said that Samkhya deals with the total human structure, which is comprised of a number of different compartments and each compartment gives birth to a particular experience, a particular state of being, a particular understanding and realisation. The Samkhya system spans both the unmanifest and the manifest dimensions, which are experienced by us and of which we are a part. These various levels or dimensions of human experience are classified as numbers, which is the Samkhya system. It begins with the unmanifest and ends with the combination of the entire unmanifest and subtle components that make up the form of the body. According to this darshana, the body is not just comprised of bones and marrow; the body is everything which is used by the individual to experience the manifest reality.

66

There are two levels of the Samkhya system. One level deals with the consciousness, or Purusha, which is pure and impure at the same time; which is unmanifest in its transcendental nature and manifest in relation to time, space and object. The other level deals with the movement of energy, or Prakriti, which is also unmanifest in the transcendental nature and manifest in the gross dimension. These are the dimensions in which a human being interacts.

According to modern psychology, the broad classification of the human mind is into four different levels: conscious, subconscious, unconscious and a speculative superconscious. The darshanas speak of twenty states of consciousness and mind, not four. Each state is easily identifiable. This gives an idea of the concept that we are dealing with in relation to our life; to our interactions in the world, in the society; to our body, mind, nature, qualities and attributes. Each of these twenty states is defined and identified with a state of consciousness and transformation of the energy field, functioning within the human body in the manifest dimension.

Ishwara/nashwara

The most subtle and transcendental aspect of Samkhya is the ishwara concept. *Ishwara* means the undecaying principle, the eternal principle that never changes, that is homogeneous. This principle is represented by the three Oms. The reason why we chant three Oms is because we recognise those attributes of ishwara within ourselves. In the first chanting of Om, it is Ooomnipotent. In the second chanting of Om, it is Ooomnipresent. In the third chanting of Om, it is Ooomniscient. These are the attributes or the qualities of ishwara, which is the transcendental, eternal, undecaying principle or reality. At the opposite end of the spectrum is another reality which is known as nashwara. *Nashwara* means something that changes all the time, that decays, that is bound and limited by the various attributes of personality which have manifested somewhere in the middle between ishwara and nashwara.

The Patanjali system of raja yoga is not taken from the Tantras, but is considered to be an offshoot of the Samkhya system. Here we can see how the different darshanas integrate themselves with the concepts and the practices of yoga. Those who have studied the *Yoga Sutras* of Patanjali will know that nowhere in the entire text has a word referring to God or the Supreme Being been used. He has not used the word God, but the term ishwara is given.

Ishwara, the undecayable principle, is the real nature of consciousness, and nashwara, the decayable principle, is simply an extension of the ishwara energy in the realm of Prakriti. So, that realm, where there is purity, light, and transcendental experience, is known as ishwara, and from that point onwards, different manifestations take place. We do not know how or why these manifestations which have resulted in our being here, have taken place. However, the fact remains that a certain transformation has been seen in the spectrum of ishwara and nashwara. Whether it is the process of growth and evolution or the process of involution, we do not know.

Purusha and Prakriti

When the first transformation occurs in this transcendental field, then the concept of Purusha evolves. Purusha means something which is contained in a form, in a shape, which is identified as having a boundary. Suppose there is a body of water, a lake or an ocean, and inside that large body of water you submerge an empty bucket. What do you see? There is water all around the bucket and there is water contained inside the bucket too. There is a division. The form of the bucket which is seen as having a shape or boundary is the Purusha aspect. From the moment that a form has manifested or a boundary has been defined in the realm of ishwara, then Prakriti also becomes involved.

So, Purusha and Prakriti come together. Prakriti is the catalyst for defining a definite form and shape. Our thoughts have a form and shape. Our feelings have a form and shape. The world in which we live has a form and shape. We live in the dimension of form and shape. We recognise form and shape. The entire interaction of a human being takes place in the dimension of name, form and idea. We see a form; an idea is created; a name is given. We have an idea; a form is created; a name is given. A name comes in; an idea is created; a form is given. They are all interlinked processes.

Once Purusha evolves from the transcendental ishwara, then the tattwas also evolve and give a definite form and shape to the expansive energy of ishwara. We know these tattwas or *bhutas* in the manifest dimension as elemental manifestation. Even in relation to the yogic system of chakras, we have space, air, fire, water and earth. Prior to the formation of tattwas, a controlling agent has to be created, a command centre, which is the super mind. This super mind is consciousness.

The word for consciousness in yoga is *chetana* which means 'continuous experience', 'continuous realisation'. Different terms like *chitta* are also derived from the word chetana. This continuous experience of consciousness, continuous experience of reality, is then further classified in the form of *mahat*, 'the supreme intelligence' or 'the supreme mind', which later manifests as *manas*, *buddhi*, *chitta* and *ahamkara*. These are the four components which control the entire activity of consciousness and energy in the realm of Prakriti.

Formation of the elements

With the formation of mahat tattwa, the energy principle also begins to manifest. Up to this point, it was the manifestation of consciousness. From this point on, energy begins to manifest in the form of the attributes and qualities of the elements. The first element to manifest is space, *akasha tattwa*. Akasha tattwa becomes the basis for all other manifestation and creation. In the absence of akasha tattwa, Prakriti would not exist. Take, for example, this building. It has grown up in akasha tattwa, in space. Buildings which go up a hundred storeys, such as the Empire State Building, the World Trade Centre or Centrepoint, exist within akasha tattwa.

Matter manifests within the space element. In the absence of akasha tattwa, the space element, creation would not take place. It is the akasha tattwa which gives creation the three-dimensional effect. In the absence of akasha tattwa, we would have two-dimensional creations, like photographs. A statue or a human body is three-dimensional. The body which you see in the photograph does not exist in space, but the physical body exists in space. So, akasha is the first important element of Prakriti, the basis of every other manifestation.

After akasha come the element and the attributes of air. After air come the elements and attributes of fire, water and matter. This is also represented in the chakras: mooladhara, representing the earth element; swadhisthana, representing the water element; manipura, representing the fire element; anahata, representing the air element; vishuddhi, representing the space element, which is the realm of energy; ajna, representing mahat or the mind element, and sahasrara, representing the transcendental aspect.

So, in this respect also, there is a very deep integration of Samkhya with yoga. I hope you are catching on to the point that in yoga, and specifically in the practical application of yoga, we see the combination of Samkhya, Tantra and Vedanta. In fact, one cannot be a yogi without the knowledge of these three systems. There has to be a proper implementation and combination of these three darshanas with yoga in order to experience yoga fully.

Body and mind

With the formation of the elements, we move into the physical manifestation which is perceived as the body of matter, or *annamaya kosha*. This body is also composed of the organs of action and of sensory organs, certain components or instruments which feed the mind. Then we move into *manomaya kosha* in which the organs of cognition are very active. The components which feed the mind from annamaya kosha are related to manomaya kosha. The eyes are physical organs, but the experience, the visual cognitive faculty, is actually perceived, analysed and categorised by the mind. If there is a disconnection between mind and body, then this cognition will not take place. One would

70

see, hear, taste, smell or feel something, but there would be no cognition of it.

So, just as the body has the five organs of action, the mind has the five organs of cognition which are fully active inside, and which use the medium of the external indriyas, or senses. Along with the physical dimension, there is the dimension of prana, or *pranamaya kosha*, the dimension of higher intelligence or *vijnanamaya kosha*, and beyond this, the dimension of beatitude, total harmony or *anandamaya kosha*. This is the basis of the Samkhya system without going into too much detail.

Multi-dimensional awareness

In yoga, Samkhya plays a very vital role, because yoga is not just a mechanical performance of techniques, whether they be asana, pranayama, pratyahara, dharana, or a yogic lifestyle. Rather, it is incorporating the awareness of these various dimensions, attributes, qualities and mental states, and giving them a direction in which they can manifest in a creative form. There are many levels and dimensions of human experience. What we feel in the physical dimension, in the form of pain or pleasure, causes a change in our subtle dimensions also. In the same way, the state of depression affects the physical as well as the mental system. It affects the feelings, the thoughts, the pranas, the rationality. So, one thing which is happening affects all these various dimensions, right from the most gross to the most subtle. If we consider something to be purely external then that is our misconception. It is only the manifest mind which says, "This is external", but the effect and influence of that affects the entire personality.

So, Samkhya says, do not consider yourself to be just the body which you can see. Do not consider yourself to be just the mind which you can experience in parts. Every action in life, every thought in life, every interaction in life, influences the entire human structure. For this reason, I feel that Samkhya is a system of knowing the human personality. It is much more than a philosophical system. It is a system which is comprised of the physical, the psychological and the spiritual dimensions. Awareness of these three dimensions is Samkhya.

71

Bhagavad Gita

Dhyana Yoga (Part II)

MAY 5, 1994

In the Gita it is said that in meditation there has to be acceptance of the self, and along with that, one should make an effort
to experience serenity. The third verse of chapter six says:

*Karma is the means for those desirous of obtaining
yoga and harmony. Serenity is the result of mastery
over the karma and attainment of yoga.*

In this verse, Sri Krishna has made an important statement: that karma is the means for those desirous of attaining
harmony and yoga. What does this statement mean? It means
that along with the normal karma which is performed, one
needs to develop an attitude of observation, of knowing that
I am performing karma. With this knowing, this observation
of the karma, one spontaneously enters into a meditative
state. Meditation begins as a process of observation and
culminates in the state of serenity.

Therefore, it has been emphasised here that meditation
in the form of self-observation has to be a part of each and
every moment of the day. One cannot isolate the meditative
practice from the normal day-to-day involvement. If this kind
of isolation takes place, then it will be similar to taking three
steps forward and two back. The growth or the progress in
one's spiritual life will be very slow, without any inspiration.
The human tendency is to be unaware of the karmas and to

72

allow the ego to govern and direct the karmas. The ego comes forward as a selfish quality and manifests as something which is non-expansive and restricted to the conditionings of our own mind and nature.

Twelve hours of this kind of involvement in life is followed by half an hour or forty minutes of a meditative practice in which we try to become aware of the thoughts, release the stress and anxiety, and focus ourselves. This does not really balance the amount of externalisation we have faced in our active day. Twelve hours of intense, externalised activity and half an hour of meditation, pratyahara or dharana, are not compatible in any way. So, yoga considers it important to make every moment of the day a part of our spiritual effort, a part of our sadhana. When every moment of the day has become meditative, then serenity is attained.

Dynamic and passive karma

There are two aspects to karma. The first aspect involves movement, activity, going forward, and the second aspect involves sitting back and observing. We have identified karma with movement, activity and going forward, but we have not been able to associate karma with the passive state of mind. Imagine being a farmer. First, we prepare the ground, till the earth and enrich it with natural composts. When the ground is ready, we sow the seeds and take proper care of them. When the seeds begin to sprout, then we can sit back. There is no need to work as hard as before; we just have to be aware of whenever care is needed to be given.

In the same way, these two aspects have to be considered in respect to karma. Initially, there is active involvement, and at a later stage, there is passive involvement. So, there is dynamic involvement and passive involvement in the same karma. These two aspects of karma actually colour our mind. Our mind is like a clear crystal ball, but we cannot see the clarity, because this mental crystal ball is always being placed on a different coloured cloth. The colour of the cloth reflects in the clarity of the crystal ball. So what has to be done? Either the cloth has to be removed to allow the clarity of the crystal

73

ball to manifest naturally, or the crystal ball has to be placed where it is not reflecting any kind of colour.

In both cases, you will find that there is a combination of karma, activity, action, clarity, meditation, observation and analysis. In order to remove the coloured cloth which is beneath the crystal ball, the senses and the body perform the physical karma of removing the cloth. If you are picking up the crystal ball and putting it in another place, then again, the body and the senses perform that physical action. So, karma should never be isolated from meditation. Once this realisation is attained, once the mastery of action is attained, then that is the attainment of yoga. Fulfilment of action, completion of action, is fulfilment in yoga, and that fulfilment is the attainment of meditation.

No peace in the Himalayas
In the fourth verse, attraction and repulsion are again emphasised:

Do not be attracted to or repulsed by the senses,
sense objects or actions related to them.

In the state of serenity, one goes through a natural process of renunciation, leaving behind, not needing. This renunciation is a symptom of a person who is attaining the state of serenity. Renunciation is not an external act, rather it is a state of inner awareness. Paramahamsaji used to say that there is no silence or peace in the jungles, forests and Himalayas, and there is no noise in the middle of the city or the town market. What we perceive to be noise and silence are external movements in the environment. The real noise and silence are experienced internally.

If you are not able to stop the chatter of the mind, you will not find peace even in a cave in the deepest, remotest part of the Himalayas. However, if you are able to stop the chatter of the mind, then you will find total peace even in the middle of a busy city, and you will be unaffected by the noise and distraction. So, when the mental chatter stops, then there is an automatic switching off of the identification

74

with the senses, the sense objects and the actions associated
with them.

Developing simplicity

Therefore, the initial aim of meditation is to stop the
chattering of the mind, to become aware of what is happening
within, and not to create a further desire to have a sublime,
divine or transcendental experience. Those people who want
to see lights and colours in order to feel that they are evolving
are not actually experiencing a meditative state; rather they
are further conditioning their minds to see or expect something. Seeing lights, hearing music internally or having a
vision of angels does not mean that you are on the right track.
Do not have this expectation at all. Be aware of the simple
experience; see what is coming up from inside.

Allow simplicity to take over your personality. Experience the simple nature of your inner personality guiding
your mental states, and your actions. Do not allow ego in the
form of desire or ambition to take over this conscious effort.
When you have come to the point of not allowing the ego to
govern and colour the effort which you are making, then the
mind renounces certain traits and tendencies naturally and
spontaneously. What is renounced? The sense of pleasure
and pain, of satisfaction and dissatisfaction, of right and
wrong. Then one begins to live in the continuity of the Self,
in the continuity of consciousness.

Mind as friend and enemy

This idea is again further emphasised in the fifth verse:

Mind is both friend and enemy to the self.
An undisciplined mind leads to downfall.
After controlling the mind, one can know the Self.
One can remain self-disciplined and serene in opposites.
One can obtain knowledge and wisdom.
One who obtains the above remains supreme.

The mind is both the friend and the enemy of the self.
When is it an enemy and when a friend? When the mind is

subject to different emotions, conflicts, fears and insecurities, then it becomes an enemy. It does not befriend the self at that moment. It does not allow friendship to be established with itself and the higher Self. For example, many people commit suicide because they are frustrated with life for some reason. Having a fight with a companion can lead to a state of mind where life has no meaning. Low self-esteem can lead to a state of mind where life has no meaning. Total frustration and depression due to some event or circumstance can lead to a state where life has no meaning.

When the nature of the mind changes because of these circumstances, then the mind becomes the enemy. It goes against the principles of evolution and growth. When the mind experiences contentment, then it becomes the friend. This contentment is not external only; it is internal and spiritual. When the mind experiences contentment and is able to persevere, then it becomes the friend, because in that state, there is no conflict of any kind. Life opens wide and you become the master of all you survey.

Openness, clarity and contentment make the mind your friend. Conflict, insecurity and fear make the mind your enemy. So, it is important to first know the structure within which the mind moves, what are the states of mind and which conditioning is most predominant. An undisciplined mind is an outgoing mind, desiring, wanting. A disciplined mind is an inward going mind, which is more stable, which does not desire as much as the outgoing mind. An undisciplined mind is like a mad dog which can even bite the owner. A disciplined mind is like a pet dog which protects the owner. It is as simple as that.

Spontaneous, inner discipline
So, there has to be a process whereby we are able to train the mind properly in a system of discipline. This is not an imposed discipline, it is a spontaneous discipline. The first sutra in Patanjali's *Yoga Sutras* is *Atha yoga anushasanam*. There have been different commentaries on this sutra, but the real meaning is, 'Yoga is a form of discipline'. If you ask a person

what yoga is, and they begin by saying that controlling the modifications of the mind is yoga, then they have missed a very important and basic principle of yoga. Controlling the mind is very difficult.

Paramahamsaji used to tell us a story about a wild horse. A king received some beautiful, wild horses, fresh from the jungle. There was not a trainer in the kingdom who could tame those wild horses. Many people came and tried but they all failed. Eventually one person came and said, "Let me try to tame these wild horses." One year passed, two years passed, then one day this trainer came riding in upon the wildest horse, in total control. The king asked him, "How did you do it?" The trainer said, "Look, my approach was different. I did not try to instantly control the horses. First I had to get to know the nature of the horses. I let them roam free and they got used to my presence. Then one day I put my hand on the back of one. That horse flinched, jumped and ran away, but after a few months, the horse became used to me putting my hand on his back. Gradually, in this way, over a long period of time, I made friends with the horse. I did not try to control him at any time, but made myself a friend. Because of that deep friendship, I was able to saddle and bridle and eventually ride him." That is also how mental training has to be done.

So, yoga is a form of discipline in which one becomes aware of the subtle nature. When there is an awareness of the subtle, dominating nature, the subtle dimensions and realms of the human personality, then, after obtaining that knowledge, one can eventually control the mind and the vrittis. Discipline is not an imposed, external rule. Rather it is a state of balance, it is a state of harmony. It is saying to the mind, "Okay, do not go out and be mad, just remain in your own space and be a friend." We have to understand that the disciplined mind is able to remain uninfluenced by the sensory inputs. The undisciplined mind cannot remain isolated; rather it becomes deeply involved and engrossed in the sensory inputs. It gets caught in that spider's web just like a fly. Then the spider comes and eats the fly. The karmas become overpowering and dominant and the mind cannot free itself from them. So, discipline is the control of the mind. The natural discipline which arises from deep within, after recognition of the human nature, is the means to control the mind and to know the Self.

Vedanta

MAY 5, 1994

We have been discussing a specific approach to our yoga practice and to our life of sadhana related to spiritual development. Yoga is just a part of our own spiritual evolution and the practices and techniques of yoga have to be combined with other systems which will give us an in-depth understanding of our own nature and personality. The aim of the various, progressive stages of yoga is to help us find harmony and balance in the body and mind, and to attain that clarity of consciousness in which the knowledge of Self is automatically experienced.

The different practices and branches of yoga provide an approach to working with the various expressions and imbalances of the body and mind. This is the practical aspect of our spiritual development. In order to realise yoga's potential, we need to combine different systems. One of these systems is Samkhya, through which we can gain an insight into the transcendental and the manifest nature of which we are a part, an extension and an expression. There are two other systems which also have to be understood. One is Vedanta and the other is Tantra.

Vedanta is another darshana. Please remember that darshana is not just philosophy. Darshana can have a philosophical aspect, just as we can create our own philosophy in life. Apart from this, however, there is also a practical,

79

attitudinal aspect. Therefore, *darshana* means 'a vision', 'a state of experience', 'a state of cognition'. Vedanta is a system which has a philosophical as well as an attitudinal aspect combined together. The philosophical aspect deals with the transcendental and the manifest nature of consciousness.

Brahman

How does Vedanta view this transcendental conscious-ness? There are two concepts. In Samkhya, we talk of Purusha and Prakriti; in Tantra, we talk of Shiva and Shakti. In the same way, Vedanta speaks in terms of Brahman and Maya. These concepts actually define the state of consciousness which is experienced in a very systematic way. Those who are familiar with the vedantic philosophy will have heard the term *Brahman*, which means 'the ever expanding state of consciousness'. There can be no limit, no boundary for the growth of human consciousness. This aspect deals with the omniscient, omnipresent and omnipotent consciousness. This particular transcendental or supreme state of consciousness is something to strive for and to attain in our lives.

Vedanta clearly defines four different stages of Brahman or expanding consciousness. The first stage is known as vaishwanara which is in the gross dimension. The concept of *vaishwanara* means 'consciousness which is undergoing con-stant change'. *Vishwa* represents 'the manifest dimension', and *nara* represents 'the change in the manifest dimension'. This state can be related to the *jagrit* or conscious mind, which is actively involved in the world. We are experiencing this state of vaishwanara in our day to day life. The conscious mind which perceives, recognises and analyses, in the state of wakeful activity, is the manifest state of Brahman, the totality of consciousness.

The next stage is *tejas*, 'the self-luminous consciousness', which is related with the subconscious. We are not fully aware of the subconscious dimension, but we know the concept behind the subconscious mind, what it is, what kind of experiences arise in this state. Then comes *prajna*, 'the aspect of knowing', where one becomes the knower, the *drashta*, the *sakshi* or the witness. The concept of drashta and sakshi is found in yoga also. One becomes the seer and the experiencer of what is happening. After this comes the state of Brahman.

Maya

The second aspect of Vedanta is *Maya*, which is literally translated as 'illusion', but it also means 'that which is measurable'. Maya is the same as Prakriti or Shakti. What can be measured? Where there is a beginning and an end, point A ending in point B, that state can be measured. Thoughts have a beginning and an end. Situations have a beginning and an end. Life has a beginning and an end. Experiences have a beginning and an end. Anything that can be measured, that falls somewhere between the beginning and the end, is known as Maya. What is the limited nature? The limited nature of consciousness is the conscious, the subconscious and the unconscious, where cognition takes a different form.

Just imagine swimming in an ocean. While we are on the surface, there is sunlight from above. When we dive down into the ocean, the intensity of light gradually reduces as we go deeper, until we reach the bottom where there is no light, only darkness. Just as while diving into the ocean, we see the light gradually diminishing as we go deeper, in the same way, the externalised, cognitive faculty of consciousness gradually diminishes as we go deep into the consciousness. Cognition of the senses through the senses is known and recognised at the conscious level, the surface of the ocean. Although we are not aware of the different currents and waves, cognition is there. We are not aware of all the experiences on the conscious level at the same time, but we know that we are conscious and we have the ability to become conscious of different things that are happening. The information is being received; it is simply a matter of focusing on that information and going deeper into it.

When the light, cognitive faculty or the cognition which is recognised by the senses gradually loses its intensity, then we enter the subconscious state, the twilight zone between the

81

external and the internal world. This is known as *swapna* or 'the dreaming state', where the senses are not active physically but they are active mentally. Going deep into the subconscious, into the unconscious, there is total darkness: *shoonya*, 'void', nothingness. Beyond the unconscious, we find the base of consciousness, supporting the other states, which is *turiya*. In vedantic terminology that is Brahman.

Brahman is the base which supports the other states of experience. Once we find this base, Maya ceases to have any kind of influence on the individual. Right up to the unconscious dimension there is Maya, the current, the flows which are encountered when we dive deep into the ocean. The fish that live on the surface of the ocean are the sensory inputs. The fish that live in the twilight zone where there is less light, but where cognition is still possible through the senses, are the thoughts, the desires. The fish that live in the depths of the ocean and have their own luminosity in them, the light fish, are the samskaras and the karmas which swim in the dark recesses. When we reach the bottom, there is the experience of solidity. This is the description of human consciousness, according to Vedanta.

Recognition of consciousness

Vedanta emphasises that a change has to take place in the philosophy of human consciousness by which one can have total recognition. According to Vedanta, consciousness is not defined as having a specific boundary or barrier; rather it is defined as decreasing states of awareness. It is like moving from one end of a ruler to the other. The area where we start is the conscious and the area where we want to go is the superconscious. This is not a vertical journey. It is a horizontal journey and the awareness gradually decreases.

It is here that through a combination of Yoga, Samkhya and Tantra, instead of the awareness decreasing as we go deep into our own mind, we are able to experience the totality, not just the partial consciousness which is restricted and limited to the senses and the mind. In the experience of the totality, an attitudinal change also takes place through having a broader vision, concept and sense of identification with the world around us. When the human or individual dimension is transcended, the individual mind merges with the universal mind. This cannot be attained through rationality. Here rationality and intuitive ability have to be combined.

'Aham Brahmasmi', I am Brahman

Once a person very much like us came to Paramahamsaji and said, "Give me a method, a mantra, a means through which I can experience the higher reality, and I want it immediately." Paramahamsaji said, "No, I don't think you are ready for it. Do your yoga practices and come back in a few years." The man insisted and ultimately Paramahamsaji gave in and said, "Okay, I will give you a mantra. Contemplate it and think about it. Once you have perfected that mantra and are able to experience it to the fullest, then you will be able to know the turiya state."

The mantra was *Aham Brahmasmi*, 'I am Brahman', 'I am That'. Paramahamsaji said, "Repeat this mantra until you can identify yourself totally with the environment, the world and the cosmos. When you feel one with all creation, and you are able to see the entire cosmos in a grain of sand, when you have the experience that all are part of the same spirit, then you will be well on your way." The man said, "Very simple, no problem at all," and he started in earnest with his mantra. 'I am that supreme consciousness,' he thought, 'I see that supreme consciousness in everything, in this tree, in this plant, in this leaf, in this flower, in this animal, in this insect, in this person. I am one and the same with all that." He was very proud of his achievement and said to himself, "Now, I have that vision in which I can see the spirit as one."

One day, in order to test him, Paramahamsaji called him, gave him a jhola and some rupees and said, "Go to the Munger market and buy vegetables for the ashram." The man said, "No problem at all. After all, it is one Brahman going to meet other Brahmans." On his way to town, he saw everybody running away from the market. One person stopped and said to him, "Look, there is a mad bull elephant who is destroying everything in its path. Run for your life!" After hearing this, the aspirant thought, "Now is a good time to put my theory and experience to the test. I am Brahman, the supreme consciousness, the elephant is also Brahman, the supreme consciousness. How can one supreme consciousness harm another supreme consciousness? It is like having water in a bucket and in a tub. The water is the same and if you pour the water of the bucket into the water of the tub, they both mix and merge and cannot be separated." This was the logic of the aspirant.

So, he continued walking until he came to the elephant. He stood in front of the elephant with his chest out and chin up and said, "You are Brahman, I am Brahman, we are both one and the same." Unfortunately, the elephant was not in a philosophical mood. He lifted the man from the ground with his trunk, twirled him in the air and threw him far away. So, this spiritual aspirant ended up in the Munger hospital all bandaged.

He came back from the hospital after a week, seething with rage and fury. He marched up to Paramahamsaji and started abusing him, saying, "What kind of Guru are you? You did not give me the right mantra." Paramahamsaji said, "Calm down and tell me what happened." The aspirant told him the story: "I was going to the market when a man stopped me and said that a mad elephant was coming my way, so I should run for my life. I thought: "How can a Brahman harm another Brahman; how can a body of water harm another body of water?" After listening to the whole story, Paramahamsaji simply said, "You forgot that the person who warned you was also Brahman. You should have listened to him."

Well, this is a story which shows that our minds tend to become so linear and logical that we can pretend to be what we are not and believe in that pretence. Vedanta has been understood as this kind of a system by many, but actually it is not. An attitudinal change has to take place within, in which the limitations of human nature and personality have to be transcended by viveka and vairagya.

Discrimination and non-attachment

Viveka means 'discrimination' and *vairagya* means 'non-attachment'. Non-attachment may not be the correct word usage, but it explains what I am trying to say. The objects are there, but you are not attached to them, nor does the mind cut itself off from them. There is a simple acceptance which is free from attachment. Viveka is discrimination, knowing how to move according to the situation and circumstances. These are the two important aspects of Vedanta: discrimination in life and non-attachment, or acceptance. Through these two qualities, an attitudinal change is brought about in our own perception, in our own mind.

The components of Vedanta, discrimination and non-attachment, when combined with the knowledge of Samkhya, can work wonders encompassing the entire spectrum of human experience from transcendental to gross. Along with Samkhya, the combination of yoga and the effort which we make on a physical level eventually alters and changes the inner level. It is like tying one end of a fifteen foot rope to the handle of a door and holding the other end. The end of the rope which you are holding in your hand represents the physical aspect with which you are connected. The part which is tied to the door handle represents the continuity of consciousness which is connected to the unmanifest, the transcendental dimension over which you have no grip. You are just holding one end of the rope. Physically when you begin to move the rope up and down, what happens? Standing waves are created which travel right up to the end.

So, when a physical system like yoga is combined with Samkhya, the understanding of the complete range of the human spectrum, and with the attitudinal changes prescribed in Vedanta, we can influence the entire range of the human personality, the manifest and also the unmanifest, that which is beyond the range of the unconscious. This is an important aspect which we should consider adopting, implementing and experiencing with our yoga practices. So, in brief, this is the theory and the practice of Vedanta, to overcome the limiting qualities of life and to have a vision of the universal qualities.

85

Bhagavad Gita

Dhyana Yoga (Part III)

MAY 6, 1994

In order to connect the outer life with the inner life, it is imperative that we become observant and aware of the inter-action between karma and consciousness. A human being is continuously performing actions and the impressions of those actions are being received by the consciousness. It is the mismanagement of the impressions in the field of consciousness, which creates inner conflict and dissipation. The dissipated states of mind are a symptom of this disharmony between the external and the internal states of action, interaction and awareness. This has to be observed by gaining knowledge of the different dimensions in which one experiences and performs action.

Jnana and bodha

Knowledge is known as *jnana*. Initially knowledge becomes an intellectual process: analysing and understanding through the mind, through the intellect. When we get caught up in the analysis of what is happening within the internal and external environment, that is simply a state of mental gymnastics. This is a handicap of our personality, because we tend to get caught up in the linear, intellectual analysis. There is always the expectation that we have to go from point A to point B in order to complete the level of understanding. Upon reaching point B, we have to progress further to points

C and D. This linear perception, or expectation, does not allow our nature and mind to experience what is happening in the subtle levels.

This is where the discipline of yoga comes in. It develops the awareness of the linear thinking, while training the mind and consciousness to become observant of the subtle influences and areas of the deeper consciousness. This discipline eventually leads to bodha, realisation. The word buddha, with which we are familiar, is derived from this word bodha. *Bodha* means 'realising internally', 'knowing experientially'. *Buddha* means 'the realised one', 'the enlightened one', who has come to know the process experientially and not intellectually.

So, jnana, which is knowledge, culminates in bodha, which can be translated as 'wisdom', although wisdom is a very inaccurate translation of the word bodha. In this process we have to deal with two aspects: firstly, knowledge of the interaction between the senses and consciousness, and secondly, conversion of that knowledge from an intellectual to an experiential understanding. This is where the effort has to be made in meditation, in dhyana yoga. Until we reach this point, dhyana or meditation can never be complete.

Drashta—the witness

The process of observation, the *drashta* or *sakshi*, has to be awakened within the aspirant. Literally, we have taken drashta to be a person who is constantly observing what is happening. Here we find a peculiar state of mind. Who becomes the drashta, the seer, the observer? One part of the mind is dissipated and likes to go out to the realm of sensory experience. This is the largest part of the mind. About ninety percent of the human consciousness tends to be totally extrovert, to identify with the senses and the objects which represent name, form and idea.

It is difficult for us to identify with something which cannot be named, to understand something which has no form, to realise something which is beyond a conditioned idea. This is just a small example of how the external mind,

87

or the impure mind, latches on to an object by way of identifying that object either as a name, a form or an idea. When we try to awaken the drashta, the aspect of the seer within, then we have to begin to work with the ten percent of the mind which is not externalised. This is the part of the mind which is not attracted to the world of object, name, form and idea, and which does not desire an attachment with the manifest dimension.

So, the aim of yogic practices, according to the *Yoga Sutras* of Patanjali, is to work through this ninety percent of the mind, which has been defined as the *vrittis*, the outgoing nature, the currents and movements within the mind. When we know what the vrittis are and how the mind functions in relation to the senses and sensory objects, then we come to the point of serenity, where one aspect is stable. When there is no dissipation or distraction, then the seer is awakened. In the outgoing ninety percent of the mind, intellectual knowledge in the form of linear thinking, linear acceptance and linear recognition, is predominant. In the remaining ten percent of mind, bodha, experiential knowledge, is active.

Realisation

So, the meditative process must combine these two efforts. The first effort is knowing the interaction of the senses and the second effort is coming to the state of serenity. When these two are combined, the interplay of the senses with consciousness, and the state of serenity, then realisation takes place. In this way, the concept of realisation is simple to understand: knowing the interplay of the senses and consciousness, and finding the state of serenity within. However, this is actually quite difficult, because in the process of meditation, one has to make an effort to go beyond that linear, analytical mode of knowledge.

Therefore, Lord Krishna has been quite firm in saying: "Remain self-disciplined and serene in the awareness of duality, the opposites." This has also been the statement of all the yogas and the masters who have come to this realisation.

We know the opposites quite well; the swing of the pendulum from one side to the other, from pleasure to pain, satisfaction to dissatisfaction, craving to fulfilment. This is the knowledge of the opposites. The knowledge of the opposing poles of the personality can be achieved with a proper combination and understanding of karma and the meditative state of consciousness. One who is able to maintain this awareness through jnana and bodha remains supreme.

Environment for meditation

The Gita also speaks on the practical aspect of how to attain this knowledge, harmony and balance in the interplay between karma and consciousness. It emphasises the environment for meditation in two different ways. Firstly solitude, meaning to live alone, and secondly, knowing when to apply the brakes in life. These two aspects are quite important. Solitude here, does not mean isolation from the external environment, leaving the hustle and bustle of the city and going to a calm, quiet place in the forest, jungle or mountains. Rather, it should be understood as a state of mind and personality, where the aspirant, the sadhaka, remains unaffected by the interplay of the mind.

Everything exists within the mind. Recognition of that nature of mind which identifies with the world and the senses and also with the serenity of the self is known in yoga as solitude, the observation and balancing of the mind. This internal environment is necessary and can be attained by learning and perfecting the states of pratyahara and dharana. The second point is learning to apply the brakes. A driver must know when to apply the brakes. Brakes are a very important part of the car. Just as a driver knows when to apply the brakes by observing the situation, in the same way, one should be aware of the environment which influences the mind and consciousness. That is how the mind has to be trained in pratyahara and dharana.

Even in our personality, we cannot take things for granted, because we do not know what kind of samskaras or karmas exist within us. Our basic philosophy in life contradicts our

89

desires, and our desires contradict our actions. There is no compatibility between the three, and one has to become aware of all the three simultaneously. Actions are the externalised movement of body and mind in all its glory. The senses, brain, emotions, feelings, thought processes, ambitions, the entire spectrum of human nature which interacts with the world, is part of the action belonging to the self. Desires are different. Desires are aspirations which are influenced by the ego, the 'I' identity, or by external factors in the the environment.

Our basic philosophy in life totally opposes the karmas and the desires. So, it is in this area that we have to fully extend our senses, and the extension of the senses is an aspect of pratyahara. In pratyahara, one has to withdraw the senses from outside, but this withdrawal cannot take place until we are aware of where the senses are attached. We get in a boat which is tied to the jetty. In order to move the boat away from the jetty, first we have to undo the rope. Undoing the rope is more important than actually starting the engine and moving away. In the same way, pratyahara emphasises the need to know the areas to which the mind and senses have attached themselves in the manifest world. Only then can we release the knots and move forward. The release of these knots and the effort to allow the boat to move freely is known as the extension of the senses before withdrawal.

Attaining harmony and serenity

In the Gita, the method that has been described to attain this harmony between dhyana and karma is threefold: (i) become one-pointed, (ii) channelise the thoughts, and (iii) channelise the senses. The aim of this channelling is to obtain inner purification. When one is going through the process of channelling, one has to be serene and fearless. One must know how to manage the fears and insecurities that come up.

So, let us look at these three components. One-pointedness means focusing the mind in order to stop the dissipation and distraction which prevents the mind from experiencing its own serene nature. One has to discipline, educate and train the mind to become one-pointed. How does one become one-pointed? This is achieved by channelling the thoughts, the senses, the sensory inputs, the emotional inputs, the behaviour, the entire range of mental activity, which is the external manifestation of the mind, with the aim of obtaining inner purification.

There is a beautiful statement in the Gita which says that a yogi performs karma through the mind, intellect, speech and interaction, with only one objective: to obtain inner purification. Awareness of the activities of the mind, of the intellect, of the normal interactions, and channelling them, helps one to attain purification.

In this process, as we go deeper into our nature, into our subconscious and unconscious dimensions, many insecurities and fears come up, which are so strong and powerful, in a negative way, that they can shake even the most stable personality. The opposing forces, the good qualities, also manifest and they are so strong and powerful that they can bind the mind in another kind of conditioning. If one begins to experience an immense love in meditation, which is manifesting from the deeper mind, that positive quality also holds the entire attention fixed on the experience of love. So, the positive and the negative qualities both come up.

The Gita says, "Be serene when the positive qualities come up and be fearless when the negative qualities come up." Serenity at the time of experiencing the positive qualities makes one aware of either the limited nature of the positive qualities, or their magnetic force which pulls the mind in another direction and diverts it from the aim of self-purification. We all know how the negative qualities function and how we react to them. So, serenity and fearlessness should be obtained.

Therefore, the sixth verse states:

Serene and fearless, maintaining Brahmacharya,
be firm in contemplation of the supreme.
Thus the yogi attains Shantih and Nirvana.

91

Brahmacharya

One has to be firm in contemplation of the supreme and this is known as brahmacharya. In this context, brahmacharya does not mean celibacy. *Brahmacharya* means 'one who is established in the nature of the expanding consciousness'. This word has been derived from the word brahman. Brahman does not mean divinity or God. *Brahman* means the 'expanding consciousness', the continuity of consciousness, without division, without demarcation. *Acharya* means 'living that state', 'experiencing that state', that is, the contemplation of the supreme. This means that, despite the attraction of the positive qualities and the repulsion of the negative qualities, one has to be firm in the aim of meditation. Meditation has been described here as being firm in the contemplation of the supreme, thus attaining shantih and nirvana.

Shantih means 'peace'. Here it refers to the stopping of the dissipated nature of the mind, to the conflicts. Then peace or serenity is experienced on the conscious, subconscious and unconscious levels at the same time. The state of passive acceptance and observation is shantih, peace. *Nirvana* is going beyond or rising above the ground level of consciousness. When we are at ground level, our vision is limited. If we go up to the top of a one hundred storey building, our vision, our perspective changes. The visual experience on the ground floor is different to that on the hundredth floor. So, rising above the normal conditioning of life and obtaining a different vision is known as nirvana.

The aim of a yoga aspirant

The yogas speak of freedom, of transcending or overcoming the limited, expressed, manifest nature. They speak of overcoming conflict, pain and suffering; of understanding attraction and repulsion to the manifest world. The different approaches can sometimes separate or isolate an individual from the realities of the external world. There may be pain, conflict or suffering, but the aspirant creates his own space in which there is peace and tranquillity, and in this way, prevents the external reality from altering his state of consciousness.

In this process, even samadhi seems to be a very individual experience: something which I am feeling, which I am experiencing, that no one else is feeling or helping me to experience, that aspect of universality which I have or feel deep within. Even 'I', as the experiencer of samadhi, am not able to express that to another person. When yoga becomes an individualistic experience, the 'I', which is trying to negate itself, becomes even more powerful than before. We are trying to remove that notion of 'I' identity, of the ego identity, but unfortunately, in the higher states of dhyana and samadhi, that 'I' becomes even more powerful.

Yoga is a technique and a system which has to accommodate itself as per the need and limitation of every individual. The mentality and the personality of an individual expresses itself in different ways, according to the depth of the yogic practices. So, what should be the actual aim of the aspirant who is practising yoga? This is a big question mark. We have been exposed to certain practices of yoga, but we have not been able to convert that individual experience into a universal experience which is supported and understood by others, because we have not allowed that experience to alter our lifestyle. This is the key to understanding how our efforts can make yoga either an individual experience or a universal experience.

Changing the lifestyle does not mean that you renounce the world. It means that you allow the benefits of the yogic system which you are practising to alter your external perceptions. When your external perceptions and interactions are positively and constructively influenced by the yogic practices, then that change in your personality begins to reach outwards.

There are two approaches which the yoga practitioner eventually experiences in life. The first is an inward approach and the second is an outgoing approach. We tend to think of that inward approach as the final state, going to the source of being. On this inward journey, there is isolation from the external environment and the manifest prakriti. When this inward movement of consciousness is harmonised with the external influences, altering the natural pattern of mind and consciousness, then creativity starts to express itself externally and spiritual life begins.

At this point the lifestyle changes, the behaviour changes, the mentality changes, the entire dimension of human interaction and experience undergoes a drastic change. It is this change that we are actually looking for in our own practices of yoga: the conversion of our nature from a tamasic state to a sattwic state of being. It is the process of becoming established in this state of being that has been clearly defined in the Bhagavad Gita. So, the message that I want to give you all as sadhakas and as aspirants, is to combine the meditative awareness with the normal activities of the body and mind. When you are able to do this, then you will be well ahead in your spiritual journey.

Tantra

MAY 6, 1994

Most of us have evolved our ideas about Tantra from different sources and from Paramahamsaji's discussions. One important aspect which we have adopted is acceptance within the tantric lifestyle. This acceptance is free of guilt. Learning to accept life and not feeling guilty about how we have experienced it, that is the basic theory of Tantra to which we have been exposed. There are many aspects of Tantra and there is a theory which one must understand before trying to incorporate or understand the practicality of Tantra.

Three components of Tantra

The three components of Tantra are: Shiva, Shakti and jiva. *Jiva* is the individual person or identity. *Shiva* is the consciousness, the controller, and *Shakti* is the agent through which consciousness can act. The individual, or the jiva, is in the state of *tamas*, inertia; this is the key concept of Tantra. Shiva is also known as *pati*, or master. Shakti is the agent who controls the manifest nature, the individual being. Jiva is the instinctive person, living, working, and interacting in the realm of Shakti.

A simple analogy can be given in order to help you to understand this concept. The individual being is like a dog on a leash which is being held by the master. They are out on a walk. While the master, who is holding the leash,

95

continues to walk along a straight path, the dog runs here and there sniffing and barking at different things, wagging his tail and running backwards and forwards. The dog and the master are two different entities. The master is walking the path that he wants to walk and he leads the dog with the help of the leash. The leash is Shakti. The dog is the jiva, or individual being, who tries to chase stray cats and the tyres of passing cars. He tries to find a bush to lift one leg up against. He pulls the master here and there, barks at people and other dogs, and is very much involved in his own expression and enjoyment of life.

It is exactly in this way that Tantra views Shiva, Shakti and jiva. According to Tantra, the individual who is bound by the leash of Shakti is in the state of tamas or ignorance and does not know what bondage or freedom means. For the individual or for a dog, freedom is simply the loosening or removal of the leash, but this does not change the activity or the personality of the jiva or of the dog in any way. It continues to do the same things without the leash. When the dog is running around without the leash, the master is doing his own thing. We can apply this analogy to ourselves in order to understand our own lives. We are in the state of doghood. We might have a body and mind which make us different to the dog, but in the scheme of creation, we are still at that instinctive level, looking for that kind of expression, according to our nature.

In order to become disciplined, the individual being, or jiva, has to be bound by the leash of Shakti. When a well-trained dog wants to go out, he takes the leash in his mouth and shows it to the master, who then knows that the dog is ready to go out for a walk. Whenever the master picks up the leash, the dog thinks that he is going for a walk. So, there is a recognition of the leash as something which makes the dog act and behave in a certain way. When that recognition of Shakti takes place within us, then we begin to act and behave in a certain way, with more optimism, "I am going to go for a walk with my master." So it is the instinctive nature of the individual, who is in a tamasic state, that has to be altered, changed, transformed and transcended.

96

Pashu bhava—state of instinct

Keeping this idea in mind, the Tantras have described progressive stages in the development of the human mind or personality which are known as *bhavas*, 'states'. The state of instinct is known as *pashu bhava*. Here the individual craves pleasures in the tamasic state. Our own cravings, wants and desires are tamasic by nature and directed towards the fulfilment of certain aspirations and ambitions. We humans have something which helps us evolve beyond the instinctive nature, the tamasic nature, which is known as awareness. Tantra aims at using the faculty of awareness in order to elevate the mind and nature.

This awareness makes an attempt to override the component of guilt which arises due to mental conflict. When there is a clash between ambition and the philosophical aspiration, then guilt comes forward. Not everyone is aware of the internal, philosophical, personal concept of spirituality. There is an unconscious acceptance of it from which comes the recognition of right and wrong, what is just and unjust. We know that something should not be done, yet still it is done. We know that an action is wrong, yet situations arise in such a way that we still do it, and a feeling arises from within which is the aspect of guilt.

Managing this aspect of inner conflict between the spiritual aspiration, the ambition and the performance of action, is achieved through awareness. This awareness is not only a recognition of what is happening; it also takes the form of a meditative process. It helps us to adjust with the changes that are happening, and to learn how to adjust when the tranquillity of the mind and inner nature are disturbed, so that some form of mental clarity is retained. This clarity helps us to evolve, and it is the component of awareness which helps overcome the aspect of tamas.

Veera bhava—the warrior state

When the tamasic nature is somehow managed, then comes the second state or bhava, known as the *veera bhava*, the state of the warrior. In the first state of tamas, the instinctive

97

state or the pashu state, we are generally not aware of the qualities or the strengths that are within. Even if we are aware, we do not know how to use those qualities or strengths positively, constructively or creatively. So, after going through this process of meditative awareness and coming to the state of warrior mentality, the veera bhava, there is an equal recognition of the strengths and the weaknesses within. With this recognition, it is possible to make an adjustment between the two which results in the fine tuning of the personality. When we are able to fine tune our rajasic nature, then the sattwic state, which is known as *divya bhava*, the divine state is experienced. So, the aim of Tantra is to take one from the tamasic to the sattwic state.

Moving from tamas to sattwa

Therefore, the understanding of the tantric concept in relation to one's life, needs to be given a different dimension. Initially, we have understood that in the process of Tantra, all of our interactions, behaviour and thoughts are acceptable. Once this broad acceptance has become a part of our mentality and lifestyle, by which we view events, circumstances, people and situations, then we can begin to work on ourselves.

It is like trying to maintain our space in a noisy room. What do we do? First there is awareness of the noises in the room, then there is recognition and adjustment. After that we say, "I want to maintain my space without being disturbed, affected or influenced by the noises." So, we concentrate on our own internal space and make an effort not to be disturbed. This broad recognition takes place outside and an adjustment takes place inside. Once that adjustment has taken place, we are then able to maintain the tranquillity and harmony within our own mind and nature. The state of peace which is experienced at that time, where there is no dissipation of any sort, is sattwa. In this context, noise or the external environment is tamas. Being aware and wanting to maintain our own space is rajas, and finding tranquillity and harmony in that space is sattwa. This is the process of Tantra, in a broad sense.

Management of insecurities

As we go deeper into the practices of Tantra, there are different aspects which have to be considered. We have covered two of these aspects: alert meditation and recognition of the environment in which we live. Next we should consider the four instinctive aspects to which our life is subject. The first is our insecurity and fear which we constantly project onto other people regardless of whether or not they want to know about them. Most of the time other people are not interested because they have their own problems and difficulties, but we want to have that interactive outlet. This aspect can easily be controlled or channelled through a process of discrimination and detachment. If the mind and consciousness are clear, and the priorities are defined, then everything falls into place. So, in order to overcome fear and insecurity, Tantra says: Define the priorities; have a direction, an aim, and an instrument or tool by which you can help yourself in this state. Know that this is the state and these are the tools: discrimination and detachment.

Maithuna—the primal urge

Another aspect which manifests very strongly in our life is the primal urge which is known in Tantra as *maithuna*. Manifestation of this instinctive nature has come down to us through the generations from our original father who happened to be God himself. God was feeling lonely up at the top and he had the desire to become many. It is this desire that represents the instinctive nature of the human being. It is not the sexual act which represents the original desire, it is the wish to become many. This wish originally came from God right down to us; it is in our DNA.

Management of this powerful instinct and converting it into a force to sublimate the mind takes place through the process of jnana yoga, where one is taught to see and recognise the passions within. When recognition of passion takes place, the self is seen as a separate entity to the actions and senses. Right now, there is identification of the self with the actions and senses. When observation of passion takes

99

place, there is separation of the self as the pure entity from the actions and senses which are directing the flow of consciousness. In jnana yoga, dispassion is attained by following a meditative process.

Ahara—craving for satisfaction

The third aspect is *ahara*, craving for personal satisfaction. This is something which is deeply rooted in the depths of the unconscious. When people are frustrated, anxious, depressed or tense, they eat constantly. They begin to grow and expand in every direction. This is the urge to find contentment and satisfaction in life, especially in states of anxiety and depression, which we are not able to work on at the conscious level. This craving manifests in the form of an instinct. I am suffering from anxiety, nervous tension or depression, so I go to the fridge and search for some satisfaction.

This search for satisfaction is distorted in our lives. The search for mental satisfaction can manifest as something physical, because there is no recognition of it. We suffer mentally, but we overload the body. We suffer emotionally, but we overload our intellect. We suffer spiritually, but we overload the family environment. This is ahara, the unconscious and uncontrolled overloading of the self with things that are not really necessary. Although there is no recognition of the search for satisfaction, there has to be an outlet. What is the simplest outlet? We recognise the body and the body is easy to satisfy. In order to control this imbalance, a method of self-observation has to be adopted by which we are able to harmonise the mind and awaken and experience contentment in all the dimensions of our being.

Nidra—areas of blockage

Nidra is the fourth aspect. *Nidra* generally means sleep, but in the tantric context, it means a state of blocking out. When we do not want to recognise something consciously, we block it out. In the state of blocking it, we create a limitation within upon which our life revolves. For example, if we do not want to see what is happening on the other side of a big room, we just close the partitions. This act of closing the partitions limits our vision, perception and cognition, which is generally what happens in nidra. We block out the reality and live in our own world. Living in our own world without any forward vision is known as nidra. In this context, nidra does not mean lying down, going to sleep and waking up in the morning. That is another aspect altogether.

There are areas in our life where we definitely experience nidra, the block. The three main areas of nidra are: (i) in the head, (ii) in the heart and (iii) in the unconscious, where the cognitive faculties limit themselves. In the unconscious state, nidra is generally experienced as a total blackout of the senses, similar to sleep at night. There are some people who sleep very deeply, and I used to be one of them. I used to sleep so deeply that I could have been carried from Australia to Timbuktoo without even knowing it. Fortunately, I have overcome that tendency and now my sleep is like dog's sleep. With the slightest noise, one eye opens—what's that?—and within a moment I am back again into deep oblivion.

When nidra relates to the unconscious field, it is definitely a vritti. The *Yoga Sutras* define the five vrittis as follows: (i) *pramana*, cognition; (ii) *viparyaya*, false knowledge; (iii) *vikalpa*, conflict; (iv) *nidra*, sleep, and (v) *smriti*, memory. The nidra which is referred to in the *Yoga Sutras* relates to the unconscious field, governing the area between mooladhara and manipura. Another area of nidra or blockage is the heart region, between manipura and vishuddhi. When we are unable to clear the blockage in this area, suppression takes place, which acts like a timebomb.

Suddenly, there is an explosion, and that explosion is shattering. If you are emotionally sensitive, your life can be shattered. However, if you are balanced, then it makes no difference. It is only a big bang which deafens your ears for a few moments; it does not blow you to bits. This is why Tantra says to avoid suppression, because the heart area is very sensitive. The emotions which govern the heart are raw energy. They are not transformed energy; they have not gone through the different transformers. The emotions are

101

pure, raw energy which cannot be channelled or controlled through logic and intellect. This raw energy is there and it can only be channelled through bhakti. This is the process as described by Tantra.

The third area of blockage is between vishuddhi and sahasrara, within the field of consciousness itself. In the external sense, it would be blockage of the logical or analytical aspect which is generally termed as cloudiness of the mind, unclear thoughts and irrational actions. At a deeper level, it relates to not being able to come to terms with oneself. When one is not able to come to terms with oneself, new karmas and samskaras develop.

In Tantra, an effort is made to overcome these four instinctive aspects of our nature: bhaya, ahara, maithuna and nidra, by harmonising the inner being and removing the three blocks. This is a broad description of the tantric system. As spiritual aspirants, our practice must incorporate the components of Tantra, Yoga, Samkhya, and Vedanta.

An Integrated
Understanding

In the course of our life, the different experiences that we gain become an aid to understanding the process of our development and making us aware of our interactions. If we wish to pursue the yogic path, there has to be a recognition of our own performance in the multi-dimensional life that we lead.

In order to harmonise this multi-dimensional life, there has to be an understanding of the karmic aspect, the emotional aspect, the intellectual aspect and the psychic aspect. These are the four areas in which we are able to express our nature.

The performance of karma should not be isolated from the aim of awakening the consciousness. The emotions should not be isolated from the aim of attaining inner purity. The intellect should not be isolated from the aim of developing a broad vision of life. The psyche should not be isolated from the aim of experiencing transcendental awareness. I have mentioned before that Paramahamsaji was asked whether or not it is possible to attain realisation in one lifetime. He replied, "No, it is not possible, because realisation is a transcendental state, and we, as individuals, are surrounded by our limited nature which is not transcendental."

Making an effort
    In order to experience the transcendental consciousness, it is necessary to have a transcendental brain and mind. The

103

effort that we make in life, by following different practices, systems and techniques, should be directed towards changing the present state of brain and mind. The aim should be to make the human personality transcendental. There has to be some form of co-ordination in this process. We can have a plate of good food in front of us, but in order to feel satisfied, to feel the fullness in the stomach, we have to use the hands to bring the food to the mouth, then we have to chew the food and swallow it. Just looking at the food and thinking, "I am being filled", is not enough. Just by thinking about food, one cannot overcome hunger.

So, it is the process and the effort that we make which are important. We have to concentrate upon the effort. Therefore, a good combination of sadhana must be adopted in life which can fulfil the needs of the different aspects of the human personality. Along with the physical practices and the external involvement in the world, we can incorporate some aspects of bhakti yoga and karma yoga. There should be an integration of the different sadhanas in relation to the body, brain, mind, emotions and the intellect. When this integrated approach has been adopted, there should also be clarity of the spiritual direction; this is very important.

What is clarity in the spiritual direction? The drive or aim to attain realisation is a very broad concept. To be more than what we are at present is a very broad concept. It is like saying, "I want to be perfect and for me perfection means this." The moment we say it, we are conditioning that perfection. How can we ever decide what perfection is? We cannot, because the moment we move from one stage to the next, the idea and the experience of perfection take on a different dimension. So, we cannot define perfection, and in the same way, we cannot define the state of realisation or transcendence. We can look at it from a very simplistic point of view. Growing up is the simplest way of describing transcendence. Attaining emotional, intellectual and psychic maturity is something that we cannot really understand.

Attachment

One day a man came to me in Munger and began to cry saying, "I have worked hard in order to have a good life. I have tried to be happy and satisfied, but I have seen many things crumble around me. Now, towards the end of my life, I feel that I have not gained anything. I have lost my job. My family is separated. My children have grown up and do not live with me any more. I feel isolated and left behind." He was describing all the usual things that can happen to a person. I tried to give him a satisfactory answer, but he was still feeling sad for the things that he had lost.

When he left the room, he saw some children playing a game outside in the garden. While they were playing, one leg of a clay toy broke and the child to whom it belonged began to cry. The man went straight to the child and comforted her saying, "Look, it is only a toy. Do not be attached to it. You can always get another one." I was watching this interaction from the verandah of my room. After the man said this, I called him back and asked him to apply this same principle to himself.

When we see something objectively, in which we are not involved, then we are able to remain detached and guide the other person. However, when attachment is felt in the form of joy or frustration, there is very deep karmic, emotional, intellectual and psychic involvement. In this state, we tend to lose our clarity of mind. We get sucked further into a state of anxiety and inner conflict, and make things more complicated than they actually are.

Diseases are not that much of a problem. One can have asthma, diabetes, AIDS, cancer, arthritis, stomach problems or hypertension. One can generally find a way to manage these different illnesses. However, there is one disease known as FIDS, which has no cure. An effort can be made to cure cancer, AIDS, hypertension or diabetes, but FIDS is a disease which has no cure, because there is no recognition of this disease. FIDS means Fear Induced Disease Syndrome. We are constantly looking for some way to identify our problems, physically, emotionally, intellectually, but the real cause cannot be rationalised in the outer dimension, and a similar thing occurs on the inner level as well.

Clarity of aim and direction

When we think of realisation, we create an aim which is composed of different symbols. Realisation of what? God, spirit, Self, higher consciousness or any other name we want to use. This idea in our mind takes a form which we move towards. When this idea has been given a particular name, form and attribute, then there is an emotional and mental identification with that concept or idea. So, in this process, we still remain in the field of our mind. The actual aspect of realisation is this process of growing up, maturing and transcending, where we go beyond the self-created concepts and ideas and develop a broader vision.

This is something which is hard to incorporate in our life, because the structure is there only up to a point. Beyond that, there is nothing, no structure; that is *nirakara*, the formless state. In the structure that we follow, we go through the process of becoming. When we become that, when we begin to experience the state of being and not becoming, then every atom, every pore, every hair of the body, experiences that reality, not just the emotions and intellect. When every atom of the body experiences that reality, then it means our nature has become transcendental.

In our own life, we need to give ourselves a clear aim which can help us evolve from this limited structure of personality. In order to find this clear aim, along with the practices of yoga, the first practice should be of Tantra: recognition of the two aspects of consciousness and energy. Then we should apply the Samkhya system: furthering the awareness of the subtle nature of consciousness and energy. Once this is attained, we should apply the Vedanta system: experiencing the unifying factor, the force which links the individual with the higher Self. This concept is not limited to the individual only, but extends to the entire world.

So, during this week, I have presented two important concepts. First, there must be a proper integration of the

106

systems of Yoga, Tantra, Samkhya and Vedanta. The process involves the aspects of discrimination, non-attachment and recognition of the subtleties of the personality. The second concept is moving from the rajasic and tamasic states to a state where sattwa is experienced. This is the direction in which we have to develop.

PART TWO

Discourses during the
Karma Sannyasa Week

Yoga and Spiritual Life

MAY 10, 1994

We are here this week to learn about yoga and spiritual life. The way I have experienced yoga and come to know about spiritual life is what you are going to learn from me. I learned yoga and developed my concept of spiritual life after coming into contact with my master and guru, Paramahamsa Satyananda. The yoga that he taught was not hatha yoga, raja yoga, karma yoga, bhakti yoga, jnana yoga, kriya yoga or kundalini yoga. Rather, he taught the yoga of common sense. In this common sense yoga, every aspect of yoga was included, from the physical to the spiritual. This combination of yogas has to be understood in terms of our own growth and evolution in life. Generally, we tend to identify more with the body than with the mind or the spirit, because the body is physically perceived as an object. Therefore, we have developed the aspects of hatha and raja yoga, and incorporated them into our lifestyle, in the form of an external, physical discipline.

In-depth study of the theories of hatha yoga and raja yoga shows that they cover more than just the physical aspect of human nature; they also deal with the subtle aspect of the personality. Hatha yoga aims at harmonising the pranic structure, the flow of pranas within the physiological systems. It harmonises the body, brain, prana and mind, in order to experience the evolution of these different levels. Raja yoga

111

provides a structure of discipline in the psychic body. It is these two aspects of yoga which seventy per cent of the people who practise yoga around the world have accepted and adopted. Paramahamsaji has clearly taught that, along with an awareness of the external structure, there should also be an in-depth awareness of the subtle, psychic structure, so that a proper combination of the qualities of head, heart and hand can take place. It is this combination which starts our quest into spiritual life. This point is often misunderstood.

Spirituality

What is spirituality? Spirituality is regarded as awareness of the spiritual dimension. The concept which we have evolved of the spiritual dimension is neither specific nor understood. If you ask me, "What is spirit?" I will not be able to give an answer, because spirit is a state of experience which transcends name, form, concept, time and space. How can we understand or experience something which is not comprehensible to the present state of mind? Therefore, spirituality is seen in the form of an awakening of certain faculties in life which make us more centred, balanced and aware of our own internal and external expressions and interactions. The concept of spirituality which develops is that of universal awareness which gives us a broader vision of life and of the cosmos in which we live, of the individual self and of a speculative, unknown, higher being.

However, yoga has a different idea about this. Yoga says that once you are able to control the subtle expressions and experiences of your nature, the gunas and Prakriti, then you can awaken the aspect of *drashta*. It is this drashta, the seer or witness, which ultimately experiences the source of light within, the undecaying nature and the inner consciousness. According to yoga, this is not just a concept, but a reality, which can be experienced by recognising and working with the different levels of human nature of which the body, the mind, the gunas, the qualities and the attributes of life, are just parts. Paramahamsaji has given us an understanding of yoga from a practical viewpoint. It is a continuous process of

112

experiencing, realising and evolving, which does not stop with meditation, kriya yoga, the awakening of kundalini or visions of divine beings.

With this concept of experiencing, realising and evolving, we are going to look into yoga and spiritual life. We should forget about the practices we are accustomed to, but continue to practise something in order to experience the higher dimension of human consciousness. The example which was given to me in order to understand the process of yoga and spiritual life is the lifestyle of Paramahamsaji. In him I can see a constant evolution of yoga, I can see a continuous experience of spirit. What did yoga mean to Paramahamsaji? For him, yoga was not the end but the means to transcend, to sublimate the tattwas of the body, brain and mind.

Developing awareness

The practices of asana, pranayama, mudra, bandha, kriya, kundalini, mantra, nada, laya and the other yogas, simply guide the aspirant through a specific process of becoming aware. This process of becoming aware is the most important aspect of yoga. The awareness is an integral part of human consciousness. Generally, people think that it is awareness and consciousness which evolve, but that is wrong. Consciousness does not evolve. It is a state of being which is there. It is like sitting in a boat, in the middle of the ocean, and being aware of the body of water for as far as the eyes can see, and thinking that is the entire span of the ocean.

There is a story of a frog who decided to see the world. He was hitch-hiking inland from the ocean. During his travels he fell down a well, where he met another frog, who had never been outside the well. After the preliminaries were over, the well frog asked, "Where have you come from?" The ocean frog said, "I have come from the ocean." The well frog asked, "How big is your ocean?" The ocean frog said, "It is huge. I cannot express how big it is." The well frog went to one corner of the well, took a big leap and said, "Is the ocean this big?" The ocean frog said, "No, it is much bigger." The well frog went back to his starting point, took a deep breath

113

and made a bigger leap. Then very proudly he asked, "Is the ocean this big?" The ocean frog said, "No, it is much bigger than that." The well frog thought for a moment and said, "Anything bigger than where I live does not exist. You are not telling me the truth."

That is how we express our nature also. The reality in which we live is the entire universe for us. When we are exposed to or told about a different reality, then it is either speculative, conceptual or non-existent. We cannot conceive of a reality which is different from the one to which we are accustomed therefore experiencing the totality of consciousness is difficult for us. We have the concept of transcendental consciousness, but due to the internal barriers of samskaras and karmas which manifest very strongly, sometimes we begin to doubt whether we are on the right track, or if it is possible to attain that transcendental awareness in this lifetime. These doubts arise because our intellect tries to understand and compartmentalise that which cannot be categorised, according to the conditioning of our consciousness, in the world of Prakriti, the manifest reality.

Yoga adopts a different method. It says, perform an action and meditate upon it. For example, while practising asana, pranayama or meditation, be in a meditative state and experience it. This meditative state is the most important aspect of yoga. The meditative state means continuous awareness of the actions and interactions which are going on in the body, mind, senses, emotions and feelings. The entire human nature is involved. When we practise different meditation techniques, this is not the meditative process of consciousness. The practices of pratyahara, dharana and dhyana are just techniques which follow a linear direction. There is no awareness of what is transpiring in the subtle and psychic levels of our personality.

For example, in the practice of antar mouna, we sit down and begin to witness the thoughts. We go through the different stages of seeing the thoughts, recognising them, trying to stop them and making the mind blank. In this process, we try to go to the source of the thoughts. If we experience *shoonya* or momentary blankness of mind, then we feel that our practice of antar mouna was perfect. We have achieved what we wanted to achieve. However, this has not taken us anywhere. It has only shown us one compartment of the mind, the thought process. By this practice, we were able to momentarily stop the activity of the thoughts and experience shoonya, the state of thoughtlessness, but that state is not permanent.

When we come out of that meditative practice, again we are confronted by the same conflicts, the same nature, the same mentality, and the same environment where we become agitated. The stress, the tension, the anxiety is experienced again. So, for many people, meditation becomes a process of escaping from the external realities, for maybe five or ten minutes, half an hour or one hour, but this is not meditation. I am giving you this example in order to point out that meditation is something else. Development of a meditative attitude in the performance of action is the real thing.

The meditative attitude

Actions are not only physical. Actions are performed by the mind, senses, feelings, intellect, ego, rationality and psyche. Everything that happens to us in this life is subject to the experiences of action and reaction. The meditative attitude means finding that inner stability and strength, where the actions and reactions are witnessed. That is the concept of drashta. Those of you who have studied the *Yoga Sutras* of Patanjali will be aware of the statement in the third sutra: *Tada drastuh swarupe avasthanam.* 'Then the seer is established in his own nature'.

The manifest nature is not the real nature. What you write on a piece of paper does not reflect the totality of your concept. You might try to write a book and go through the laborious process of putting down in black and white the concepts or ideas which have evolved in the subtle level of your personality. That laborious process of writing words down only represents one aspect of the ongoing mental process. It does not represent the totality of mind or the

115

mental concept which has evolved. In the same way, the manifest nature which we experience through the entire personality, the senses and the ego, the intellect and the emotions, simply represents one state, an extension of the consciousness which is huge and transcendental.

An artist can never put all his ideas onto one canvas. Each and every canvas is a different expression of those ideas. A yogi can never experience the totality of consciousness in one glimpse. A human being can never understand the entire reality in one thought. So, it is the awareness which has to evolve from the most basic and fundamental level to the most sublime and transcendental level. In this process, the vision of life, the entire interactive process of life, has to be seen. This is the aim of yoga: to see the interactive process of life in the physical, mental and psychic realms, and to be in a continuous meditative state where there is constant observation and awareness. Once we are able to reach this stage of yoga, then the journey into spiritual life begins.

Importance of an integrated sadhana

Coming to this state from our level in life, through the practices of yoga, is a very lengthy process. It involves a lot of determination, effort and sadhana. Sadhana has to be properly analysed. Sometimes people come to me and say, "I have been practising the same techniques for the last fifteen years. What should I do next?" In sadhana, there has to be a good integration of the different aspects of life along with yoga. In the physical aspect, there are the practices of asana and pranayama, combined with bandha, mudra, relaxation and specific meditation, starting from the first step and gradually evolving.

Sadhana is not just something to be done for half an hour in the morning or half an hour at night. Eventually it has to become part of the entire life. There has to be an awareness of sadhana twenty four hours a day. The moment this change takes place in our normal, mental pattern, we begin to move very fast on the path of sadhana. Along with

116

this external sadhana, there has to be a recognition of some other aspects of human nature which are then incorporated into the sadhana.

During this week, I request all of you to stop whatever sadhana you have been doing, as I wish to take you through an integrated process of sadhana. Our entire day will be part of that ongoing process of sadhana. Certain disciplines help us on that path, so there are some things which you will need to observe.

Mouna—silence

It is important to maintain *mouna*, 'silence'; in the evenings after dinner from 6.00 pm until breakfast time, 6.00 am: twelve hours of total silence. It is not a big effort, because you will be asleep most of the time. While you are awake, with your eyes open, moving about, maintain mouna, silence. Continue your normal activities: making your bed, getting ready to sleep, looking at things, but incorporate the aspect of continued awareness of mouna. Not a single movement of the body should be unconscious or unrecognised. When walking, be aware of how you walk. When thinking, be aware of what you are thinking. When brushing your teeth, be aware of that. When getting into bed, be aware of that. Even when you sleep, be aware that you are sleeping. Try to develop and awaken that aspect of alertness in total silence. That is very important.

Mantra chanting

When you go to bed, do not just go straight to sleep. Sit down or lie down and practise mantra chanting. Chant Gayatri mantra: *Om bhuh bhuvah swaha tat savituh varenyam bhargo devasya dhimahi dhiyo yo nah prachodayat*, twenty four times. After this, practise one mala of Om chanting, with normal breathing during inhalation and verbal chanting of Om during exhalation. Then practise twenty seven rounds of the Mahamrityunjaya mantra: *Om trayambakam yajamahe sugandhim pushti vardhanam urvarukamiva bandhanat mrityoh mukshiya mamritat.*

117

Review the day

Then lie down and review your entire activities of the day from the time you woke up in the morning until the time you went to bed and did your sadhana. What did you do? With whom did you speak? When did you have your breakfast? How did you interact with other people? When were you in a tamasic state of mind? When were you in a rajasic state of mind? When were you in a sattwic state of mind? Go through the whole day and classify all your actions and interactions into these three categories: tamasic, rajasic and sattwic. Once you complete this review, say goodnight to the external world and sleep well.

When you wake up the next morning, before getting out of bed, focus on your eyebrow centre and inhale deeply seven times. With each exhalation, relax yourself. See the entire body, the state of body, then chant Om three times. Concentrate on the vibration of Om. Feel as if it is creating a force field or a pranic field around the body. Take another seven deep breaths and just relax. Then get up and go about your daily business.

The Four Darshanas

(Yoga, Vedanta, Samkhya, Tantra)

MAY 12, 1994

In our spiritual experience, we need to follow four different systems of practice in order to overcome the idea of right and wrong. Generally speaking, right and wrong are the attorneys at law which deal with our life. The entire spectrum of human understanding and acceptance is based on these two opposite principles. Either you accept and what you accept is right, or you reject and what you reject is wrong. These two are powerful forces in our understanding of the self. Initially, we take them to be intellectual concepts which arise out of mental conditioning through the influences of society, culture, family, and our own ideas in the course of life.

According to yoga, it is this aspect of duality which eventually must be isolated from the deep, spiritual realisation. We become aware of this aspect in our own sadhana. Sometimes, during meditation practice, we may experience a state of mind which is very positive, creative, even transcendental. In that state, we may experience identification with our inner self. We may see visions of angels, demi-gods and gods. At the opposite end of the spectrum, we may be confronted by hell, demons and all the negativity. At times like this, we tend to desire the positive experiences more than the negative. We want to have the nice experiences continuously. If we have a bad experience, we reject it and create another mental

119

conditioning to satisfy our mind, such as: "Perhaps this vision is coming because the practice is not right for me; I am going in the wrong direction".

Therefore, according to yoga, we need to isolate and then move away from the mental conditioning of right and wrong. This right and wrong has been described in the yogic tradition as attraction and repulsion. The *Yoga Sutras* clearly state that whenever there is attraction, we will desire pleasure, happiness, contentment, satisfaction and fulfilment. Whenever we encounter rejection, there is bound to be pain, separation, suffering and dejection. This happens to the state of mind which is surrounded by objects of pain and pleasure and that is the world. This is the vedantic concept of yoga. So, in order to attain this inner freedom, along with Yoga, one needs to have an understanding of Samkhya, Vedanta and Tantra. Together these four systems cover the entire range of human life. Yoga represents a quarter, Samkhya another quarter, Tantra the third quarter and Vedanta the last quarter of human development.

Samkhya

In brief, the system of Samkhya makes one aware of the elemental forces that govern the entire personality. We live with the impure mind which belongs to the realm of nature, or shakti, where movement and transformation are taking place, where there is no continuity in any state of perception or in any state of consciousness. That is the realm of energy, the impure mind. The pure mind is the realm of consciousness, the continuity of human perception.

It is like the story of the blind man who has full use of the limbs and the lame man who cannot walk but has full use of the eyes, helping each other to go from one part of the city to the next. The blind man carries the lame man on his shoulders, and the lame man directs the blind man where to move. The lame man who cannot move at all, but has a clear vision of the direction in which they have to go, is the consciousness. The blind man, who cannot see but can move in any direction as guided by the consciousness, is the energy. So, the realm of energy is that of the impure mind and the realm of consciousness is that of the pure mind.

Even in kundalini yoga, this is the concept we come across. What is the awakening of the chakras, the rising of kundalini? The reversal of the manifestation of energy. The downward movement of energy from sahasrara to mooladhara chakra represents growth in the manifest world. The reversal of this process from mooladhara to sahasrara represents the inward movement of energy towards the unmanifest dimension. Samkhya makes us aware of this aspect of life, of the interaction between the forces, between the elements, between the mind and the elements, between the different components of the mind. If we are sincere about restructuring and harmonising our life in all of its dimensions: gross, subtle, causal and transcendental, this awareness is essential. The knowledge of Samkhya combined with the practice of yoga can make us more aware of the interaction of the forces in our personality and enable us to direct these forces in a better way, with greater control over the senses and the mind.

Tantra and Vedanta

The third aspect is Tantra. In brief, Tantra is observation, recognition and acceptance of our lifestyle, nature, patterns of behaviour and mental conditioning. Simultaneously, a system of discipline is created within, which can raise the level of consciousness without provoking insecurity, fear or mental conflict. An understanding of the tantric method is important for the yogic aspirant, in order to develop acceptance of life in its totality.

The fourth aspect is Vedanta, which emphasises the flowering of universal, human nature. Universal, human and nature are key words here. At present, our nature is limited or confined to the lower self. The universal, human nature is an expression of the divine qualities, which raise the mind above duality and give that feeling or experience of unity between the individual consciousness and the higher consciousness. The movement from duality to unity is known as

121

Vedanta. If we could incorporate these four principles into our life, every day would be a very beautiful experience. Then we could realise what Paramahamsaji meant when he said, "Life is a flowery mystery and every unfoldment is beautiful."

Bhagavad Gita

Karma Sannyasa Yoga

MAY 13, 1994

After the recognition of karma, we come to the fifth chapter of the Gita in which Arjuna says to Krishna, "You are talking about karma, that everyone performs karma, and also about renouncing karma. How is it possible to perform karma and renounce karma both at the same time?" How is it possible to perform action and not get caught in karma, to be free from the results of that karma? At that point Krishna says, "It is a simple process. One cannot avoid karma; one cannot avoid the pain and pleasure of life, and one cannot alter the nature of Prakriti. However, one can be more observant. One can free oneself from the attraction and repulsion to objects and events by following two paths.

One path is *karma sannyasa*, living in the world without expectation, fulfilling one's duties and striving to keep oneself aligned with one's inner nature without any expectation of the fruits of action. The other path is *sannyasa*, total renunciation of the karmas." However, the karma sannyasa concept, as it has been described here, is not the same as the karma sannyasa initiation. They are two different things. Karma sannyasa initiation is simply a process through which an aspirant can begin the journey into spiritual life, living according to the principles of yoga and spirituality. The karma sannyasa which has been mentioned in the sequence

123

of discussion in the Gita aims at clarifying the role, the involvement of an individual in the realm of Prakriti.

Renunciation

Karma yoga can be briefly defined as renunciation of the results of action. In this context, karma sannyasa should be understood as the renunciation of doership, the concept of doership. This is the basic difference. In karma yoga, there is renunciation of the result, the fruits of action. This renunciation is preceded by the awareness and recognition of karmas that are happening at different levels of one's being. Whereas karma sannyasa is renunciation of the identification, that 'I am performing', 'I am the centre of all activity'. This is often a cause of worry for us. When we become the centre of activity, then worries arise.

This identification is the veil of ignorance in the life of an aspirant, which makes him an *ajnani*, 'unknowledgable'. An ajnani, or the aspirant who is under the influence of misconception about the Self, thinks that he is the actual performer of all actions. What should the proper attitude be? At this level, the proper attitude has to be that all actions pertain to the realm of Prakriti. There is no voluntary or conscious control by anyone over the actions. How the mind and the gunas function and act is beyond the cognitive field of an individual. Every action that is performed in the world, in the various dimensions of the human personality, is according to the nature and attributes, or gunas.

When I see a line of ants, I wonder what they are thinking. If we could read their thoughts, I am sure many of them would be thinking, "I am indispensable in this world", just like we all think that we are. In our own minds, we not only become the centre of all activity, but we also make other people believe that we are the centre of all activity. It is like one ant saying to the other ants, "Look, I am the centre." The human being who is observing the ants and reading their thoughts has a good laugh, shows them his thumb and says, "You may think that you are the centre, but I have the ability to squash you at any time." This is what God does with us too. His thumb is death.

124

Somewhere above our heads this thumb is waiting, seeing how far we can go with the game of believing that we are the centre, that we are in control of our actions and karmas, that we are able to channel our samskaras. Then suddenly, when God has had enough, he brings the thumb down and we live no more.

Ego

There are a few times when God actually smiles. The first time He smiles is when a doctor says to the patient, "Don't worry, I am going to save you." The second time is when we say, "This is mine and that is yours." The third time God smiles is when we begin to tell Him our plans for the future. These are the three times when God smiles, and there may be other times also. Our own relationship with ourselves is a relationship of ego. It is not a relationship of spontaneity or freedom, a free expression. What is our concept of freedom? Breaking down all the norms that have existed.

Many times the swamis get tired of the ashram discipline. I remember in the olden days, they went to the restaurant which used to exist up the road from here. That was the place where they would express their freedom, with milkshakes. This concept of freedom is peculiar. We tend to express our freedom in the market place, but we are unable to experience it within. This kind of attitude is formed under the veil of *ahamkara*, ego. Anyone who acts in such a way is considered to be an *ajnani*, a person who is not aware of himself. A *jnani*, or a knowledgeable person, is able to eventually renounce the concept of doership, by recognising that nature functions in a particular way. The gunas have their own direction. Throughout our life, we live according to the influences of nature and the gunas. It is learning to live according to these directions, to flow with life, which is the aim of karma sannyasa.

Miracles

Many times we evolve certain theories, such as, life is like a boat on the ocean of *samsara*, the world. The spirit is the passenger, sitting in the boat, trying to cross the ocean of the world. We pray to God, "My life is in your hands. My boat is

125

without an oar or rudder. Take me where you will, but please remember that I am holding on to you." This is our approach to God and spirituality. We try to make God our servant. We pray, "Do this and do that for me", "Give me this and give me that". When something we wish for actually happens, we call that a miracle. For example, we pray for money and when we win the lottery, we say it is God's grace or a miracle. That is the concept of a miracle. When what you want happens, is that really a miracle?

My understanding is that when we live according to the desires and wishes of God, when we become obedient servants of God, instead of making God our servant, then that is a real miracle. This is the concept of karma sannyasa: to overcome the ego by developing simplicity; to overcome the concept of doership, that I am doing, I am acting, and without me the world would be a very nasty place. Overcoming this concept is actual sannyasa of the karma. Learning to flow with the currents of life and nature, destiny and karma, without losing our inner equilibrium and clarity, that is sannyasa.

Attraction and repulsion
Another idea which is conveyed in this fifth chapter is that a sannyasin who is able to renounce doership neither hates nor desires. Hate and desire should not be understood within the intellectual framework. When we speak of hate and desire, it becomes a very intellectual concept. What do we hate? That which is not in conformity with our likes, ideas, thoughts, beliefs and aspirations. Anything that does not conform is hateful. The same applies to desire. Whatever conforms with our aspirations is what we normally desire. So, hate and desire are the two aspects that have been emphasised.

In order to understand this, we must go through a process of self-observation, self-analysis, and try to recognise how many kinds of hate and desire there are in our life. We can hate one person and desire to be with another. We can hate one kind of environment and desire to live in a another.

We can feel repulsion for some things and attraction to others. The entire human life swings between the two opposite poles of attraction and repulsion, like the movement of a pendulum which constantly swings from left to right. When it swings to the left, repulsion is experienced in different stages and when it swings to the right, attraction is experienced in different intensities.

Jnana, karma, bhakti

This pendulum is managed through recognition of the personal desires and aspirations. This involves incorporation of wisdom or jnana. Karma culminates in jnana, jnana culminates in bhakti and bhakti culminates in realisation. Karma is something physical with which one can easily identify, because it is happening continuously. When the recognition of the karma takes place, that is jnana, knowledge.

Jnana is a non-intellectual experience; it is the realisation that 'I know'. This state of 'I know' is not influenced by people, events or circumstances. It is based on the principle of truth, not on the superficial reality which we are constantly trying to change to suit our needs. Jnana is the inner realisation of the underlying principle of reality. First there is awareness, next acknowledgment and then the realisation that this principle exists in relation to the karmas. When this acknowledgment has taken place with clarity of mind, jnana is converted into bhakti.

The first aspect of bhakti provides a clear direction for the channelling of the intellect. The second aspect is the channelling of emotions, and the third aspect is the channelling of actions. 'I am an instrument which is being played.' So, once there is awareness of the intellect and emotions, and realisation of ourselves as a tool, instrument or medium, which is expressing our own nature, then bhakti is converted into realisation. Karma, jnana and bhakti go together. One cannot be isolated or separated from the other. The moment we try to separate them, a split takes place in our life, disharmony is experienced, and we go off the path of evolution.

Re-educating the mind

Evolution is not a process of continuous progression, rather it is coming to a stage of life, then standing still and harmonising that area before taking another step. There is no continuous progression; it is stop, go, stop, go, stop. This evolutionary process is very natural and spontaneous. In order to be educated, to get our degrees and diplomas, we have to go through kindergarten, primary and secondary school, college and eventually university, moving in sequence from one class to the next. In the same way, we have to go through different stages in spiritual life, in relation to our karma and our awareness of karma.

The most important thing to remember is to keep *ahamkara*, the ego or 'I' identity, in check and free from the influence of the gunas. There are two aspects of ego. One is the 'I' identity and the other is the simple 'I'. This simple 'I' is the *drashta*, or seer. When there is identification with the object of cognition, that is ahamkara, the 'I' identity. For example, a beautiful flower can be seen in two ways. One way is to see the beauty and shape and to appreciate it. That is the simple 'I', an acceptance that the flower is there. The other way is to desire the flower, pick it, take it to our room and put it in a vase. That is ahamkara, where there is no appreciation of the flower in its natural form, but the desire to take it and keep it with us.

It is keeping this aspect of desire in check, which has been mentioned in the fifth chapter of the Gita. We must begin to observe and appreciate the natural form, not only of the world, but also of ourself. An effort has to be made to change the direction of the mind. In order to overcome that aspect of 'me' identifying with the objects and situations, we must re-educate the mind to appreciate, and not to want, desire or crave. This is a part of sadhana which has to be understood and realised in meditation.

Re-education of the mind can only be done through the stages of pratyahara, because in this state there is already dissipation and we try to focus and centre ourselves in that state of dissipation. So, this mental education is to be provided in pratyahara and not in the stages of dharana or

128

dhyana. In dhyana, we are experiencing the continuity of consciousness. In dharana, we are experiencing the one-pointed, focused state of consciousness. In pratyahara, we are educating and re-educating the mind, the nature, the gunas and the vrittis, the tendencies of mind.

Renunciation

Therefore, pratyahara is a very important aspect of life. It is in the state of pratyahara that renunciation actually takes place. I feel that it is easy to renounce home and family. With some effort we can even renounce the lifestyle to which we are accustomed. However, it is very difficult to renounce the passions that arise in the mind, at the conscious, subconscious and unconscious levels. What have we renounced? Many have renounced one thing and adopted another, renounced that and then adopted something else.

We constantly see this concept of renunciation in external situations, but we have never observed or applied the concept of renunciation in relation to our passions, the forces which come from inside, which are involved with the world of the senses and objects, in the dimension of time and space. There has to be renunciation of the passions, the forces which guide the human personality in the external dimension, so that eventually we are able to experience the inner purity of the Self.

When one is able to experience the purity of the Self by overcoming the attraction to passion, and when one is able to remain uninfluenced by and accept the karmas, the gunas and the attributes, then one can be called a karma sannyasin and a sadhaka. An aspirant who is able to channel the forces created by the attraction and repulsion of Prakriti is a real karma sannyasin. This karma sannyasa is definitely different to the karma sannyasa initiation that we have received. The culmination of this attainment is when one is able to see God and good in the immediate environment.

When this attitude of seeing God and good arises, it means the passions have subsided and then one attains purity of heart. When purity of heart arises and is experienced, then

129

one becomes established in spirit, or '*atmabhava*', as Swami Sivananda used to say, 'the feeling of the Self', knowing that you are. When one is established in the nature of spirit, then God and good are seen throughout the universe and the expansion of consciousness takes place. This is one way of looking at renunciation of doership and renunciation of the results of action.

Sadhana

Sadhana means a practice which is done regularly for an extended period of time, with a firm conviction that one will be able to perfect and derive benefits from it. This is the broad meaning of the word sadhana according to the yogic tradition. The aim of sadhana is to purify the mind and the human nature. Purification of the mind is necessary if we want to harmonise our personality. So, the means to harmonise the personality is through sadhana, which can take different forms depending on one's level. A beginner will have a basic sadhana, and as he or she evolves, the sadhana will become more advanced.

Sadhana can be classified in three broad categories: physical, mental and psychic. In physical sadhana, we have the practices of hatha yoga, asana and pranayama, for the maintenance of health and harmonising the body. In mental sadhana, we have the practices of mantra, yantra, pratyahara and dharana, for harmonising the mind. In psychic sadhana, we have the practices of kriya yoga, kundalini yoga, nada yoga and laya yoga. These are meant to balance the psyche and increase the sensitivity and receptivity, in order to experience the non-mental or transcendental states of consciousness, where we see the interplay between energy and consciousness.

There has to be a good combination of practices in our sadhana, not only physical or mental but also psychic. The

131

sadhana must evolve progressively, as one outgrows a particular sadhana after some time. It is like anything to which one becomes habituated. For example, when one enters a room full of cigarette smoke, initially the smell is very strong, but after spending fifteen minutes in the room, one is not as aware of the smell. This also happens in sadhana. We get habituated to a form of sadhana and lose the awareness needed to complete that process.

Postal Sadhana

For these reasons, we have introduced a postal sadhana programme with an accompanying questionnaire. Every two months you return the questionnaire and, in that way, we are able to keep track of your achievements, shortcomings or difficulties, and suggest ways around them. This sadhana is mainly for those who have been involved in yoga for a long time. People used to say, "I have been practising this sadhana for the last ten years. What should I do next?" I could never accept that. It is like taking one step forward and staying there until someone tells you to take another step. I feel more comfortable with an interactive sadhana. Write down your problems and difficulties and I will suggest what to do and how to incorporate that into your life and practice.

The postal sadhana is a combination of postures, breathing techniques, bandhas, mudras and shatkarmas. As you progress, the components of kriya and kundalini yoga will be introduced. The entire sadhana takes about an hour. You are asked to observe the different states of mind and body, the level of energy, how and what you are feeling, and where there is greater sensitivity towards oneself. So, in this sadhana, we are covering the physical, the mental and the psychic aspect of the human personality. That is the general concept.

Types of Mantra

There are two types of mantra which aspirants are given. One is the personal mantra and the other is the special mantra which is used for some time in certain practices. Using the personal mantra is one thing and using other mantras is another. The personal mantra is selected according to our personality and need. It helps us to tune in with the subtle dimension of our being. For example, in the mantra *Om Namah Shivaya*, there are six syllables. *Om* is the sound of ajna chakra; *Na, Ma, Shi, Va* and *Ya* all correspond to different centres. So, through this mantra, we are working with ajna, vishuddhi, anahata, and swadhisthana chakras.

At the same time, other mantras are also incorporated into our sadhana programme. Some are Shakti mantras and some are Shiva mantras. Shakti mantras stimulate and raise the level of energy, and Shiva mantras raise the level of consciousness. So, there are times when one may be given a bija mantra like *Om Klim* to use for a month or so, along with the personal mantra. The bija or one syllable mantra works specifically on the energy level. Hammering the pranic aspect of our personality with one sound vibration stimulates the prana, which in turn awakens the mind. There are times when another mantra can be given to raise the level of consciousness. So, the personal mantra and the mantra which is used for some time in our sadhana, both have to be combined.

The Gayatri mantra is one of the Shakti mantras. It has twenty four syllables which work at different levels of the pranic structure. The Mahamrityunjaya mantra is a Shiva mantra. It raises the level of consciousness and sensitises it for the projection of healing energy. When we begin to project this energy outside, the healing takes place within. In the sadhana that we are doing in the evenings, these two mantras have been used. Gayatri raises the pranic level, and Mahamrityunjaya utilises that pranic stimulation for self-healing, rebalancing and also to help others, by creating a positive, creative environment which is conducive for growth. Om is the seed mantra which touches and balances the entire range of the personality.

When you return home, if you are so inclined, you can practise this meditation, but not continuously. Practise it for a month, then stop for a month, then again practise for a month, then again stop for a month, so that you do not get into that state of habituation. When you practise for one month, you are psychically active, alert and reaching out. Then you stop for a month and again become aware of the normal perceptions, so that the intensity of stimulation gradually reduces. When you begin again, there is a push, and in this way, you should continue. Please remember that when any form of sadhana is practised for many years consecutively, there is no attainment or achievement.

Symbol and Yantra

The personal mantra is often accompanied by a symbol. The concept behind this is that the symbol begins to take on a visible shape as the mind becomes more focused. Initially, concentration on the symbol takes place through a process of imagination; we cannot see it. As the concentration deepens, the symbol is gradually seen like a photograph inside the mind. First, we see it as a two dimensional photograph, and later on, as a three dimensional image, like a hologram. So, perfecting the symbol awareness is an important aspect of the mantra. We should not move into yantra meditation until we are able to see that symbol as a holographic image within the mind.

In the course of time, yantras should also be incorporated. Yantras begin with one simple symbol like a candle flame, a star, a cross, a trident or the third eye. After one has outgrown that, more complex symbols can be used. The easiest yantra to use in advanced stages of meditation is Shiva yantra. The hardest yantra is Sri yantra, because it is more compact and complex. After the yantra aspect, we move into mandala. So, there is a progression in the system of yantra and mandala also. This is the general concept of this sadhana.

Karma sannyasa sadhana

Karma sannyasins, poorna sannyasins, jignasu sannyasins and yoga aspirants are all given different sadhanas. If you were not told about this when you took karma sannyasa, maybe it was too early at that time. Now, karma sannyasins are required to follow a specific sadhana. Understanding the interaction of karma and consciousness is the sadhana of a karma sannyasin. How should this sadhana be performed? At night, before sleep, sit down for ten minutes. With total intensity of mind and with faith in yourself, begin to observe the body. This is something which you can start even tonight.

Sit in a comfortable posture, close your eyes, stabilise yourself and begin to observe the body. See the areas of pain and pleasure, comfort and discomfort. You may become aware of a slight muscle, knee or back ache, or of a pleasant sensation in your body. After recognising what is happening in the physical structure, say to yourself, "I am observing the body, but I am not the body. I am feeling the state of discomfort in the body; I am feeling the state of comfort in the body, but I am not identifying with either the state of comfort or discomfort." This should take no more than five minutes.

After disassociating yourself from the body, apply the same process to the mind. Recognise the states of discomfort and comfort within the mind. When this recognition has taken place, disassociate yourself from the mind with the thought: "I am not the mind, nor am I the experiences of pain and pleasure associated with the mind." Then the big question comes, "If I am not the body or the mind, then what am I?" At that moment, focus the awareness either in chidakasha, the region of the eyebrow centre, or in hridayakasha, the region of the heart centre, wherever you feel comfortable initially. Do not fight with yourself, because by doing so, you are again identifying with the mind.

When you are comfortable in either chidakasha or hridayakasha, visualise a point of light and identify yourself with the light. See a flame and identify with the flame; see a white light and identify with the white light. With the attention firmly fixed on the white light or on the flame, say to yourself, "Light is my real nature. I am not the body; I am not the mind. I am not the experiences related with the body or the mind. Light is my nature." Identify with the light for ten minutes, not more than that. Keep it short and sweet.

Once you begin to focus on and identify with the light, begin chanting the mantra Om. Whether you chant a few times or for one complete mala does not really matter. It depends on how long you feel comfortable with the practice and how much time you can afford to spend on it, without disturbing your companion who is trying to sleep. Each time you chant Om feel the mind merging with the vibration of the mantra and the light. Then stop the practice and gradually begin to identify with the mind and body again, stretch out your legs and go to sleep.

This sadhana contains several aspects which can be enumerated as follows: (i) gradual disassociation of the mind from the body, (ii) awareness of the interaction between the mind and body, (iii) gradual disassociation of the consciousness from the mind, (iv) awareness of the nature of consciousness, which is a pure state of being, a state of harmony with no dissipation. I am sure you will not have any difficulty with this practice. However, I would like to give you a word of advice: eventually, not from the very first day, the focusing of consciousness should take place in the heart centre.

Yoga has emphasised chidakasha awareness, recognising that we are caught up in our head. Therefore, an effort must first be made to stabilise this area with concentration in chidakasha. After some time, bring your awareness down to the heart centre. Get it out of the head space and into the heart space. Initially, it may not be a very comfortable feeling, because you have to harmonise your heart space. First, harmonise the head space and become comfortable with concentration on the symbol in chidakasha. When you move down to hridayakasha, you have to start afresh, to balance the heart space and focus yourself in that space. So, do not be disheartened; just keep on trucking!

PART THREE

Discourses during the

Yoga Festival Week

and

Yoga & Meditation Weekend

Yoga of the 1990's

MAY 18, 1994

Greetings to all of you from the land of Bharat. Bharat is not India. The word *Bharat* means 'a land which is immersed in light'. I am not referring to present-day India, to the socio-political structure or to the pseudo-religious culture. I am referring to a land which has evolved a unique method of understanding spirituality, of experiencing the nature of the human personality. Bharat is the home of an ancient culture which has made every effort to concern itself with the preservation of vidya. In 1976, when Paramahamsaji came to Sydney for the World Yoga Conference, he made a pronouncement that we sannyasins are concerned with vidya and nothing else. Generally, *vidya* is translated as 'knowledge', but that is not the concept that I am trying to convey here. The concept that I want to tell you about will become clearer in the course of this discussion.

Cultural dichotomy

In human civilisation we find two types of mentalities, and these are seen very clearly by the impressions and samskaras that have evolved in different countries of the world today. One type of mentality geared itself to manipulate nature, to make nature suitable to the lifestyle which that group of people wanted to live. From this group of people and this mentality, we see a trend of great technological achievements. Another

139

mentality and another group of persons directed their efforts towards living according to nature, not towards manipulating nature. This group went in another direction of discovery and that was the spiritual discovery. So, in the course of time, one type of mentality became technologically oriented, externally oriented, with the emphasis on sensual satisfaction. The other type of mentality became more introverted, in tune with the inner nature, spiritually oriented.

These are the two distinct cultures which have evolved in the world. The so-called Eastern cultures from Japan, China, India and the Middle East became adept in their methods of attuning with the external nature, the internal nature, and the cosmic nature. The western cultures that evolved represent the outward drive to make nature suitable to their lifestyle. This is where an imbalance took place in both the mentalities. The extrovert culture lost touch with the inner self and the other, the introvert culture, lost contact with the external realities. Thus, a disparity is seen in both.

Let us compare this with a person who goes surfing on the ocean and another person who goes swimming in the ocean. The waves on the surface of the ocean are different to the currents that are within the ocean. The person who catches the waves remains on the surface; he moves with the water but is not aware of the undercurrents. The other person who dives into the ocean has absolutely no idea of the surf but is more in tune with the undercurrents. Now which person has a full vision of what the ocean actually is? Neither.

The person who remains on the surface, who is always extrovert, knows how to ride the waves. But when an undercurrent catches that person, there is a panic attack, there is a loss of direction. He does not know how to react in a balanced and controlled way. I remember once while body surfing in South America, the wave caught me on the wrong foot. I did about fifty somersaults. I had sand in my mouth, in my nose, in my eyes, in my ears. I totally lost my sense of direction. I was pulled under. I did not know which way to go or whether my head was down or up. I did not know whether I was going towards the shore or away from the shore. This incident made me aware of my own responses to the undercurrents that generally come up from deep within our own personalities.

When a person who is on the surface encounters the undercurrents of the human personality, there is loss of direction, there is a panic attack. That is one reason why we go to a psychotherapist who teaches us how to behave, how to act, and how to confront different situations, emotions and feelings, which we have no knowledge or concept of, which we have not recognised as a natural part of our being. The cultures which evolved a spiritual tradition were able to overcome this problem. They did not need psychotherapy to learn how to behave, to learn how to feel their emotions. They needed to experience, to undergo the process of experiencing those feelings which come up spontaneously from within, and to integrate those feelings with the external interactions. This is the aim of spiritual traditions. By 'spiritual' I do not mean 'religious'. A spiritual tradition is comprised of certain systems and methods which can make one aware of the spirit, not just of the body, of the external environment, of the various situations which surround one all the time. This is where yoga comes in.

Yoga festivity

We are celebrating a festival of yoga. What does 'festival' actually mean? What do you feel when you are in a festive mood? Just think about it for a moment. What do I feel, what do you feel in a mood of festivity? How do we recognise that? I believe that when one is in a festive mood, the body is in tune with the mind. When you are in a festive mood, your body does not jump up and down while your mind is depressed. There is a tuning of the body, mind and intellect, of the rationality with the emotions and feelings, with the inherent qualities of life such as love, compassion, oneness and wellbeing. In a festive mood, the entire personality, right from the nervous system or the physical body, to the intellect, the emotions and the spirit, are all tuned as one unit. That is my definition of festivity.

We are celebrating a festival of yoga here, but it is just the beginning, because this festival has to continue. External festivals may last a few days; they do not go on forever. But a yoga festival must continue forever and ever, because yoga is a festive mood. It is a mood, a way of life, a way of experiencing oneself, which is in tune, in harmony. If that harmony, that integration stops after some time; if the experience, the awareness, the understanding of this harmony stops after some time, then we can definitely say that we are not in tune with yoga or with the spirit of yoga. So, this yoga festival is the beginning of a life-long festival. It is the time to make a sankalpa, a resolution, that we will strive for this harmony, we will strive for the experience of oneness which is both individual and cosmic. If we can do that, then we can be proud to say that this yoga festival has been a success.

We are also in a very special place, not because of the scenery, not because of the location, not because of the ashram, but because this place has been given a definite direction and blessings by Paramahamsaji in our first Festival of Yoga in 1976. At that time he said, "Mangrove Mountain is a mountain where man grows." I have always remembered that statement of his: a place where one learns to grow. It is to this special place that we have come to learn how to grow, and yoga is going to be the basis of that learning and education.

Yoga education

Yoga is not a system of practice. We have been exposed to yoga as a system of physical exercise, therapy or meditation, but this is not what yoga is. You cannot say that this arm, this eye or this head represent the entire human body. Hatha yoga is not the complete yoga. Raja yoga is not the complete yoga. Kriya yoga is not the complete yoga. They are simply parts of a greater structure, and we have to recognise that.

There is a story which explains this very well. Four blind men wanted to know what an elephant was. They all went together to the zoo and there they started touching the elephant. The first one grabbed hold of the tail, the second grabbed hold of the legs, the third grabbed hold of the trunk

142

and the fourth grabbed hold of the ears. Then each one described the elephant. The first one said, "An elephant is like a small piece of rope." The second said, "No, an elephant is like a pillar." The third said, "No, an elephant is like a python." The fourth said, "No, the elephant is floppy and flat."

Now, there was a fifth person present who was watching each one of the blind men and listening to their descriptions. Finally, he said to them, "Look, you have it all wrong. What you are describing is not the elephant but a part of the elephant." The four blind men in this story are actually very similar to us, and the method which they used to examine the elephant is how we have adopted yoga in our life. Some have taken up hatha yoga, some have taken up kriya yoga, some have taken up raja yoga, some karma yoga, some bhakti yoga, some jnana yoga, and we all think that this is yoga. Now, however, an effort has to be made to re-educate the mind.

The education which we receive in society today is known as job-oriented education. The educators are very correct in saying this because they are not providing the real education, they are only providing us with the education that is necessary for obtaining a job. In this real education we have to educate the mind to learn to experience and to realise the human nature. We have taken yoga as a job-oriented education and it is high time that we relearn yoga as a method of education which instils within us a sense of balance, harmony and dignity. This is what our effort is going to be during this festival.

Learn to be sattwic

There is a message from Paramahamsaji for all those who are present here. That message is, "Learn to be sattwic! Attainment of this sattwic nature should be the goal of yoga in this decade." When Paramahamsaji came here in 1976, he pronounced that the Yoga of Meditation was going to be the yoga for the eighties. Now he has given a new direction to us by saying that experiencing the sattwic quality of life has to be the yoga of the 1990's. How do we do that? The quality of sattwa, the pure quality, the inner quality of life has never been experienced by us because we have never educated and

143

disciplined the inner being to experience the sattwic nature. Either we live as a tamasic person or a rajasic person.

Living as a tamasic person means we are happy in the present state of life and we seek no further development, understanding or realisation of the inner nature. We are happy where we are and there is no forward movement in the process of discovery of the self. That is the tamasic state. In the rajasic state, we want to know something more about the self, but we want to keep the 'I' concept, the individual concept, alive, predominant and active. This 'I' becomes powerful and it also diverts the growth of human consciousness from the evolutionary aspect to an aspect of stability and contentment in the world that is created by our own mind and sense of logic. These are the two states in which we have been living all our life. Most of us are tamasic or rajasic, very few of us are sattwic.

Sattwic here means tuning with the inner Self where one dies to live again. Our paramguru, Swami Sivananda, used to sing a song in which the words were, "Die to live, kill the little 'I', lead the divine life." This was not his speculation; this was his experience. When the aspirant comes in tune with the inner nature, then he experiences divinity. This divinity is not becoming God. We all like to play God, but the real divinity is to experience the continuity of consciousness, going beyond the self-made limitations of the human personality and mind. This has to be the direction of yoga in the 1990's. It is with this message of Paramahamsaji that we take a pledge, a sankalpa, to experience yoga as it is. I hope that during this yoga festival you will gain a good understanding of it.

You know, I am having a hard time with all of you because I am dealing with two generations here: one generation of Paramahamsaji's and another generation which is my own. It was easy for Paramahamsaji to deal with his generation and it is easy for me to deal with my generation, but here I am trying to grab hold of both and move them in the spirit of yoga. You will all have to help me in this process, even those of you who have come here for the first time, because it is the spirit of yoga which we have to experience and imbibe. So, let us see how things unfold in the coming days.

Cellular Enlightenment

We were talking about the attainment of harmony and the necessity of re-educating our mind and personality. This has been the basic aim of yoga from the outset. Sage Patanjali, one of the early exponents of yoga, codified the yogic system. In the beginning of the *Yoga Sutras* he stated that yoga is a method by which the yogic practitioner can control, alter and direct the *vrittis*, the modifications of the mind, thus allowing him to experience the inner self. However, before this, he made another statement which is the first sutra, *'Atha yoga anushasanam'*. Generally, this sutra has been translated as, 'Now we begin the instructions in yoga', but the real meaning of this sutra is, 'Yoga is a form of inner discipline'. The word *anushasan* means 'discipline', not the external, imposed discipline, but the discipline which follows the knowledge of the subtle, unmanifest and unknown areas of human personality.

Understanding this first sutra is very important for yoga aspirants, because until and unless we understand this statement, we cannot progress further in the yogic system. It is not easy to control the mind because we do not have that training. In yoga the training which is given to control the mind and the vrittis is the fifth and sixth stages of raja yoga, in the form of pratyahara and dharana. What about the previous stages? Sage Patanjali has mentioned asana and pranayama. Although there is no reference to mudra, bandha, shatkriya and

145

the other physiological practices, they have all been incorporated in the description of asana and pranayama, because yogis have always believed that the body is a vehicle by which one can experience the unknown. Therefore, attainment of physical balance and harmony is necessary before learning how to deal with the mind.

Harmonising the physical structure

The body is definitely linked with the mind. It is easier for us to identify with the various states and conditions of the body because it is something physical which can be seen. If there is a cut, a pimple or a boil in any part of the body, no matter how small and insignificant it may be, our attention is automatically diverted to it, and we make every effort to treat that condition. However, we do not do the same thing in relation to the mind until a major, mental biopsy has to be done. We cut and bruise ourselves many times mentally, but because it is not visible, we ignore it. So, the body is a very important medium for understanding the human nature and personality.

The classical yogic texts have emphasised the importance of first knowing what the body actually is. The practices of asana and pranayama, no matter how simple or how complex they may be, alter the present state and condition of the body. The *Yoga Sutras* have defined asana as a posture in which the aspirant is able to remain steady without experiencing pain in the body. There is total ease and comfort. Although this particular statement has been associated with meditative postures, it refers to the normal functioning and performance of the human body.

How do we see our body? We see it in the form of different systems, different organs. Yoga views the body in the form of a neuro-muscular and neuro-cellular structure, incorporating all the organs and systems, such as respiratory, cardiac, digestive, muscular, endocrinal etc. Asanas aim to provide this understanding and control over the entire physical structure, the body and the brain. This is the purely physical side of yoga which has to be understood properly. When we

146

begin to work with asana, pranayama, mudra, bandha and shatkarma, then we are stimulating, altering and harmonising the neuro-muscular and neuro-cellular structure of the body.

Five physical modes

The body moves or functions in five ways. The first is a natural state of activity. The second is more playful and dynamic activity, for example, the difference between walking and running. Walking is a state of activity in which there is no effort or strain on the different systems controlling the body. When you run, the body enters into another mode and changes are felt in the various systems. We call this the dynamic, playful nature of the body.

The third function of the body is adaptability. The body adapts itself. We are sitting in a position which bends or folds the body, yet we are comfortable. When we sit on a sofa, on a bed or in a meditative posture, our body is not upright and straight, it is not aligned, there is always a fold. So, this is adaptability of the body to a particular condition of bending itself forward or backward. The fourth function of the body is balance, and the fifth is stillness, motionlessness. These are the five functions or states of the neuro-muscular and the neuro-cellular body.

Yoga has always emphasised that you should begin with the most simple and basic practice, so that you come to know your body, not just how you feel in your tibia, in your stomach or in your lower back muscles. "Oh, I did that practice and now I feel a bit more relaxed," that is only the superficial aspect. Rather, experience and know how the body adjusts, adapts and enters into different modes from the normal state, from the first mode to the fifth. Study the motionless, quiet, silent mode and go through the other modes, the dynamic, playful mode, the adaptation to a certain condition mode, the balancing mode.

In an asana class, awareness of the movement is always emphasised; each movement must be conscious and not unconscious. This becomes part of life in the course of time: "I am aware that I am moving my hands", "I am aware that I am moving my head", "I am aware that I am looking at people". This awareness, which is gained through the practice of yoga, becomes a natural, spontaneous part of human nature and life. This process represents the progression in the neuro-cellular structure of the physical body.

Effect of asana

So, when we begin with any asana or posture, what is actually happening in the body? At the neuro-cellular and neuro-muscular level, the body is being altered. This alteration of the body is definitely not felt externally. We remain the same, but the cells and the muscles are being processed. Whether we practise pawanmuktasana, dynamic postures such as surya namaskara, intermediate postures, balancing or advanced postures like sirshasana (headstand), mayurasana, (peacock) or vrischikasana (scorpion), all these different types of asanas actually transform the neuro-cellular structure of the body. When the neuro-cellular structure is changing, what is the first experience? The first experience is the state of relaxation. This is defined as the free flow of energy, "I feel relaxed". There is a release of tension and blockage from the muscles and joints. The organs go into an active functional mode without any blockage or imbalance in them. This result is seen in the form of therapy.

Many investigations have been conducted which have proved that, in certain conditions, the practice of asana is helpful in the management of asthma, diabetes, essential hypertension, arthritis, digestive disorders, even cancer. Last year it was also shown that being HIV positive could be controlled through the practices of yoga. One HIV positive case has become HIV negative after one year of yoga practice. This work with yoga and AIDS is being done by the ashrams in England. Yoga is not a miracle cure for every problem, but under certain conditions it can work. If the timing is right, if the application is right, then it will work. If the timing is wrong and the application is right, it is a lot of effort. If the timing is right and the application is wrong there is no result. So, both timing and application have to be considered.

In the asana group we have dealt with the basic, intermediate and advanced practices, to go from mode one to mode five. Along with asana we have also used the basic shatkriyas which help to purify and balance the body by eliminating toxins and blockages. When we go deeper into the neuro-cellular structure, we come to the group of pranayamas.

Pranayama, mudra, bandha theory

The yogic texts describe pranayama in four aspects: (i) the process of inhalation, (ii) the process of exhalation, (iii) the process of internal retention, and (iv) the process of external retention. So, pranayama is generally related with the breath. Patanjali was not trying to make us believe that just by closing the nostrils one can attain enlightenment. He has used the word *pranayama* to mean 'enlarging the dimension of prana'. All the pranayamas that we do, such as nadi shodhana, bhastrika, bhramari, ujjayi, kapalbhati, surya bheda, chandra bheda, sheetali, sheetkari or any other form, are not pranayamas in the real sense; they are prana nigraha techniques. The word *nigraha* means 'control'. Controlling and moving the breath with a specific purpose, direction and aim is not pranayama. Enlarging the dimension of prana is the literal meaning of pranayama. How does this happen? In order to answer this question, first we must have an understanding of the neuro-cellular structure and the three compartments which yoga has classified within it.

The first compartment is the perineum which deals with and controls the various instincts and urges which are both physical and psychological in nature. The second compartment is the chest and here the functions are also physical and psychological. The third compartment is the head where the functions are physical, comprised of the senses, eyes, ears, nostrils and mouth; and also mental, comprised of the thinking process, rationality etc. These are the three distinct compartments which are created by yoga to understand the various activities and manifestations of the body in relation to the external world, and to the feeling aspect of the inner

149

world. These are the areas which initially have to be known, controlled and harmonised.

These three compartments are known in yoga as *granthis*, blocks or confined space dimension. Each of these granthis relates to a specific *karmendriya*, organ of action. The perineal block, perineal space, between the region of manipura and mooladhara, deals with the organ of reproduction. It is an indriya, an organ of action, which also affects and stimulates a corresponding state in the mind. Is the sexual urge only physical, or is it mental and emotional too? Is hunger only physical or does it have a mental and emotional link as well? Is fear only mental or does it have a physical link also? These are interlinked conditions. So the indriyas, the organs of action and perception, of the body and mind, are all inter-related. The aim of pranayama, along with the practices of mudra and bandha, is to activate a movement in the field of prana in the cellular structure, which is then experienced as a physical and a mental state.

There are three bandhas: (i) *moola bandha*, the perineal contraction, associated with the perineal space, relates to *brahma granthi*, the first neuro-cellular space; (ii) *uddiyana bandha*, contraction of the abdominal muscles, associated with the space between the abdomen and the chest, relates to the control of *vishnu granthi*, the second neuro-cellular space, and (iii) *jalandhara bandha*, the chin lock, controls the third neuro-cellular space in the head, the *rudra granthi*.

Physical harmony
The neuro-cellular brain, the organs of action such as the arms and legs, the organs of reproduction and elimination, the organs of sensory perception such as the eyes, nose, mouth, ears, and skin, all have a very close connection with each other. In fact, if you see a cross-section of the brain, there is a part which is known as the homunculus, meaning 'the little man'. Different indriyas or organs of action and perception relate to specific centres in the brain. Each indriya has been assigned a particular location in the brain. This cutout picture is very grotesque. When I first saw a picture of

150

it, I thought that the artist, Salvador Dali, had drawn it because his drawings are very similar. So, there is a link between the organs and the brain.

In the practice of pranayama a third link is seen, that of impulses and stimulations. In the practice of bandhas another link is seen: energy, prana moving in a different direction than its normal state. If you are able to understand the pranas, you will be able to understand your behaviour. These four: the brain, the organs, the impulses and the pranic energy, intermingle with each other and go into a hyperactive, turbo mode. Just as in a computer one can change from twenty five mega hertz to thirty three by pressing the turbo button, in the same way, in the real practice of pranayama one can change the normal mode and go into turbo mode. Then what happens? Sparks begin to fly inside.

However, pranayama here does not refer to the breathing techniques with which we are familiar. As I have mentioned, those are the prana nigraha techniques. We have not yet practised pranayama. It is for the first time in Australia that I am creating a distinction between pranayama and the prana nigraha techniques that we have been practising. I hope to explain to you what pranayama is and the fine distinction between prana nigraha and pranayama. Then you will understand what I am saying now. Sparks begin to fly and this hyper-mode of the body is actually the tuning of the body, the harmonising of the body with itself. The body becomes in tune with itself. The body harmonises with itself. We have not brought mind or spirit into the picture yet. We are talking about the concept of physical harmony, which is the beginning of yoga.

I am using examples of practices with which we are all familiar: asana, pranayama, shatkarma. We have all done these practices, but we have never looked at them from a broad angle. That is because we have never been exposed to classical yoga. In our tradition, Swami Sivananda used to speak of yoga in an orthodox way. The second generation, Swami Satyananda, Swami Vishnudevananda, Swami Satchidananda and Swami Venkatesananda, spoke about asanas and pranayamas in a scientific way. With the third generation, I hope to inspire people to speak of yoga in a classical way, which is a different approach and understanding of yoga in relation to the total human nature. So, what I am speaking about now is classical yoga, not the traditional or the scientific approach. Classical yoga combines both the scientific and the traditional approaches.

State of festivity

After completing the practice of asana and coming to a mode of steadiness and harmony in the neuro-muscular structure, there are five different stages of pranayama. The first stage begins with learning how to breathe properly. The second stage is controlling and directing the breath. The third stage is understanding the states of body and mind in relation to the breath. The fourth stage is becoming aware of the impulses which are being generated in the neuro-cellular structure of the body, becoming aware of the physical and the pranic link between the body and the brain. The fifth stage is allowing the pranas to dominate the functions of the body. These are the five stages of pranayama. The first three are known as prana nigraha and the last two are the actual pranayama.

In the fourth and fifth stages of pranayama, the perineal space, the thoracic space and the head space are linked in one unit. Fusion of pranas takes place, and I have used the plural here, because prana is not one. There are different kinds of pranas, for example, the *apana* force which is situated in the perineum, is a downward moving prana. It is responsible for the elimination of waste products from the body, for excretion and urination, for the discharge of everything from the body, so that the body maintains a state of wellbeing and harmony. Now, when the flow of this prana is altered by the practice of pranayama, along with the practices of bandha and mudra, the dissipated energies are rechannelled and focused internally.

In this way we work with the different pranas, focusing them and experiencing the opposite activity of those forces.

When the opposite activity of the prana is being experienced by the aspirant, then the resulting hyperactivity or the increase in the generation of impulses and pranas, totally controls the mind and brain function. The body then enters the state of ecstasy, euphoria, festivity. In this state every cell is dancing and vibrating with joy. Every cell is pulsating with life. This is the physical festival attained through the right practice of asana and pranayama.

The Pranic Dimension

Now we will continue with our topic about how the cells of the body become enlightened. For this, yoga has described two practices, asana and pranayama. We are dealing with the subject of pranayama here, but before we go into our discussion, I would like to make it clear that although the techniques are physical in nature, they are also pranic, mental and psychic, and interaction takes place on all levels.

Just imagine that for a moment you are placing your finger on top of a candle flame and then you remove it. Now this was just a physical act of placing the finger near the candle flame and then removing it. However, in the course of performing this simple act, many things have happened. An interaction has occurred between the finger, which is a physical part, and the brain, involving sensory input, past experience, intellect and the pranic effect. All these have merged into one interacting movement. When we take the finger to the flame, we feel the heat. What is feeling the heat? Who is feeling the heat? Is it the finger, the nerve endings or the brain that feels the heat? Is it the intellect or the memory that recognises the heat, or is it prana that experiences the heat? We do not know.

If we take one approach, then we can say that the finger feels the heat. If we take another approach, we can say that the brain feels the heat. We may be happy with any one approach

154

but, in actual fact, there has been an interaction from the most physical to the most subtle level of our being. This is the interaction which we have to become aware of in the practice of pranayama. Prana in its cosmic manifestation is just pure energy. In the causal manifestation it takes the form of kundalini energy. In its subtle manifestation it takes the form of *nadis*, channels, flows of energy. In the physical manifestation it takes the form of the breath and the prana, which are responsible for governing specific parts, organs and senses of the body. This is a very broad topic, and we are going to start from the beginning with the physical dimension.

Five pranas

The prana in the physical body has been classified into five different groups according to its function. The first is *apana*, the downward moving force, situated between the navel and the perineum, responsible for the expulsion, excretion and removal of toxic matter, which is physical, mental and psychic. Sometimes people get diarrhoea because of a mental conflict, and people also get diarrhoea because of a viral attack. When the diarrhoea is caused by some form of inner conflict, that is a form of mental expulsion, toxins of the mind are being removed. When one is under emotional tension, emotional stress, at that time also certain forms of elimination take place physically and at other levels as well. This is the function of apana energy.

The second energy is *samana*, situated between the navel and the diaphragm. This prana has lateral movement and it is responsible for assimilation. After we eat, the food is assimilated by the body, not only in the physical context but also in the pranic context. Whatever has been assimilated and digested is distributed to other areas of the body and to the pranic dimensions.

The third prana, situated between the diaphragm and the throat, is known as *prana*. It is an upward moving force which is responsible for the maintenance and the functioning of the organs in the chest cavity, the lungs and the heart. The fourth prana is *udana* which moves in a circular direction and

155

is located in the arms, legs and the head. It is responsible for the functioning of the brain, the sensory organs and the co-ordination and movement of the arms and legs. The fifth prana is *vyana* which is also known as the second breath, the reserve force. It is an inter-penetrating force and is located throughout the body.

These are the five different pranas and their functions at the gross level. At the subtle level they also govern the psychic centres which are located along the sushumna passage in the spine. Apana, the first, controls mooladhara and swadhisthana. Samana, the second, controls manipura. Prana, the third, controls anahata and vishuddhi. Udana, the fourth, controls ajna, and vyana, the fifth, controls sahasrara.

Awakening and merging the pranas

These five pranas are also linked with the breath. When we learn how to breathe properly in the initial stages of pranayama, the prana nigraha techniques, an effort is made to change the flow of three pranas: prana, apana, and samana. The flow of apana, the downward moving force, is reversed and made to move upward. The flow of prana, the upward moving force, is reversed and made to flow downward. These flows are then merged in the samana area and this is the awakening of the pranas. The aim of pranayama initially is to activate the pranas through breath control, and later on through the practices of mudra and bandha.

Therefore, mudra and bandha are incorporated in the later stages of pranayama. Initially, when we are dealing with the normal breathing process, we do not practise bandha or mudra. For example, in nadi shodhana, we begin with simple breathing in and out through the nostrils. Gradually we lengthen the ratio of inhalation and exhalation, and we add the ratios of inner and outer retention. As we progress further, we incorporate bandha and mudra into our nadi shodhana practice. After inhalation we practise jalandhara bandha and moola bandha while holding the breath inside, then after releasing the bandhas, we breathe out and practise the three bandhas: jalandhara, uddiyana and moola, while holding the breath out. This is how the simple breathing technique is combined with bandha and mudra.

When the combination of prana nigraha with mudra and bandha takes place, the pranas change the direction of their flow and they meet in the centre at samana, which is known as the agni mandala. Here we are not talking of manipura chakra. The word *agni* means 'fire' or 'vitality' and *mandala* means 'zone', 'dimension' or 'area'. So, agni mandala is the 'dimension of vitality', 'the zone of fire'. These three pranas actually merge and become one in agni mandala.

Expansion of pranas

Now we move into the classical side of yoga. Classical yoga is not a theory of yoga. Rather, it is the next step in our own practice which we have to consider, experience and realise. Classical yoga becomes an aid to the furthering of our own understanding of yoga, and this yoga talks about expanding the dimensions of prana. First is the awakening of prana, second is the merger of prana, and third is expanding the dimensions of prana.

Now we move into the subtle personality. We experience the effects of ida and pingala on the human personality, the body, the mind, the emotions and the intellect. Here swara yoga, the science of brain breathing, comes in. There is a book on swara yoga, published by Bihar School of Yoga, which will give you a better understanding. All the five pranas divide into the ida force and the pingala force. The active or dynamic aspect of prana is the pingala force and the passive or subtle aspect of prana is the ida force. Ida and pingala are the areas on which we work in our own practice of pranayama.

I have seen very extrovert, dynamic and outgoing people, suddenly become quiet and introvert, many times even entering deep states of depression, by the simple practice of pranayama. This is an indication that the ida aspect of prana has become overactive. From hyperactivation it takes one to a state of total withdrawal, isolation and even depression. The opposite can also happen. People who are totally withdrawn and depressed suddenly become overactive and do not know how to control their body. Their fingers never remain quiet; they are always doing something, moving something. This is hyperactivity of the pranas, either in the ida or the pingala range. Some of us have gone through these stages as well.

Then, in the third stage, when we have attained some kind of balance in the ida and pingala pranic performance, and the body and brain have come into attunement with the pranas, work begins with the mind on the causal level, the chakras and kundalini. We have taken the practice of nadi shodhana as our example. If the process is correct, this pranayama can awaken the chakras and stimulate the kundalini energy. When the kundalini energy is activated, changes take place in the field of consciousness, and we experience altered states.

To attain altered states of consciousness is not really difficult. We undergo different states practically every hour during the day. For example, sleep is an altered state of mind. Emotional hyperactivity, depression and anxiety are altered states of mind. An altered state of mind does not mean something spiritual or beyond our comprehension. It simply means becoming aware of another dimension, another area of interaction in our own personality and consciousness. With the awakening of kundalini and the chakras, the mind undergoes certain changes, because kundalini is cosmic prana and the chakras are centres of prana in the causal body,

The perceptions change, visions change, and this interaction takes place on the physical, pranic and mental levels, including the level of ego. This is why the yogic texts have emphasised the practice of asana and pranayama as a means to harmonise the external, physical organs of the body with the pranic field and with the emotions, feelings, mind, intellect, samskaras and karmas. If we begin to look at our own practices of asana and pranayama from this viewpoint and try to understand them, we will find that in a very short period the experiences of our body will change. We will be able to feel the need of the little finger and this need is not an intellectual process. We become the little finger, we become

158

the whole body, we become an integrated unit, and that is the enlightenment of the physical body with the practice of asana and pranayama.

Practical note

So, there are certain things you should do at the time of asana and pranayama practice. On the first day, when you practise your asana and pranayama, just have the outer vision of the body, of the muscles and the joints being exercised. During pranayama, feel that the lungs are being exercised. Do not go any further than this.

On the second day, drop this awareness of the muscles, bones, joints and limbs, and move into a deeper level of your body, maybe into the atomic structure. While you are practising asana and pranayama, see yourself as an atomic being. The body is not to be viewed as something made up of skin, blood vessels, bones, marrow. Have the concept of an atomic structure within the body and see the response of the atoms to the asanas and pranayamas. Do not go beyond this.

On the third day, practise this same set of asana and pranayama, but be aware of the neuro-cellular structure of the body. See the interaction of asana (the movement), pranayama, (the breath) and prana (the energy) in that dimension.

On the fourth day, practise the same, but go deeper into the dimension of energy, pure energy. Visualise your body in the form of light; the arms, the legs, the trunk, are made up of different patterns of light. When you practise an asana or a pranayama, see the sparks fly.

On the fifth day, go into another level. Experience your body as consciousness only, not as a physical structure. Experience the body as a feeling, as an emotion, and see the change in the state of emotion and feeling within the body.

On the sixth day, see yourself as pure logic, *buddhi*, and experience that dimension at the time of asana and pranayama practice.

On the seventh day, disassociate yourself completely from your body and mind. See them as a separate being

159

practising asana and pranayama. Do not associate yourself with the pains and pleasures of the physical, mental, emotional or rational states. Just see the natural spontaneous performance of the body and mind.

Like this, move from one stage to the next and if you complete this process, in seven days, then on the eighth day your perception about yourself and your awareness of your body will have changed. When you reach this state through sadhana and continued effort, where you are able to see in one glimpse the actions and interactions of the entire neuro-cellular structure with prana, with consciousness, then you will know that you are ready to move on into the stages of pratyahara and dharana. Try this method. It is very fascinating and it will give you a new dimension of understanding within yourself.

Re-education of the Mind

MAY 20, 1994

Before attempting to know more about the pratyahara and dharana techniques of mind education, it is necessary to understand what the mind is from the yogic viewpoint. The yogic approach to the mind is very clear and systematic. It recognises the various areas and dimensions of mind function. Only after attempting to know the areas of the mind will we be able to appreciate and understand the techniques of mind education. I am not saying 'mental' education, I am saying 'mind' education, because it is here that restructuring and reformatting of the mind take place.

Generally, yoga has divided the total structure of the mind into four compartments, which are known as: manas, buddhi, chitta and ahamkara. *Manas* has been translated as the rational aspect, *buddhi* as the intellectual aspect, *chitta* as the aspect which perceives, and *ahamkara* as the ego. But the actual yogic concept is slightly different. There are two aspects of human nature: one is pure and one is impure. The impure mind relates with the world of name, form and idea, and that is our normal mind. The pure mind relates to the cosmic mind, the cosmic link between an individual and the Self.

Three areas of the functional mind

We function at the level of impure mind. Here 'impure' means distorted, not having the purity, the clarity, that is the

161

inherent nature of the Self. The impure or the distorted mind functions effectively in the dimensions of time, space and object; name, form and idea. It recognises them. It also functions under the influence of the three gunas: tamas, rajas and sattwa. This is the mind which we deal with every day. Now we will look at the three areas of the impure mind: (i) time, space and object; (ii) name, form and idea; and (iii) the gunas.

This distorted mind is limited by the concepts of time, space and object. Time represents states of continuity and stoppage, going forward and stopping. This sequence of moving forward and stopping is seen in the form of time. At one given moment we stop; at another given moment we move. Where do we move? We move in space. Our body moves in space. The sequence of life, from birth to death, moves in space. Thoughts move in space. This space is the area of our interaction. What is meant by object? When identification or recognition of a situation, an event or a person takes place, that is awareness of the object. Pleasure or pain can be an object of identification when we become aware of it. So, objective awareness is a state in which identification is experienced, known, perceived, and realised.

The second dimension of the mind is name, form and idea, which relates more with the aspect of buddhi, intellect. Intellect or the faculty of recognition moves in these three areas. When we see something, we perceive the form. That form conveys an idea and the idea a name. That is how recognition takes place, "I am the body." Body is what? It is a form and that form has been given a name, 'body'. The name is conveyed by an idea that the body is like this; it has a certain shape. This is how buddhi, the intellect recognises the manifest dimension.

The third area is the influence of the three gunas: tamas, rajas and sattwa. These three gunas are very much related with the normal day-to-day expressions. For example, when one becomes possessive about something and there is an attachment to it, whether it is a friend, a relative, a piece of cloth or any item, such as a ring, then that is the rajasic quality. Possessiveness is rajasic, because that is where 'I' becomes the dominating factor; "It belongs to me", "I am the owner". We always express the rajasic tendency more than the tamasic or sattwic tendency. Even the craving for satisfaction, fulfilment or attainment, is very much a rajasic trait. In fact, our whole upbringing and education is rajasic, whether individual or social. We live in a rajasic environment, and it is very difficult for us to move from this state into a state which is more subtle, more sattwic.

Tamas represents stagnation or fixation in one condition, state, perception or belief in life, and it also represents deep aggression which is self-destructive. For example, a fourteen year old boy walks around with a pack of beer. That may be a very ordinary thing for an adult to do, but what is the moral and ethical concept of that young boy? Is beer good for a fourteen year old boy, especially if he drinks a few packs? This type of self-destructive behavior, whether it is due to a reaction, a compulsion or to acute aggression, is tamasic. Aggression in the rajasic state is not as self-destructive as it is in the tamasic state.

Stagnation, being satisfied and content with our position, with our understanding of life, and not having the drive to develop a broader vision, that is tamasic. The mental and creative faculties stagnate. One hundred percent of humanity functions within the area of these two gunas, rajas and tamas. So, these are the three areas of the mind.

Four classifications of the mind
Now, let us come back to the different classifications of the mind. Manas, the rational power, which thinks, which creates thought processes, is very much subject to the influence of events, people and circumstances. If somebody tells you many times that Swami Niranjan is very bad, then, without having met me, you will believe what that person has said. You will be influenced by that person. After a month, if somebody tells you ten times that Swami Niranjan is a very good person, then, without having ever seen me, you will find that you are changing your ideas. Again you are being influenced by someone else's input.

What does that mean? It means that manas, the rational mind, is not capable of recognising and assimilating information on its own. The assimilation of information normally takes place at a very superficial level, because the mind is influenced by the gunas, by people, by events and by circumstances. This aspect of the mind shadows buddhi, the intellect. We all have the same intelligence. It is how we apply it that makes the difference. Some people are very intelligent and yet totally gullible, while others may not seem to be so intelligent, but it is impossible to take advantage of them. Conditioning of the intellect, of buddhi, takes place.

The third classification of the mind is chitta, the aspect which perceives. Chitta has another function too, which is *bhavana*, feeling, emotion. Yet nobody speaks of chitta in terms of bhavana. Yoga speaks of chitta as the ability to perceive by a rational process as well as by an emotional process. You walk into a room and suddenly you feel uplifted; that was chitta experiencing and assimilating the environment of the room. You come across a certain person on the road and you get the shivers. Suddenly the thought comes, "Gee, I really don't like that guy." That is chitta, feeling out the vibrations of that person. You see another person and you feel very happy; again, that is chitta, feeling out the projections of that person.

So, chitta functions more on the level of feeling and emotion, natural emotion, not projected emotion. Projected emotion is anger, anxiety, frustration. These are the feelings we project very well. If we try to project our love, we go all gooey eyed. We can project anxiety, but we cannot project compassion, because projection of a distorted state of mind and emotion is more natural to us than projection of a natural and spontaneous state. When things come up from the depths of our personality, a feeling, an emotion which cannot be rationalised, then we have to run to a psychotherapist who teaches us how to accept and define that feeling and how to behave with it. Small things can totally alter the human perception. I will tell you one small story which illustrates this point.

164

There is a person here who is a very close friend of mine. I do not have many friends, and I have very few close friends. He was and is one of the close friends. We both respect each other a lot. When I was in Australia last, that person asked me, "When are we going to see you again?" I gave a shrug, and this shrug actually meant, "Whenever our paths cross again". But, the shrug was taken in a different way, "Get lost". This friend became so upset with me that for three years he was angry. Aggression came out, and eventually, he had to go to a psychotherapist. Whatever happened with the psychotherapist is another story, but the final point was: What is there to be angry about? Why the aggression? It was a normal human interaction, but when an idea, an expectation overpowered the state of feeling, then he wound up a mental case. That is what happens to many people, and that is how the psychiatrists collect their rent. The neurotic builds a castle in the air, the psychotic lives in it and the psychiatrist collects the rent. That is the range of our mental interaction, and we have never moved beyond it.

Ego or ahamkara, the fourth aspect of the mind, is the overpowering one. Ego can represent many things: the need for security, for recognition. It can mean many things to many people. This is the area of the impure mind.

Pratyahara

Now, when we practise yoga and begin to re-educate ourselves, what do we do first? There is a process of recognising what is happening in the body and in the mind, in the visible part of the mind, not the invisible. Modern psychology says that there is a conscious, a subconscious and an unconscious aspect of the mind. Interactions take place in all the three levels, but it is recognition of the first level, the conscious, which is important initially, and that is the meaning of the word *pratyahara*.

Tradition says that the state of pratyahara is similar to a turtle withdrawing all of its limbs inside the shell. In the same way, in pratyahara, we withdraw the senses from outside and focus them inside. Why is this comparison with a turtle always

165

used? Why not with any other animal or condition? It is because the turtle has six limbs: two arms, two legs, one tail and one head. In times of attack, it withdraws those six limbs. The arms, legs and tail represent the five indriyas, and the head represents the mind. So, this is a very apt description of the state of pratyahara.

The senses and the mind constantly interact with each other. In order to educate and to sublimate them, it is necessary to withdraw them from the impure mind, from the world of time, space and object, from the world of name, form and idea, from the world of tamas, rajas and sattwa gunas. This process starts in the beginning stages of pratyahara where we practise, for example, the technique of antar mouna. What do we do in that practice? First we become aware of the senses. Later on, we become aware of the thought process, and finally, we try to disconnect the senses and the thought process by observing them and eventually stopping their activity.

This is the first stage of pratyahara. There are many other techniques of pratyahara which have not yet been taught, published, or even discovered. This stage deals only with the conscious area of mind. The pratyahara techniques which are utilised today in yoga, such as yoga nidra, antar mouna, ajapa japa and trataka, are techniques that deal with the conscious area of the mind. The practices which deal with the subconscious and unconscious have not yet been discovered or brought to light. In the future, a new book is going to come out, describing all the techniques of pratyahara, and you will see that those practices go much deeper into the mind than the ones that we know now. One of these new practices is known as *Hamsa Dhyana*. This is a very fascinating technique, because here we become aware of the various traits of the human personality.

I have a special theory which can be used for understanding the human personality. It is called the SWAN theory, not 'swan' meaning the bird, it is an acronym. S stands for strength of mind, W for weakness of mind, A for ambitions in life, and N for needs in life. We all have certain strengths, in some they are more active, and in others they are less active. We all have weakness, such as lack of self-confidence, fear, inferiority complex, and any kind of emotional or even deep psychic imbalance. We also have certain ambitions of which some are tamasic and some are rajasic. There is a desire for fulfilment and satisfaction, a desire to have the latest model car; these can be ambitions or needs. Is it important to have a new car? Many times we confuse ambition with need; an ambition becomes our need, and many times a weakness or a strength becomes our ambition. Recognising this and letting go of these different blockages is the culmination point of pratyahara.

Dharana

When we have released the senses and withdrawn the mind from the areas of deep attachment and attraction, then we move into the state of dharana which is one-pointed concentration. In dharana, after detachment has taken place from the areas of attachment, involvement and identification, the inherent qualities begin to manifest. It is the manifestation and recognition of those qualities which is the actual dharana. Unless and until we are able to recognise those qualities, we cannot move into *dhyana*, the meditative aspect. This is because dhyana is a state of mind; it is not a practice. The practices stop after dharana. In dharana, we become more focused, balanced, harmonious and aware, in relation to the outer mind. In relation to the inner mind, we become more active and stable in the sattwic nature. The transition takes place from tamasic to sattwic, from rajasic to sattwic.

So, it is here that the first sutra of Patanjali becomes relevant: 'Yoga is a process of self-discipline', and this discipline is a natural outcome of the balanced human personality. When we are learning how to drive a car, the teacher tells us when to brake, when to accelerate, when to change the gears. He teaches us to listen to the engine and to be alert and active. After some time we do not have to think about when to change gears, we just do it naturally and spontaneously. Similarly, when the qualities which are inherent within you manifest and

167

there is recognition and application of them in practical life, that is the culmination of dharana.

Dharana means 'to hold', 'holding onto'. It is not just a tranquil, balanced, harmonious, mental state, but also the qualities and the faculties that one experiences in this state. The experience of these qualities is not momentary. We do not experience and get a buzz out of them only at the time of meditation. We begin to experience them every moment of our life. This is the concept of discipline which one attains in pratyahara and dharana.

Meditation, Reintegration
and Initiation

MAY 21, 1994

Yesterday I was telling you about the yogic concept of mind and the range of the practices of pratyahara and dharana. In order to come to the point of self-discipline in the practices of pratyahara and dharana, we need to work with the area of mind which is known as the impure mind. In dharana the inner faculties are awakened and focused. Dharana is not just withdrawing the mind from the external world and fixing it on one point; it is also understanding and applying the result of an awakened mind in our lifestyle. This awakened mind in the dharana state is the necessary aspect prior to beginning the practice of meditation. Meditation leads on to the pure state of mind.

In the impure state, with the practice of pratyahara and dharana, we have moved from the conscious, the subconscious, to the unconscious. We have moved from the tamasic to the rajasic state, and we are learning to understand the sattwic state. We have moved the attention from the world of name, form and idea, and we have fixed it in one state where these external distinctions do not exist. When the external distinctions do not exist, then the inherent qualities of life begin to manifest. With the manifestation of these qualities, we move into the dhyana aspect, into the pure mind. What is pure mind? Pure mind is a state which unites an individual with other fellow beings and with cosmic forces.

169

Concept of self-isolation

I have never subscribed to the belief that samadhi is the culmination of yoga. In samadhi one isolates oneself from other people and from other external realities. This isolation goes against he basic precepts and principles of yoga, because the word *yoga* means 'unity', 'harmony'. In the name of harmony and unity, we isolate ourselves within ourselves, and we go on an ego trip which is a creation of our own mind. Therefore, isolation of an individual from other beings cannot be the aim of yoga.

Supposing we sit down, close the eyes and practise the so-called meditative technique. There is disconnection with the outer world, with the senses and the mind. We become lost in an inner space, which does not really mean anything except as a state or a feeling of nothingness, shoonya. When we come out of that state we say, "Oh, it was a nice meditation", when in fact, what we experienced was a nice isolation. It is like being inside one of those sensory deprivation tanks. You go in and float in space, forgetting about the body and the sensory perceptions. That is how we understand meditation and samadhi, although this is not the state to be aspired for either in meditation or in samadhi.

Process of meditation

There are two ways of understanding the process of meditation. In the meditative mode, we move from the concept of trinity, to the concept of duality, to the concept of unity. Paramahamsaji has said in his discourses that there are three aspects of meditation: (i) the practitioner, the meditator; (ii) the process of meditation; and (iii) the aim of meditation. When we are aware of these three aspects: that I am sitting down, I am following a process and this is the aim, then this diversified awareness is actually the experiencing of the trinity concept: three states or three conditions of being.

As we go deeper, sometimes one aspect drops. The self-identity or the awareness of the process may drop. One aspect drops depending on the condition of emotion and intellect of the practitioner. So, only two aspects remain, the concept of

170

duality, either me and the aim or the process and the aim. As we go deeper, even this condition changes and we simply become aware of the aim. A merger takes place with the aim, the state, the result of meditation. That is the initial stage of knowing; it is a milestone in meditation. We have come to a point where the mind is not distracted anymore.

Reintegration
There is another dimension beyond this state, and that is the aspect of unifying an individual with other fellow beings and the reintegrating of the self with the environment, with the world. This is something which we tend to miss out. We have never really considered this aspect of meditation, of reintegration with the world. This reintegration takes place in a different way.

After we have worked through the impure mind and the gunas and entered into the pure mental dimension, four qualities are experienced or seen. These qualities are: affection, love, compassion and devotion. If you are not able to experience these, then you are not practising meditation. Please do not consider the concept of self-isolation as the actual meditative process. In meditation, self-isolation does not exist. These four qualities of affection, love, compassion and devotion bring one closer to the divinity inside and the divinity outside and to other fellow beings.

The generation or the natural manifestation of these four qualities softens up the prana as well. What is 'softening up' the prana? Our pranas are very hard at present. They are conditioned. They are structured to function, to act and to interact in a certain, limited and very individual way. The softening up of the pranas is actually the restructuring of the pranic energy which controls the mind and the body, and which also links the human spirit with the mind and body. In the lifestyle that Paramahamsaji is leading now, he is spontaneously and naturally expressing these qualities and that is how I have come to understand it.

Paramahamsaji was always very compassionate towards me. When I was leaving India to go abroad he said to me,

171

"Niranjan, you are not under any form of obligation to me, to yoga or to sannyasa. You are free to choose your own way of life. If you want to settle abroad, if you want to marry, if you want to take a job, if you want to remain as a sannyasi, you can do it." He gave me total freedom. For many years I looked at him with critical eyes and compared him to other teachers and masters. I tried to find out what made him different to them. What was the quality in him which had attracted me to him? Only now I realise that what attracted me to him was his understanding of the process of sadhana. He always said that the stage which you consider to be final is not final.

Culmination of yoga sadhana

One cannot define perfection. Perfection is an ongoing process. And if one defines perfection in any way, then one has totally missed the point. If one considers that a miracle is making God do one's bidding, then that is wrong. When we pray, "Oh God, please allow this to happen," and that thing happens, then we say, "A miracle has taken place. I was able to convince God to do my bidding." But I have come to understand that the real miracle takes place when one lives according to the will of God. This is what I have seen in the life of Paramahamsaji and in his sadhana which he is performing even today, as a sannyasin, as a disciple. The flowering of that sadhana within him has gone far beyond the state of samadhi. He has reintegrated himself with the world, with the society, with people, from the other dimension of pure mind. These four qualities are seen in him, and because I am convinced that yes, this is how the yoga sadhana must culminate in our life, I am telling you this. Isolation, no. Integration, yes.

This integration is comprised of four aspects:
1. *Love*, which is not a conditioned love or an expecting love, but an unconditioned, universal love.
2. *Affection*, which does not have a motive, but is a natural state of being.
3. *Compassion*, which is not for the sake of gaining name, fame or recognition, but which becomes a natural expression of the human personality.

172

4. *Devotion* or *bhakti*, the key which links the individual with the higher being, which gives a sense of unity, a unifying force to the entire creation of which we are all a part.

The development of these four qualities is the real sadhana, the real process of yoga. We have to learn to recognise our own ego trips if we want to derive or achieve something from the practices. Possibly it is this recognition of our own ego trips which is the most difficult part of our realisation. How do we recognise what is an ego trip and what is not an ego trip?

Initiation

Many people ask about having higher forms of initiation. Do not consider one form of initiation to be superior to another. Rather, any form of initiation must be followed with an effort to change oneself. There is a stage in our lives when we all dream of changing the world. I used to dream of that too. Paramahamsaji always reminded me, "No. Instead of changing the world, why don't you change yourself." As I gain more maturity day by day I feel that yes, the change has to come and we have to strive for it. In initiation we also have to strive for that change.

After initiation, there is a code of conduct which must be followed. This code of conduct is universally applicable. Know who you are. Be honest. Be truthful to yourself. Be observant. Many times I have seen that people who take some form of initiation feel that they have become instant prophets. They behave in a funny way also, maybe with an eye for profit! A prophet with an eye for profit. That totally goes against the principles of yoga and spirituality. Many times people feel that after taking initiation they have become free, and where do they express their freedom? In the market. They go out to the market and say, "Now I have become free and I can do all the things in life which I have never done before."

Guru and disciple

There is a short story of a few disciples tagging along behind their Guru who goes out to the market. The Guru

173

enters a discotheque. The disciples look at each other and say "That is forbidden, but if our Guru is going in, let us also go and have a good time." After spending an hour in the disco they come out and the Guru walks into a pub. The disciples look at each other and say, "This is prohibited, but if the Guru is going in, let us go also ." So, they all go into the pub and have something to drink. When they come out, the Guru walks into the red light district. Again the disciples say, "It is prohibited, but if Guru is going, let us go also." During the course of their wandering and enjoyment, they come to a factory where molten glass is being poured. The Guru goes inside, picks up a cup full of molten glass and drinks it. The disciples look at each other and say, "Only Gurus can do that."

Step by step

What you should understand from this story is that, after initiation, your perceptions have to change. Initiation does not just mean wearing geru and feeling part of the elite club, feeling divine and sublime. You have to make an effort to follow the code of conduct, which will enhance your own sensitivity, receptivity and creativity. It is better to take one step at a time; do not try to jump. Along with this code of conduct, which enumerates the qualities which you need to develop in your life, there are certain other things that you need to study to gain greater clarity of thought and to know what you are actually doing with your life. You must be true to yourself, not true to me, and go step by step.

In my mind, poorna sannyasins, karma sannyasins, jignasu sannyasins and the yoga students, are all on an equal plane. It is your sincerity and your commitment which makes the difference, not the initiation. If you are initiated as a poorna sannyasin and you are not committed, not sincere, what is the use? You are duping yourself. You are not being true to yourself. You have made the first mistake of your spiritual journey. You are trying to drive the car without getting into it. So, take it step by step.

174

Emergence of a
Paramahamsa

MAY 21, 1994

This is the last session of the Yoga Festival and tonight it is my wish to tell you about the present lifestyle of Paramahamsaji who has been a source of inspiration to us all which we can never forget or ignore. The more I think about Paramahamsaji, the less I see him as a Guru and the more I see him as an eternal inspiration, lighting up the path. In fact, from the very beginning of his ashram life with Swami Sivananda, he has been a very special person.

In "Sankalpa", one of the early poems which Paramahamsaji wrote when he first took sannyasa, he said:

> *"I shall run into the desert of life*
> *with my arms open and a smile on my lips,*
> *sometimes stumbling, sometimes falling,*
> *but always picking myself up,*
> *a thousand times if necessary."*

This has been the way of Paramahamsaji all along. He has lived this sankalpa throughout his life and it becomes clearer as we watch him evolve into the paramahamsa stage of sannyasa.

What is sannyasa? We have seen people with shaved head wearing strange, roman type robes and wondered, "What is this kind of spirituality? What is sannyasa and where does it end?" Of course, Paramahamsaji has talked about sannyasa in his lectures, but talking about something and living something are two different things. We also talk about many things, but we don't live them? There is always some form of ego trip in our life, and this ego is a very funny thing also. The more we think about ego and how to get rid of it, the more we tend to latch onto that ego field.

Ego identity

Ego can take many different forms and shapes. It is like the hydra. You cut off one head and another head replaces it. You cut off that head and you see a third head and a fourth head, ad infinitum. This is because in the manifest dimension, ego identity is the root of life, and if that ego identity is lost, then life as we know it no longer exists. It exists as light; life becomes light. That has been the aspiration of all the spiritual seekers in the course of history: to overcome, to transcend, to sublimate this aspect of nature. However, very few have been able to do it. Very few, through their effort, have been able to come out of the gravitational field of ego. You may think that as you move away from the centre of the ego, you are getting away from it, but the attraction, the gravitational force becomes more powerful as you move away from it.

Normally, in our life, this ego manifests either in the form of fear and insecurity or in the form of desire for power and recognition. That is the crude form of ego. Even in the most content and sattwic state which we can perceive through our impure mind, there is always some desire for appreciation and recognition. I will give you an example. A person carries with him, in his wallet a newspaper cutting with his picture, maybe of an interview which happened thirty years back. Whenever the opportunity presents itself, he shows that newspaper cutting and says, "Look, this is me thirty years back." This is a very simple thing, but it represents an aspect of ego, desire for recognition.

In the body and mind, ego manifests as the glue which holds the personality together. In the crude form, the tamasic form, it is destructive. In a more refined form, it boosts and

176

increases the self-image and makes one adopt an identity which one is not. That is the rajasic state of ego. Even in sattwic state, there is ego. As long as the 'I' awareness remains, ego is there.

Ego in the spiritual process

So, when do we come to the point where the influence of ego can be eliminated from our consciousness? It happens in the meditative state, but even here we have to work hard on ourself. During meditation, if we see a vision of a demon or some bad thing, we feel uncomfortable and we say, "This practice is not right for me; I should not see such a vision." Then we try to block out that negativity which is coming up from within; we suppress it. At that time, the ego looks at us, smiles and says, "You are doing fine; you are coming into my grip." This is because the ego creates a conditioning of perception, of seeing, of understanding. The opposite can happen too. We may have a vision of God, of angels or of light. After that, the purity of the vision is lost, and in future meditations, we begin to crave more and more for similar experiences.

Even this positive experience which is manifesting naturally creates a conditioning, so ego smiles again and says, "Good, you are in my power." It is here that we have to be careful in the process of sadhana, always remembering that the aim must be to attain purification first. Only when purification is attained can we evolve further. This idea must remain alive all the time in our mind. When this idea dies down, we miss the path, we confuse our priorities, and we become obsessed with another idea, another style of living. That becomes our realm of existence once again. We may have changed from one type of life to another, but no evolution has taken place.

Many people attain *siddhis*, psychic powers. They think, "Now, we are well on the path", and they begin to use it. This kind of refined mental state which is experienced in the form of siddhi, of control over the natural elements, again becomes a force which pulls the consciousness down. So, actually, there is no end to ego manifestation in our spiritual process. Forget about life, ego is always there, but even in the spiritual process, this continues.

Jnana, karma and dharma

It is here that three things come into play. One is *jnana*, knowledge. This knowledge is not intellectual or intuitive; it is clear perception or understanding of the state of being. We may have knowledge, we may have excelled in the field of our studies, we may have attained degrees and diplomas, but where has that knowledge taken us? It has not helped us to change our lifestyle or our perception. We have not put into practice what we have learned. Even in yoga I find that people learn many things but they are not able to live them. Paramahamsaji has taught us many things. All we have to do is look at the collection of his teachings. He has said everything, but we have never applied it consciously in our life. We have taken the teachings as words of wisdom, that is all, without trying to apply them.

When this knowledge is applied, it becomes jnana, all encompassing knowledge. This jnana then takes the form of karma. The behaviour, actions, ideas, thoughts, all change and one lives life according to one's dharma. If we want to understand what an egoless state is, this is the key: living life according to one's dharma. What is dharma? Dharma is understanding of the natural state of being and living according to the natural principles governing the human personality and the cosmos. It is knowing the interaction and the process of interaction which is an inherent part of our life structure. Dharma is not responsibility, duty, or even moral and ethical knowledge and understanding. It is learning to flow with the current of life rather than against it. Jnana and karma help to provide this understanding.

Therefore, please remember, when you reach a meditative state where certain experiences begin manifesting spontaneously from within, do not get caught up in them. Try to understand them from the aspect of jnana; try to see their influence on your total structure as a person, as an individual.

178

Notice and observe what kind of desires and emotions come up, what kind of perceptions you encounter, and convert them into action. Let them not remain just a mental experience; let them become physical and interactive. It is possible for us to experience this, and if we try, we will know it for ourselves.

Bhakti

When jnana becomes karma, then another transformation takes place. That is the unfoldment of bhakti which is the real sattwic state of letting go. This letting go has to be understood in the right perspective. Letting go does not mean that we loosen all our screws. Rather, it means tightening up of the screws and becoming more centred and firm in our direction. When we become more centred and firm in our direction then bhakti evolves. Bhakti is experienced in the form of oneness with the entire creation. In this context, bhakti does not mean devotion, chanting, dancing or even the states of joy. It means the state of *Ishwara pranidhana*.

Those of you who have studied the *Yoga Sutras* of Patanjali would have come across the sutra on ishwara pranidhana, belief in God. What is this God that yoga speaks of? The power of Generation, the power of Organisation and the power of Destruction; G-O-D. These are the powers that are inherent in every individual. But this power of creation, of generation, is generally utilized externally in a limited way. The power of organisation is also used externally, in the manifest world, in a limited way. The power of change, transmutation, transformation, destruction, changing of the old into the new, takes place in the external world, in a limited way.

Man with a cosmic vision

Imagine what would happen if you were to become cosmic. All this would happen, but in an unlimited way. I will just give you one example. Where Paramahamsaji stays now, we started some social work for the people at his instruction. I am telling you this instruction, because it was a mandate which he had received from high above in meditation. The

179

mandate was: "Provide your neighbours with the same facilities that I have provided for you." What are the facilities that Paramahamsaji has at present?

He is over seventy now, yet still very dynamic, and I would say, even younger, more powerful, more piercing, more loving and more compassionate than he was in his earlier days. This is usually the age where people look for comforts and stability in life. But it was at this age that he renounced everything he had created. He could have lived comfortably in the ashram; he could have come here every year and spent time with you. He could have gone any place in the world and lived well, continuing with his teachings and interactions, but he had a call.

In fact, we have known him as a guide, as a teacher, but we have not really known the depth of his life. Many times he has said that his life cycle is divided in twenty year periods. He was born in 1923. He left home when he was twenty and became a sannyasin in 1943. He started his mission in 1963 and he left his mission to become a royal mendicant, as he used to call himself, in 1983. Before he started his yoga mission, which was a command that he had received from Swami Sivananda, he had prayed to God for help and guidance. At that time he had a vision in which it was confirmed to him that he would have divine support for a specific period of time until he was able to establish his mission properly. After the completion of this sankalpa, the divine support would leave that work, and this happened in 1983.

Paramahamsaji said that all his life he had met with success wherever he went. But after 1983, obstacles began to come up everywhere, in his ashrams, with his disciples, because he had forgotten his pledge to God. But, at that time, he could not figure out what was happening, why the obstacles were coming. When he returned from Australia in 1984, he happened to go to the place where he had made the pledge earlier, and there he suddenly remembered that vision. It came to him in a flash, that pledge, and he said, "Now I know why I am being obstructed, why things are not going as I had expected, because that support is gone."

It was at that time that he decided to leave the ashram. But, as I was new and still learning the tricks of the trade, he conceded to my request and stayed for five years longer. He finally left in 1988 for destinations unknown. In the course of his wandering, he went back to the place where he had first received the inspiration, the vision and the support for his mission. There he removed everything he was wearing, his dhotis, malas, watch, and placing them in a bundle at the feet of his ishta devata, he said, "Now, I remember my pledge. I have fulfilled my work. Tell me what I have to do next." After performing sadhana for some time in that particular spot, the message which he received was to lead the life of a *Paramahamsa*, a person who does not work for his mission or flock alone, but who has a universal vision.

Paramahamsa lifestyle

In sannyasa, there are different stages or progressions. From the first stage of sannyasa, which is known as kutichak, one progresses to bahudak, from bahudak to hamsa, from hamsa to paramahamsa, from paramahamsa to turiyateeta, and from turiyateeta to avadhoota. These are the different progressions. So, at that point, Paramahamsaji entered the state of avadhoota, the unclad sannyasin. He does not wear clothes, only a small kopin, and that he wears only when people come to see him out of respect for their mental, social conditioning. He lives alone, sleeps outside, and remains outside the whole day and night. He says that, "Previously I used to be a five star swami, now I am an infinite star swami."

He does not sleep on a bed; he sleeps on a gunny bag. Even in winter, on the coldest night, he never covers himself. His sadhanas vary. In summer, when the temperature ranges between forty five and fifty five degrees centigrade, he sits under the burning sun, surrounded by four fires, doing tapasya. This is not a ritual. It has been stated in the tradition that only those can perform this sadhana who have controlled the five fires within. Believe me, it is a tough sadhana. I know, because one day I put a thermometer where he was sitting in

181

the middle of the fires, and in five minutes the mercury rose to ninety degrees.

There he sits oblivious to everything, surrounded by four fires in the midday sun of India. I tried sitting for one hour in front, out in the open, under the sun, and for three days I had a splitting headache. So, you can imagine the resistance he has developed, physical as well as mental and psychic. This is the sadhana he performs in summer. In winter, his sadhana changes. He sits for about eight hours at one stretch, practising japa. His diet consists of one chapatti, one bowl of milk and maybe some boiled vegetables, that is all.

Global consciousness

Now this lifestyle may sound strange to you, but, I wonder, is it strange or is our way of living strange? Because what we are seeing here is a person who is undergoing a process of deep inner transformation. Those who have seen him will agree with me that his energy has changed; it has become sharper, more focused and more piercing. When you enter into the energy field, it is just incredible. As he performs his sadhanas, he becomes more in tune. He never leaves the boundaries of the place where he is, yet he knows what is happening all around him.

When we took up the project of providing his neighbours with the facilities that he has, we started constructing small mud houses for the villagers who have nothing. One day he got up from his sadhana, called Swami Satsangi and said, "In a nearby village there is a widow with six small children, and her house has burnt down. They are all sleeping under a tree. Find her and help her." It took us three days to locate the village of that woman, but he had seen what was happening just sitting there. There was a widow whose house had burnt down about a week back. She was absolutely destitute. The family had not eaten for four days; they were only surviving on water. This came to Paramahamsaji's attention during his sadhana, and he gave the instruction, "Go and help that person."

So, as you move into deeper states of meditation, your consciousness does not remain confined to yourself only, it

182

becomes one with the environment. When your consciousness becomes one with the environment, you feel what other
people are feeling. You let go of your own in-built props
which have supported you until that point, and you live in a
different dimension altogether. We call that the dimension of
siddhas, the perfected ones. But from the perspective of
Paramahamsaji, it is not a siddha state, it is a state in which he
is letting himself go. He is losing the identity of 'I am', and
fusing himself more and more with the environment, not just
the local environment, but the global environment. I can
definitely assure you that, in the course of time, you will also
see him here, not in the physical body, but he will come to you,
and you will recognise him.

A new vision of life
    That linking with every aspect and object of creation is
taking place in his life now, and since this process has started,
he has become much more simple internally. This is what
happens in meditation, too. One has to become more simple
and natural internally. One has to drop the ideas that have
supported oneself throughout life. Clean the blackboard of
the impressions that it has received in the course of life. When
the blackboard is clean, then one sees the things written there
which are not of human origin, and that is the state of
realisation. Believe me, I am not saying this because I have a
feeling for Paramahamsaji or because I am his disciple. I am
saying this from your perspective, as a person who is watching
the transformation and the emergence of yoga in the life of
one individual. He is showing us another path, that, yes, it can
be done, one can change, one can have that realisation, one
can come to terms with oneself, one can attain that purity, that
sattwic state and allow things to just happen.
    This time Paramahamsaji has also given an invitation to
everyone to go to his place and be with him for maybe a day
or two or three. It is an opportunity to reconnect with him, not
on a physical level but on a cosmic level, to get the inspiration,
the energy, and see what it does to you. I am sure that if you
accept this invitation, it will be a very uplifting experience. It

183

will give you a new vision of life, a glimpse of the sattwic state which you all aspire for, in a very simple and practical way. Do not go there to see the work that is being done, go there to connect with him, to receive that inspiration, that energy which will move you. Then you will see what the egoless state is. Because, as one becomes sattwic, one surrenders to God, and this God is not the manifest God, it is the unmanifest God.

The actual and the apparent reality

The manifest God can have name, form and quality, but the unmanifest God is just pure spirit, Ishwara, the undecaying reality which never changes. There are two kinds of reality: one is the apparent reality and the other is the actual reality. What is the apparent reality? Suppose your body is filthy, but you are wearing a clean pressed suit. You might wash your face and comb your hair, but the fact remains that the body is still filthy. Externally you may appear to be a clean person, but in actual fact you are not. There is mud clinging on underneath the clean clothes. When does the apparent reality change? When you remove the clothes and see what is actually there.

That is *maya*, illusion. This is what Vedanta has said. In a dream somebody is chasing you. You are trying to run but your feet are glued to the ground and you cannot move. You feel that intense fear, that urgent drive to run away, but you cannot. Suddenly, as the hand is coming nearer to grab you, you cry out. Then you wake up and say, "Thank God, it was only a dream." In the dream, what you were experiencing was real. But when you came out of that state, you thanked God that it was only a dream. Similarly, when you are in a tight situation, caught in the shifting sands of maya, then you think you are really trapped. However, another person sees you and says, "Look, go that way and you can come out of the quicksand. Hold that vine and pull yourself up." It is as simple as that, and you come out. Suddenly you feel yourself overtaken by exhaustion, anxiety and fear, then you just let go and relax.

So, in a situation where problems, conflicts and tensions dominate the expressions of the mind, personality and nature, it becomes difficult to have clear vision. Just moving away from the problems enables you to have clear vision. This is the basic difference between the apparent reality and the actual reality. People have been known to drown in three feet of water due to the fear of not finding support, when they could have simply stood up and come out of the water. This is known as maya, the illusion which covers reality.

Vedanta has said that the whole world is simply an illusion, because it covers the reality which is not perceived in the life which we live. The moment we become aware of that reality, the dross of the world drops away. It is this dropping of the veil which is the aspect of bhakti. Jnana culminates in karma and karma culminates in bhakti. It is through these three stages that we become egoless, we become one with the universal energy. This is the aim of yoga, the direction that we have to move towards, and it is a joyful experience, not a static experience. If we begin to practise yoga in earnest, then every moment of life becomes a moment of joy. When we become aware of our physical and mental movements, then every movement becomes a movement of joy. Then we begin to dance to the tune of the cosmic harmony. That is the dance, and it is the dance of letting go. So, let us let end with this song:

"Dance, dance, wherever you may be,
I am the Lord of the Dance, said he,
I will lead you all, wherever you may be,
I will lead you all in the dance, said he."

13

Theory of Meditation

MAY 27, 1994

We have come here to experience within ourselves what yoga and meditation can mean to us, and how they can be applied in our day to day life. We all have our concepts about yoga and meditation. These are two terms which cannot be separated, nor should we try to separate them, because ultimately yoga and meditation mean the same thing. They lead the aspirant to the same experience. In this context, both yoga and meditation become tools or mediums by which one's inner nature can be experienced.

Sakara and nirakara

People have accepted yoga as a set of physical practices and meditation as a set of mental practices, but I do not see them as being different. The aim of yoga and meditation is to know the Self with a capital 'S', the Self which manifests in the external world as a personality, a mind, a body, a nature, and the Self which exists in the unmanifest dimension as pure consciousness and energy. We live in two different dimensions. The first is *sakara*, the manifest dimension, which has form, which can be perceived, known, recognised and identified. The second is *nirakara*, the unmanifest dimension, which is formless, unrecognisable and infinite. The aim of human evolution is to move from the manifest towards the unmanifest.

186

We function in the manifest dimension with our ideas and beliefs, rationality and emotion, behaviour and action. We slowly evolve and create new concepts, new understandings of life, divinity, bhakti, jnana and karma. In the manifest dimension, we discuss in great detail and go to great pains to discover the nature of reality, but we never know what is real. There is a story of Moolah Nasruddin, a sufi saint, who is called one day to give a speech. He gets up on the stage and begins by saying, "I am not going to speak the truth, because I have never spoken truth in my life. I do not know what truth is."

Of course, this statement of his can be taken in two ways: one, that he is a liar beyond compare, and the other, that he has not been able to experience the true reality which is beyond the normal range of human perception and understanding. If I were to say to you that I have never spoken the truth in my life, what would your first thought be? You would think that this swami is a fraud and he is admitting that he has never spoken the truth. This idea shows the interaction of the mind with some event, some situation, somebody with whom we are trying to relate. The other idea, that there is an esoteric meaning to this statement, that truth is something beyond comprehension, which cannot be expressed, explained or defined, would never come into our mind. Why? Because of the conditioning, the programming of our nature, in relation to the world in which we live.

Role of yoga and meditation

So, what role can yoga and meditation eventually play in our life? Do they make us feel comfortable and happy with our idiosyncrasies, or do they eventually change our nature and extend our receptors towards infinity? The second theory would be more appropriate. They are the means, the methods which bring about a change in the normal perception. It is from this angle that we have to view yoga and meditation, because we live, we express our nature in the manifest world. The aim of yoga and meditation, whether we call it *samadhi*, *nirvana*, *mukti*, or *kaivalya*, represents a

187

state of perception, a state of being, which is beyond the manifest personality.

Our concepts of divinity, of God, as a female figure or a male figure, a white figure or a black figure, are sakara concepts. However, when we enter the realm of nirakara, the unmanifest, the unknown, then these concepts do not apply. They do not give the right understanding; they do not convey the right message. The nature of the human personality has to change with the practices of yoga. If we are unable to change our nature, personality, attitude, behaviour and actions, then definitely we are not practising yoga in the right spirit.

Five questions

The entire process of yoga actually evolves from the following five questions which we may ask ourselves:
1. What is the body?
2. What is the mind?
3. What is the soul?
4. How do we interact in the manifest world?
5. How do we experience the unmanifest?

These are the five vital questions, and the answers to them can run into volumes. We have been trying to find the answers to these questions in relation to ourselves and to our position in life, but we have not been successful. We can ask ourselves, "What is the mind?" and never get a satisfactory answer. We can ask ourselves, "What is the body and how does it tick?" and not get a satisfactory answer. Science has also not been able to give a satisfactory answer. The answers and the understanding which we arrive at are very superficial and in no way convey the true meaning. We are very far from the real answers and we will not be able to arrive at them without the correct means.

Three areas of cognition

In the course of human evolution, we know that we have to go through different stages of experience. These stages belong to three main areas of cognition. The first area is *buddhi*, intelligence. I am using the word 'intelligence' because intelligence is the underlying factor, the force which controls every kind of life form. If this intelligence were not there, then plants, insects, animals and humans would definitely not exist. There is an intelligence. For example, an amoeba has no known brain. It is a single cell. However, if you put a drop of acid and a grain of rice in front of it, the amoeba will move towards the rice grain and not towards the acid. This is because it has an in-built intelligence which knows what is good and what is not good for it. The same intelligence manifests in a human being, not as intelligence, but as intellect. This intellect generally distances our perception of life, because it relates only with the manifest world, the manifest dimension. We cannot use the intellect to understand the unmanifest. For this purpose, we have to tap the source of intelligence, which is inherent in every life form, from an amoeba to a human body. Tapping this source of intelligence is one purpose of meditation.

Another area in which our cognition functions is *bhavana*, feeling, emotion, vibration, non-linear perception. Intellect is linear perception. The non-linear perception, belonging to the realm of bhavana, has to be tapped with the practice of meditation also. Here, meditation takes a different form. In order to tap into the intelligence, we have to work in the region of vishuddhi, ajna and sahasrara chakras, which is the area of *chidakasha*. In order to tap into the realm of bhavana: vibrations, feelings, non-linear perception, then we have to work in the region of manipura, anahata and vishuddhi, which is the area of *hridayakasha*.

The third area of cognition is instinctive action which is a part of the day to day expressions of the senses and mind. In order to deal with this area, we will have to work with the mooladhara, swadhisthana and manipura region which is known as *daharakasha*.

The three akashas
So, the three regions which correspond to the three areas or dimensions of cognition are: daharakasha—the lower space,

189

hridayakasha—the intermediate space, and chidakasha—the upper space. We may think that if we work in chidakasha, the upper space, we do not have to work with the lower spaces. We see them as blocks of space, one above the other; daharakasha at the bottom, hridayakasha in the centre, and chidakasha at the top. But actually they are not placed on top of each other. In the meditative process, they are placed beside each other and we begin to work with the top, chidakasha. Once we are able to tap into that cosmic intelligence, then we have to work in hridayakasha, to allow that intelligence to manifest in the realm of vibrations and feelings. Once that is mastered, we have to work with daharakasha, to allow that harmony of intelligence and vibration to manifest in the world of the senses. Only then does meditation become a complete experience which manifests through the mind and emotions into the body, a state of experience which manifests through the mind into the spirit. It is a process of total enlightenment, enlightenment of the body, enlightenment of the mind, enlightenment of the spirit, which is the actual meditation.

Theory of relaxation

In this process we have to be aware of three things. What is the theory of relaxation, of concentration and of meditation? Because they are three different stages. One cannot meditate without obtaining concentration, and one cannot concentrate without obtaining relaxation. So, this process where we sit down, close our eyes and go into the meditative state, is not actually meditation. First, we have to learn how to relax, then we have to learn how to concentrate, to focus the mind, and after that, we can move into the state of meditation. So, the crucial factor here is learning how to relax.

What is the concept of relaxation? Relaxation means lowering of the subtle barriers. This has to be understood. Relaxation here does not mean that you lie down and let go of all control over the body and mind, rather it means lowering the defences, the shields, which we put up consciously, subconsciously and unconsciously. These defences,

190

shields or barriers, which we put up, do not allow creativity and simplicity to manifest in our life. We always complicate even the simplest interaction with our head trips, ego trips and emotions. One grain of sand can become an insurmountable mountain. So first, we have to experience inner simplicity and creativity, by lowering our barriers and learning how to relax.

From the yogic point of view, relaxation deals with the subtle aspects of our personality. First of all, it deals with the awareness of movements that are happening spontaneously, without any conscious or voluntary control within ourselves. After becoming aware of the subtle aspects of our personality, we begin to recognise the areas of our strengths and weaknesses. Then we can work with our deficiencies and increase our creativity. This is the concept of relaxation. When there is no struggle, no conflict, between our beliefs and actions, we develop a strong mind, and a strong mind does not mean an arrogant mind.

Strong, awakened mind

A strong mind is not a mind which believes that, "What I say is correct and what you say is false." It is the weak mind which believes this. The weak mind can become arrogant to hide its own deficiencies. It can take a position in life and not be swayed, in order to hide its weakness. The strong mind is an awakened mind; the weak mind is a confined and dormant mind. So, we have to aspire for a strong, awakened mind, by first of all, knowing the normal expressions of this mind and how they interact in the world. Normal expressions of the mind can be indecisiveness and weak willpower. When we interact in the world with an indecisive mind and weak willpower, then nothing ever gets done, practically speaking. We allow our mind to be influenced by many events and situations. A strong, awakened mind knows when to press the accelerator, when to move into fourth gear and when to move into reverse. There is no guilt, no feeling of remorse, if you move into reverse. There is no negative thought that, "Now, I am moving backwards." It is the

191

ability to adapt and adjust in life which is the nature of a strong, awakened mind.

Mental attention

So, learning how to relax is the first step. Those who are able to relax the subtle personality are the true meditators, the true yogis. What is the subtle personality? How do we define it? Normally, we define the personality intellectually, in the form of behaviour, thinking patterns, ambitions and desires. The different expressions of the mind can sometimes be comical in nature and sometimes full of tension and conflict. So, in the process of self-discovery, we have to place a very strong emphasis on knowing what we are trying to do and being aware of every moment. Awareness of every moment is important, and for this, we will have to make an effort to be constantly alert mentally.

This is what is meant by the word 'attention'. If somebody shouts, "Attention!" we all become alert. In the state of attention ('at' plus 'tension'), we all become tense, but not in the sense of discomfort or stress, tense in the sense that all our faculties become sharp, active and ready to act. In this context, tension is a creative and not a destructive process. When all our faculties are tuned with each other and channelled in the same direction, then that tension is a creative stage. However, when the mind and nature become dissipated and distracted, and there is no control, no direction, then tension becomes destructive.

It is like riding a cart drawn by many horses. When all the horses are galloping in the same direction, in harmony with each other, and there is continuous movement, a force is created, tension is created, and evolution takes place. When the same horses all try to do something different—one tries to go left, one tries to go right, one tries to sit down, one tries to stand still, what will happen? The driver will not be able to control them. The dissipated nature of the mind is also such, and in an effort to control it, we create further stress and anxiety. That is destructive tension, destructive to the harmony of our inner being.

192

The meaning of the word *dhyana* is also similar: mental attention. When these two words, mental attention, are put together, it becomes meditation. What is this process of mental attention or meditation? The simplest way to define the state of meditation is with the example of a bulb which is radiating light in all directions. If you are able to focus all the light at one point, then what happens? The dissipated light is converted into a laser beam. The sun's rays fall all around us continuously. If we focus the light rays with a lens on one spot, what happens? Fire will be created. Similarly, the aim of mental attention is to bring together all the mental faculties. Mental attention is obtained by a process of concentration, learning how to focus the mind on one point.

Antar mouna/antar darshan

For relaxation of the mind, yoga has described certain practices such as *antar mouna*, in which you witness your inner thought processes. You become the observer, the witness, the seer, and you allow the thought process to manifest spontaneously; there is no struggle with the thoughts. When you know the nature of the thoughts, you are able to stop them at any given moment. In this way, just as you observe your thoughts in the practice of antar mouna, you can observe many other things.

Antar mouna is just a part of another technique which is known as *antar darshan*, 'vision of the inner self'. The antar darshan techniques are of a very broad nature. Antar mouna is just one technique of this group which deals with observation of the thought process and lowering of the mental resistance, the mental barriers. It also deals with the sensorial interactions and lowering the barriers of the senses. In antar darshan we incorporate different techniques which can help us understand our personality. For example, we become aware of one ambition. Just as we observe a thought process in antar mouna and try to go to the source of the thought, in the same way, we observe an ambition and try to go to the source of it. We observe an identifiable weakness in our personality, and try to go to the source of that. We observe an

193

identifiable strength in our personality and try to go to the source of that. In this way, we gain a clearer understanding of our own personality and nature.

Psychic therapy

After we have gained an understanding of our nature, it is necessary to focus the mind. This mental focusing takes place in different degrees and stages, by following a system of mantra, yantra and mandala meditation. There are specific techniques which guide us in this process of focusing the conscious, subconscious and unconscious activity of the mind on one particular point, whether it be on a mandala or a yantra. These techniques of concentration can bring up deep rooted emotions and release them, so that you suddenly start crying like a baby. They can also awaken your creativity.

The techniques of concentration can also act as a form of therapy, which deals with problems arising out of the samskaras, karmas and impressions, that we have brought into this life from past lives. In order to illustrate this, I will tell you a true story about an English lady who came to the ashram in Munger. This lady was suffering from chronic headaches and she came to the ashram to see whether yoga could help her. In the course of her life, she had gone to every specialist in the world with the hope of finding a cure for her headaches, but no doctor or medication could help. Her earliest childhood memories were of continuous headaches.

In her first meeting with Paramahamsaji, he asked her, "Do you trust me or not?" She thought about it and replied, "Yes, I trust you." He looked at her and said, "If you trust me, then stop all medications from today onward." She replied, "How can I do that? At least they provide me with some temporary relief. If I stop them, then I will have such a splitting headache that I will fall down and faint." But Paramahamsaji said, "You must stop everything", and he taught her one meditative practice. We used to get the creeps when we would hear her screaming at night because of the pain. Many times I went to Paramahamsaji and asked, "What are we doing to this lady?" He would say, "Do not worry."

194

We went through agony hearing her scream because of the pain, but we could not do anything. Explicit instructions from Paramahamsaji were not to interfere. One day this lady gave a loud scream, fell down and fainted. We thought, "Oh God, she has had a brain haemorrhage!" When she returned to consciousness, for the first time in her life, she did not have a headache. In describing her experience, she said that while meditating she went so deep into herself that she lost body consciousness and total contact with reality. She regressed to her childhood, then into her previous life and into her life before the previous life.

She saw herself in a male form, working inside a coal mine, possibly in Wales. At that stage she heard a rumbling sound and saw the man look up as the ceiling caved in. The impact on the head was the last impression, followed by pain and then death. Now that last impression, the cause of her instant death as a miner, was carried on into her next life and into this life, in the form of a samskara, pain in the head, which needed to be released. When this kind of psychic therapy is needed, no amount of medication can help. You need psychic help, and that help is provided by focusing the mind. By concentrating all the faculties of the mind in the same direction and not allowing them to dissipate, meditation is experienced.

The Spirit of Yoga

MAY 28, 1994

A lot of water has flowed under the bridge; many days have come and gone. This is a new beginning for all of us in the sense that our approach and understanding of yoga has changed according to the necessities of modern society. We can look at yoga from different angles, no doubt, but two are most relevant. One is the need of an individual as a spiritual aspirant and the other is the need of the society of which we are a part. Yoga has to cater to both of these areas. In our personal life we have aspirations for finding stability, peace and inner freedom. In our external, social life, we need to contribute to the welfare of the society which has provided us with a means of growth and brought us to this stage. Yoga has to look at both angles; the teachings and the techniques have to evolve as per the need of the individual and the society. This is the beauty of yoga. Although there are fixed structures of discipline in the various systems, such as hatha yoga, karma yoga, bhakti yoga, raja yoga, kriya yoga, there is also flexibility, and this reflects in our contribution to society in general. These are the two aspects of yoga which we need to understand.

First we will look at the personal, individual aspect of yoga. We, as human beings, follow a course of evolution. There is no doubt that we have come a long way from the times when we used to live in caves and hunt for food. In our present structure of life, there is a lot of creativity and growth, but at the same time, there are some gaps, some dark areas, and these have to be recognised. These dark areas represent states of imbalance and disharmony within our own personality and mind. Why is there suffering, pain, conflict, stress, fear and insecurity? There is only one answer. We are not able to create a balance between our external and internal life. When we are unable to strike a balance between the external and internal life, then there is disharmony between our involvement in the world and our desires and our philosophy.

Our individual philosophy describes a method of living an ideal life, but our ambitions do not allow us to lead that ideal life. Our actions are very extroverted by nature, and this is the main disharmony which creates imbalance in the body. This imbalance in the body is seen in the form of illness and disease. In fact, the word 'disease' (dis-ease, disturbed ease of the body) very clearly describes the disharmony of the body. When the body is not in harmony, not comfortable, not balanced, not able to follow the natural laws, then it is a sick body. For example, 'eat to live' should be the principle in life and not 'live to eat'. When we live to eat, stomach problems arise: constipation, indigestion, acidity, gas, stomach cramps, diarrhoea. This is an imbalance of the body which will manifest as a disease, if it is not brought under control.

The root cause of the physical, mental and emotional conflict and suffering which we experience today in our life is disharmony and imbalance. We are very familiar with mental and emotional conflicts which do not allow us to attain peace of mind. These conflicts are seen as whirlpools which can hold even the strongest swimmers in their grip. If we look at ourselves and find out the areas of imbalance, we will also notice that most of our thoughts and efforts are constantly being directed towards our problems. If there is any mental or emotional conflict, we think about it continuously and become more and more depressed. We lose our mental clarity. This is where yoga comes in, as a way, as a means, to eliminate the areas of imbalance and to obtain greater inner clarity, balance and harmony. In fact, this has been the aim of yoga, and when we practise yoga with this idea in mind, the attainment of harmony automatically removes many diseases and problems from our life.

Different experiments have also proved that the practices of yoga are beneficial for those who are suffering from disorders like arthritis, gout, stomach problems, diabetes, asthma, hypertension, cancer and even AIDS. Investigations are being conducted in different parts of the world in order to understand the healing power of yoga, but yoga does not end there. The process of yoga continues, because yoga aims at something far beyond therapy. It is directed towards an area beyond the mind and consciousness. What is that area which yoga aims to discover? That is the area of enlightenment. Please remember, enlightenment here does not mean that one attains power, knowledge, wisdom, and becomes a saint.

When Paramahamsa Satyananda came to Australia in 1976 for the World Yoga Convention, which was held at Sydney Show Ground, in one press conference he was asked by some reporters, "Your disciples call you a master, an enlightened one. Can you describe your state of enlightenment?" He replied, "What do you mean describe the state of enlightenment?" The reporter said, "Tell us some general things, for example, can you fly through the air?" Paramahamsaji said, "No, I cannot fly through the air." The reporter asked, "Can you read other people's minds?" Paramahamsaji said "No, I cannot." The reporter asked, "Can you walk on water?" Paramahamsaji replied, "No, I cannot." For ten minutes the reporter asked about everything under the sun, "Can you do this? Can you do that?" The answer which he received was always a flat, "No." Finally, he gave up asking and said, "Okay, then tell me what you can do." Paramahamsaji said only one thing, "I can stand up on my two feet, without any props." That was the most beautiful statement of his I have ever come across, and I have adopted it as my slogan in life.

That is the real state of enlightenment, because throughout our life we depend on props, whether emotional or intellectual. We are continuously dependent on such props to support us, but the person who is able to stand up without any support is truly a realised one. That is the concept of realisation in yoga, because yoga does not say that God can be found outside. Yoga says that the divine energy, which is known as spirit, is in everyone but we are not aware of it. We are aware of the body because it is seen and perceived by the senses. We are aware of the mind because it creates havoc with our lives. The mind, thoughts and emotions cannot be seen, but we can experience them on a different dimension.

In the same way, there is spirit which is the link between the individual and the divine, between the microcosmic and the macrocosmic experience. It is the realisation and experience of the spirit which links the individual with the universe that is the aim of yoga. Once the realisation takes place and you are able to live in that state, nothing else remains to know, to experience or to be a part of. You can stand on your own two feet, without any props. The different practices of yoga, whether they be karma yoga, bhakti yoga, jnana yoga or raja yoga, simply direct the human effort in the right direction, so that an understanding of our personality, and channelling of the forces that govern our personality, can take place.

Hatha yoga is a system by which one can obtain physical and mental purity. Karma yoga is not only the yoga of selfless service. It is also a system by which one can become free from the effects of actions, from the negative and the positive inputs of life, and maintain an inner balance. Bhakti yoga is not just focusing the emotions through kirtan and mantra, it is also a method of channelling the pure energy of feeling and emotion for the discovery of the Self, the inner being. Raja yoga is a system by which one can discover the dormant areas of mind and consciousness. In this way the different yoga practices simply help to direct one's efforts towards the discovery of the Self. Therefore, yoga is a process of constant and continuous discovery, in which every practitioner, every aspirant is a scientist, and the body, the mind, the consciousness are the laboratory where one works.

199

The second aspect of yoga is the social perspective. This does not mean that we become involved in social activities. There are plenty of social organisations which put up a sign saying, "Aid given here". Social work, the social approach to yoga, is different. It involves discovery of the love, compassion and affection within you, and then applying those for the upliftment and betterment of the society. In this way a very positive interaction takes place between the individual and the society, and that is the social aspect of yoga. That has to be our aim and direction, if we wish to undertake any kind of social work as a form of yoga.

The aim for which this ashram was established was to provide a heart for the work that was to go on. That is the need of today, to provide a heart. We all live in our heads which are ticking away at different frequencies all the time, but our hearts are closed and we have never opened them. We are not able to open our hearts, because every time we try, the head, the conditioning, the ego, the selfish motives take over. Opening of the heart is just a fantasy. In an ashram, one learns how to open the heart through positive interactions and application of the yogic principles in life. If we can learn to open our hearts, heaven will descend onto earth. This is the future direction for this ashram, and we hope to receive your support, encouragement and love to achieve this.

It is with this hope that I have come here, and this is the message which I have brought. Enough of dabbling with yoga in our life, what have we derived from it? Maybe some degree of health, of wellbeing, but now is the time to take a definite step. We have to experience the simplicity of life and live according to the principles of human dharma. That is the final message of yoga. I hope that the next time I come, you will be here in the spirit of yoga, so that we can work together to build a better life and a better society, by changing ourselves. We have to change ourselves; we cannot change the society. The change has to come from within us, and we have to be ready for this change, this transformation of consciousness, energy and mind, in the spirit of yoga.

A short meditation practice

Please close your eyes for a few moments. Make yourself comfortable. There should be no discomfort in your body. After you have adjusted your posture, become quiet, motionless and still, like a rock. Maintain your inner serenity. Whatever happens outside in the environment should not disturb your serenity.

Be aware of the state of comfort and motionlessness in the body and try to develop the same experience in your mind. You are comfortable in your body; you should be comfortable in your mind. You are still and motionless physically; you should be still and motionless mentally. You are balanced physically, try to find that balance mentally.

The body reflects what the mind is experiencing and the mind reflects what the body is experiencing. In this way there is harmony between the two. Be aware of this harmony that you are experiencing at present. Try to remain relaxed and comfortable, and at the same time, be still and motionless.

Apply this same principle to the body and to the mind. In the state of comfort, stillness and motionlessness, which is physical and mental both, you will experience a vibration. That vibration is the vibration of silence.

PART FOUR

Questions and Answers

Questions and Answers

You talk of non-attachment. I find it hard not to be attached in relation to someone that I love. Please comment on this.

While you were speaking, I had the image of Parama-hamsaji in my mind, because he is the only person whom I love from the depth of my being. Of course, I am not married so I do not know what attachment is to a wife or children. What you are saying is correct in the sense that it is very difficult to maintain objectivity in terms of love which changes into attachment, deep bondage. As long as the deep bondage is creative, positive, constructive, and supports your growth, I do not think you have to worry about it. Only if it limits the expression of your own faculties and creativity, do you have to start worrying about it.

If this kind of situation arises where your creativity is being restricted or limited, and your expression is not free, then there is definitely a problem with the attachment which has formed between you and your companion. So, it is here that you will have to actually work with the idea of non-attachment. There must be acceptance of what the other person stands for and desires, acceptance of what you stand for and desire. You must find a way to cultivate a compatible interaction. Have a clear-cut, open discussion with your companion, about how you can support the growth of one

205

another without disturbing each other's space. As these ideas become clearer, then non-attachment will develop.

Eventually, we will have to deal with the attachment to our body, nature and mind. How will we do this?

That is definitely the final stage. Our present concept of attachment is external and not related with ourselves directly. Attachment refers to something external which we are attracted to, which we like, want and desire. Eventually, the last attachment to be observed in the yogic tradition is to the body and mind. This form of attachment is known as *raga*, or desire for pleasure, contentment and satisfaction, which is a source of sustenance for the inner being. To be a real aspirant, there has to be a definite change of lifestyle, in which attachment must be dealt with.

The example of Paramahamsaji is clear to us. When he left the ashram, he cut himself off from all of his previous associations. He said, "I do not want to see anyone or hear about anyone. I want to remove even the thought that anybody is my disciple or that I am guru to anyone, because even in this thought, there is some form of attachment to an idea, a concept." After he had established himself in a different lifestyle, he said, "Now, I have overcome that stage and I am opening the doors again to everyone who wants to have that communication or that connection with me." Of course, that communication or connection will not be an imposition of views, rather it will be an inspiration to go further in our own spiritual life. So, this form of attachment that we are speaking of is the last form of attachment to be overcome. Where no attachment remains, only inspiration, only fire is experienced. When you go near the fire, you feel the warmth of it.

Detachment has been described in many ways which can often create confusion. Please give your explanation of detachment.

There are three terms which need to be defined: attachment, detachment and non-attachment. Attachment is being caught in the force of attraction, like the two poles of a magnet which come together, and it is very difficult to release or be free of that magnetic force. Detachment means the opposite, total disconnection, like unplugging a wire from the socket. Non-attachment is like leaving the plug in the socket with the possibility of turning the switch on or off. You do not have to strain to sever that connection; you just turn off the switch. Whenever the situation demands, you simply turn on the switch. So, having the ability to switch on or off is non-attachment.

What is the yogic definition of ego?

The word 'ego' means an identity with the self which becomes predominant in our day to day affairs in relation to the cravings and desires of the senses and mind. Yoga speaks of ego in two different ways: one is 'I' and one is 'I' identity. The 'I' identity is known as *ahamkara*, *aham* meaning 'I' and *akara*, meaning 'identity'. We all have this ahamkara. We suffer from the 'I' identity syndrome, identification of the self with everything that happens around us.

This syndrome can take strange forms. For example, you pass somebody on the road who happens to be smiling. He looks at you with a glitter in his eye, and suddenly you begin to wonder, "Why is he smiling at me? Am I wearing my T-shirt back to front? Have I messed up my make-up?" In actual fact, that smile has nothing to do with you. The other person is smiling because of a thought that has passed through his mind. You happen to catch the smile and super-impose it upon yourself, creating an intense self-awareness, "What have I done wrong?" This is 'I' identity, taking every thing upon yourself.

'I' identity is one of the main causes of suffering and conflict in the majority of people. In order to overcome this, the pure 'I', or just the aham, is to be experienced. According to yoga, the experience of 'I' happens in a very systematic way. You begin to isolate the areas of identification with the self, from the self. Once you have isolated all the inputs, the 'I' identification drops away. Then only the 'I' remains, and that

207

'I' is the self, with a small 's', not a capital 'S'. This self, this 'I', is then worked upon through the process of meditation, with the idea of uniting the individual self with the cosmic Self. The cosmic 'I' is the big one, and thank God we are not affected by that. We are affected by 'I' identity. That is the concept of the ego according to yoga.

Sometimes I feel overwhelmed when I think about the qualities which I aspire for, such as compassion, humility, attunement to guru. I do not know how to develop these qualities or which of these qualities I should aspire for.

What you are expressing is very natural. There is a rack of sweets and a child cannot decide which one to try first. Our aspirations can be divided into two groups: those which can be attained with a little effort and those which need a lot of effort. A little effort means beginning with something which you can identify with or relate to more easily and more deeply, rather than with some abstract, ambiguous idea. If you are attracted towards compassion and you would like to develop it, then you should be aware of the means by which you can become a receptacle of that quality. Just as Paramahamsaji has said, "What is our tool? Our tool is the mind." The mind becomes the medium through which we can develop different kinds of qualities and experience new dimensions.

Therefore, we have to first get to know the intricate nature of the tool which we need to use. If we want to cut down a tree, we have to know how to use the power saw, which is the tool, and not put our hand where it is not supposed to be. There is a particular way to switch on and to operate a power saw. When that tool is utilised properly, it can cut down a tree. So, felling a tree or attaining some quality in life represents an aim which we are aspiring for. Then we need to know the instrument by which we can attain what we aspire for. This is the real secret of definitely attaining what we aspire for in life more efficiently and with greater ease.

Generally, if we have an idea in our mind that we want to develop affection, devotion or jnana, then we tend to lose the awareness of the tools we need and the effort we must make,

208

because we become obsessed with the idea. That is what I want and I am not satisfied with anything else. This is human nature. A yogi, sadhaka or aspirant, however, recognises an aim as something to work for, to strive for, and so he becomes practical. We do not have the capacity to change ourselves, our mind, mentality and lifestyle, in the blink of an eye. Even if we have that ability, we tend to be afraid of using it.

So, recognition of the tool, the medium, is the most important thing in the life of a yogi or sadhaka. To see the weaknesses of the tool is necessary as well. Does my mind become obsessed with an idea? If so, it is important to know and to recognise that. Is my mind in harmony with my individual nature or does it react against my nature? If it reacts against my nature, it is creating conflict, strain and anxiety. If it is in harmony with my nature, then the whole attitude and behaviour of the mind changes; there is receptivity, openness and acceptance.

So, first it is more important to develop the tool, the medium, the mind, before aspiring to develop the higher qualities of the mind. The development of certain qualities can remain as an aim or a motivating force, which helps us to evolve naturally, but the actual work space is here in the mind and not outside.

If I want to develop humility, how should I go about it?

If you want to develop humility, the first thing which you should see is whether your mind accepts humility or not. What is your definition of humility? If you think that listening to others and not projecting your own ideas is humility, then you will be swayed by the influence of other people. If you can maintain your inner balance, stability and harmony, then it is not necessary for you to listen to another person's heart rending stories all the time. Rather, in the true state of humility, you can identify with another being on a non-verbal level.

So, again we come back to the mind. Making an effort to open one's mind is the key to success in spiritual life. Once the mind is open, all the positive qualities manifest, whether

209

humility, compassion or devotion, without trying, striving or aspiring to attain something.

Is it like a state of relaxation?

Yes, it is like a state of relaxation which is free from the influences of duality.

How do you touch the heart of an oppressor who has attachment to being in control? When do you turn the other cheek and when do you fight back? How can I stop resenting those people who have hurt me?

This is a tough question, but I have chosen a yogic aphorism for myself which says: Be friendly to those who are happy, be compassionate to those who are suffering, be joyful for those who are virtuous, and ignore the crooked. I think this is a very beautiful teaching. If we can apply it in our life, we will not need to go through any head trips about when to turn the other cheek and when not. These feelings of animosity and anger are actually our own creation. We all live life according to our nature, whether we are an oppressor or a saint. However, it is our own reaction which is of interest here, not the action of the oppressor or the saint, but how we react to that.

We tend to identify more with what other people are doing and less with ourselves. At least ninety percent of the time, we compare ourselves with other people, we see what the other person is doing, and about ten percent of the time we are aware of our own drives and motivations. There is a big disparity here which affects our thinking process, behaviour, mental stability and inner clarity. This is where the problem actually lies in our life. When we are able to live naturally and harmoniously with ourselves, such problems will have no place in our life and we will find great peace of mind

How can we control fear? When I am experiencing fear, I am very sensitive and it takes over.

Fear is a psychological process. Rather than saying to yourself, "Oh, I am afraid of this or that", first observe the physical reactions. How does the fear affect and alter the physical state? What is the experience that the body is having at the time of feeling that fear? Observe the breathing pattern, perspiration and trembling of the limbs. Begin with controlling the physical manifestations of fear by releasing the tension from the body, then regulating the breath, so that the brain is not affected by that state. Gradually, when you have the physical manifestations of fear under check, then figure out what caused the generation of fear. Identify the source of fear and then see how you can deal with it in a positive and constructive way. One thing you have to remember is that your strength is greater than the fear which you experience.

How can I develop willpower?

Willpower can be developed by recognising the areas of weakness in your personality and making a conscious effort to strengthen them. After identifying the weak areas in your personality, think about the different complementary forces that you can develop, so that you will not be affected by the weakness of your nature. These vary from individual to individual. So, sit down and make a list of your strengths on one page, and your weaknesses on another. Then decide which is the actual area of weakness. First of all, you will be imposing a lot of things from your mind. After crossing out the inconsequential things, do the same thing with the strengths. Finally, the list will be narrowed down to one or two areas only. It is that identification which will eventually help you.

Human suffering is ever present in our world, bringing sadness and grief. God's name brings joy, faith, love and trust. Someone grieves for human suffering, another laughs in God's name. Can you talk about the nature of humankind and God's will?

It is not necessary to talk about the nature of humankind. We just have to take a look at ourselves, and we will know. But, something can be said about God's will. What is God's will or

211

what is God? God is a force, an energy, which is neither masculine nor feminine, black nor white. God is pure energy which contains within itself the components of Generation, Organisation and Destruction. This is the actual meaning of the word 'God' also: the power of generation—G; the power of organisation, maintenance, sustenance—O, and the power of destruction, transformation, transmutation—D. These powers are the three aspects of life which manifest spontaneously and which we can also experience. We can experience the power of nurturing, preservation and sustenance. We can experience the power of destruction. We can experience the power of generation and creation. In our own way, we are constantly experiencing these three forces, or aspects of God.

In the cosmic dimension, God takes a universal form which is omniscient, omnipotent, and omnipresent. This energy of God governs the entire process of evolution. It is a process over which we have no control. We are constantly evolving, constantly moving. If we think that the eighty years of our life make a big difference in infinity, then we are mistaken. The eighty or one hundred years of our life are nothing in infinity; it is not even the blinking of an eyelid. In this span of life, which is not even the blinking of an eyelid, we go through so much drama. It is incredible. We become a minor god in own way, in relation to our life. We feel that we are controlling our life, but in fact, this is the time when that cosmic energy laughs at us. How many times does God laugh? He first laughs when the doctor says to a patient, "Do not worry, I will save you." Again he laughs when you tell Him all your projects and plans for the future.

God has also defined how a human being has to live throughout the different periods of his life. In the vedic tradition this structure has been called *purushartha*, self-effort, which has four areas: artha, kama, dharma and moksha. *Artha* means external security, contentment, happiness. *Kama* means fulfilment of one's desires and aspirations. *Dharma* means living according to the laws of nature and divinity, and *moksha* means continuing in the path of evolution in order to attain mukti, freedom. These are the four components of a

212

structure which governs every kind of life form, whether amoeba, plant, insect, animal or human. Wherever there is life, you will find this structure. Of course, the understanding and the experience of this structure will be different for different life forms, but it exists nevertheless.

Living harmoniously within the structure of artha, kama, dharma and moksha, is also known in yoga as the will of God. One who strives for contentment and happiness with a selfless attitude is following the first mandate. One who strives to fulfil his aspirations and desires in a positive, constructive and creative way fulfils the second mandate. One who lives according to the principles of dharma fulfils the third mandate. One who is aware of the evolutionary process in life and does not struggle with that process fulfils the final mandate. This is the will of God; these are the four components of the divine will.

The vedic tradition also states very clearly that no life form is different to God, all life forms have their source in God. The *Purusha Sukta*, a very beautiful hymn in the *Rig Veda*, states that God has a thousand heads, a thousand eyes, a thousand arms, a thousand legs, a thousand feet, meaning that this energy, which we call God, is an all-pervading reality. The spark of life is in everything. Of course, according to our understanding, we have given divinity a colour, a form, a name. In order to identify it with something, we have to give it a name, a form. We cannot identify with an abstract or universal idea. We are individuals who express our individuality. We can only identify with a concept after it has been given a name.

Without name and form, we cannot understand anything. If we did not know the word 'sun', how would we describe that fireball in the sky? We have to use some word to identify it. This has been defined as the *sakara* or the manifest aspect of God. The *nirakara* or unmanifest aspect is the cosmic nature of God. Yoga helps us to adapt, adjust and structure our life in order to ultimately understand that cosmic reality which goes beyond name, form and idea. That is the yogic concept of God. The best way to experience God

213

in daily life is to live according to the principles of dharma, strive for mukti, be aware of kama, and be content in artha. If we can fulfil these four conditions, we do not have to work very hard.

Could you please talk about the meaning of transcendence?

The word for transcendence in yoga is *mukti*. Depending on the context in which it is used, mukti can mean many things, such as liberation, freedom, realisation or transcendence. Mukti is the appropriate description of the state which we are trying to achieve and understand. The bondages in life are the various impressions, samskaras, conditionings; the different modes of behaviour, action, performance and interaction. Mukti means changing the normal pattern and adopting a new, universal, transcendental and sattwic vision of life. This new vision is known as transcendence, in which one grows out of a limited state of being, goes through the process of becoming, and establishes oneself in the transcendental state of being. So, in brief, that is the yogic definition of mukti which can also mean transcendence.

Could you speak about linear time and non-linear time?

Linear and non-linear time has to be seen and understood from the context of Purusha and Prakriti. Whatever is in the realm of Prakriti follows this linear movement. Energy follows a linear movement in the realm of Prakriti. Manifestation of energy and the reversal of this movement happens in a linear way. Our intellect works in a linear way. Whatever happens in the realm of Prakriti, in the manifest dimension, right from the level of tattwa and tanmatra, is actually linear experience. This body frame is governed by that linear activity. When I say body, I mean not only the physical, but also the entire structure of the body, mind and psyche. The only thing which is not linear is the spirit, because it is an all-encompassing consciousness. This is, in brief, the concept of linear time and non-linear time, and you can build up on it yourself.

214

What role can Mangrove Mountain Ashram play in the life of a karma sannyasin?

Karma sannyasins must come here for at least one week every year, not necessarily for a course, but to participate in ashram living and community life. There are also certain projects in which karma sannyasins will have a lot to offer. We are considering having a yoga community, an interactive, supportive community mainly for karma sannyasins. If you can become part of that in the course of time it will be a very beautiful, mutual growth; the growth of the ashram as well as yourself, because of the supportive atmosphere. Keep in touch with the ashram and you will be told of the different projects as and when they are finalised. Let us all work together to make ourselves better and more beautiful people. If we can change ourselves, then I am sure that we can also inspire others to change. Change begins with oneself, and eventually it is like a row of dominoes falling; one falls, then the rest follow. In the same way, if we let ourselves go, maybe in one or two generations the whole world will let itself go. So, let us start with that.

We have heard about the ancient tradition of ashramas where women did not get any mention. What happened in those days for the spiritual life of women?

Actually, the yogic, vedantic and tantric traditions are more matriarchal than patriarchal. It is wellknown that women have the ability to feel from the heart whereas men feel more from the head. In the olden days, women were given more importance than men. In the tradition of yoga, there were many great women saints in the past who took on the intellectual giants of their times, the rishis and munis, and who were teachers to them. Women are the shaktis; without them we would not be here. My mother was a woman. Paramahamsaji's mother was a woman.

Due to later changes in the social structure, societies became more patriarchal in their nature and there was less involvement of women in spiritual traditions. This is quite evident in India, because there were many invasions and wars. The Indian people were never interested in expanding their empires. Invaders came to India, but Indians never invaded other countries. They were very happy to lead their own lives. When the invasions took place, the Indians isolated the women folk and kept them in the home.

From that point on, the tradition of women saints diminished, because women were not able to go out and pursue a spiritual direction. It is a long history, however, Indians have always recognised women as a greater force, with more capacity for spiritual awakening, than men. If you compare the involvement of women and men in yoga throughout the world, you will see that there is a ratio of sixty to forty; sixty percent females and forty percent males. So, again, that awakening is taking place and, in the course of time, the males may be out of work.

We have heard about a sannyasa code of conduct. Could you please explain this code?

I will just tell you in brief what the code of conduct is. The code of conduct deals with a specific set of *yamas* and *niyamas* to be incorporated into the normal lifestyle. We are familiar with the yamas and niyamas through the *Yoga Sutras*, although we have not given much attention to them in our own sadhana. The *Yoga Sutras* describe five yamas and five niyamas. The five yamas are: (i) *satya*, truthfulness; (ii) *asteya*, honesty; (iii) *aparigraha*, non-possessiveness; (iv) *ahimsa*, non-violence; and (v) *brahmacharya*, celibacy. The five niyamas are: (i) *shaucha*, cleanliness; (ii) *santosha*, contentment; (iii) *tapas*, austerity; (iv) *swadhyaya*, self-study, and (v) *ishwara pranidhana*, surrender to God.

The other yogic and sannyasa traditions speak of many more yamas and niyamas. These are qualities which are to be incorporated into one's life in order to improve the experience and expression of the personality and the nature of the Self. The yamas and niyamas have been incorporated in the code of conduct to form a part of the sadhana. They are not

216

just speculative, intellectual concepts, but practical observances which, by becoming part of the sadhana, can raise the level of awareness.

A different code of conduct is devised for the jignasu aspirants, so that along with the yogic practices of asana, pranayama, meditation, relaxation, pratyahara and dharana, they are able to also experience the qualitative aspect of life. Jignasus have a set of rules which are few in number, but which initiate the aspirant into this process of self-observation and awakening of the faculties. Karma sannyasins have a larger code of conduct than jignasus, and poorna sannyasins have an even larger code, so that there is a progression or evolution from one stage to the next.

How does a humble rag-tag sannyasin earn the stripes on the forehead? Please explain the deeper significance of this mark.

The stripes represent the tradition of Acharya. Those who have been trained in the tradition and have become adepts or have had that experience of sannyasa in its real form are given this as a recognition of their determination, continuity and adoption of the sannyasa way of life, from the heart, not from the mind. It is like being part of the Captains Club. The three stripes, *tripundra*, represent the tradition of the Paramahamsas. Each stripe represents a guna or quality. Those people who are given this in-depth training are then initiated into a form of sannyasa. Jignasus are one stripe sannyasins, representing their drive and motivation to overcome the tamasic tendency. Karma sannyasins who undergo this training are given two stripes, representing their drive to overcome the rajasic along with the tamasic tendencies. Poorna sannyasins, who undergo further training, are given three stripes, which represent their motive to transcend the three gunas: tamas, rajas and sattwa, and to attain inner sublimation. This is the meaning of the three stripes. The red dot represents the aspect of Shakti, the spiritual power or energy, which gives us the strength to control the three gunas. It is the awakening of that Shakti which is the real aim of sannyasa.

The ancient texts are full of rituals for all occasions. Society today lacks such rituals, yet people are searching for a higher reality in many diverse ways. Please speak on the importance of rituals in the inner quest.

There are three aspects of inner life: (i) wisdom and knowledge, (ii) coming towards self-realisation, and (iii) performing action and knowing where that action is leading to. This is the vedic theory of jnana, upasana and karma. These are the three theories of the Vedas, which are known as *Jnanakanda*, the section on knowledge; *Upasanakanda*, the section on worshipping the Self, and *Karmakanda*, the section on rituals. I am talking about this last aspect. Performance of action with the knowledge of where it is leading to is the concept of ritual in the Vedas and in yoga.

Yoga states clearly that whatever effort, method or system is adopted with faith and conviction, for the development of the self, this is the ritual which leads one closer to the inner nature. External rituals are symbolic. They can align the mind with what is happening outside and inside. The external act of *havan* or *yajna*, performance of the fire ceremony, has this effect. It helps us to experience the same act internally and thereby elevates the spirit. This external act also alters the elemental forces, the external structure of the elements, and harmonises them with the forces which govern the human nature.

Therefore, rituals have to be looked into from a different angle, with clarity of mind. Just performing an external act is not going to change anything until we are prepared to experience that change internally. There has to be some form of understanding in the performance of the ritual, otherwise it becomes a superficial act, and when that act gives birth to a force, we are unable to handle or channel that force. Take magic, for example. We draw a star or a circle on the ground, we write some mantras, we invoke some supernatural presence. The aim of that ritual is to control the external force which is evoked. In that process, however, we are also awakening the inner dimension of that force, the devil within. If we

218

are invoking the devas, or divinities, then these subtle forces become active inside.

In ancient times, the knowledge of ritual was extant throughout the world, but today people have lost this awareness. Therefore, rituals do not really work any more; the link is lost. When there is an alignment of forces, however, ritual can become very powerful. Rituals are to be used in order to confront the forces of the personality. In Tantra, there are many rituals and they all vary. Some rituals are complicated, some are very simple, some are meditative, and some involve going to the graveyard in the middle of the night. There are different kinds of actions which are performed by the sadhaka in order to confront the forces of the personality, and one has to be ready for it.

Therefore, the definition of ritual is performance of an action and knowing what the result of that action is going to be, not only in relation to the elemental forces of the external dimension but also to the forces which are being generated within. Rituals such as havan or yajna clean the environment of negative influences. If you throw a handful of chillies into a fire, what will happen? You will feel the effect of it immediately. Your eyes will begin to water, your nose will begin to run, you will begin to sneeze, and you will want to get out of the place. Just as the act of throwing chillies on a fire can immediately affect the environment, in the same way, different forms of havan and yajna can also work wonders in the environment.

Can you talk about Tantra and its relationship to the system of yoga which you teach?

Tantra is the science of spirit which deals with the awakening of the dormant energy potential and the expansion of human consciousness. In fact, this is the literal meaning of the word *Tantra*, 'release and expansion'. The aim of Tantra has always been to provide the method and the system whereby an aspirant can awaken the dormant energy potential and expand the consciousness. Tantra has also stated that there are different levels of understanding human life. The

219

first level is recognition of the individual nature, after that, working with the personality to develop it by following a system of practices, and ultimately, attaining freedom, *mukti*. The method which is employed by the Tantras to attain this level of freedom or mukti, is the system of yoga. Of course, one has to aspire for this inner freedom.

Once a person came to Buddha and placed the following question before him. "If freedom is our aim and birthright, and the teachings of great masters show us the path, then why do they all describe different techniques, instead of pointing straight to the goal?" Buddha replied, "You must have the desire to attain inner freedom, before you can take that straight path." The man said, "Everyone in the world desires freedom and peace." Buddha said, "No, not everyone desires freedom and peace. If you do not agree with me, then go and find out for yourself. Ask the people and make a list of their desires, then come back to me."

The man spent one week going to people in different places and asking them what they really desired in life. He wrote down the answers which the people gave him, and came back to Buddha with the list. Buddha asked, "How many people want freedom, mukti?" The man replied, "As per the list, none. Everyone wants something different in life. Some want relaxation, others want a solution to their problems, each one wants something else." Buddha said, "This is why we have to approach freedom in various ways in order to train the different individuals and prepare them to experience the inner life." So, this has been the approach of Tantra.

Therefore, Tantra says, first recognise your own nature and after that recognition has taken place, adopt a system, a method, by which you can work on yourself and eventually transcend the self-imposed limitations. This is what makes Tantra a very practical system as well as a spiritual science, because it does not emphasise theory. Of course, there is a basis of theory, there is an analysis of the human nature and the process one must follow, the effort one must make in life in order to experience the divine nature. However, this theory is very practical; it is not speculative.

Tantra deals with human experience, and it has identified different areas of human development in a very beautiful way. Just as modern psychology has divided the human consciousness into four areas: conscious, subconscious, unconscious and superconscious, in the same way, Tantra has described twenty one states of consciousness. This shows that the practitioners of Tantra developed a very deep insight into the human nature. This was made possible by the practice of yoga, because yoga is the practical aspect of Tantra, which has been incorporated in the other traditions like Samkhya, for example.

Sage Patanjali, who wrote the *Yoga Sutras*, 'aphorisms of yoga', was a follower of the Samkhya tradition. Therefore, in the *Yoga Sutras*, you will find a great emphasis on the Samkhya philosophy. In the same way, in other traditions, yoga has also been adopted. In the vedic and upanishadic tradition, yoga has been incorporated as a practical system by which one can awaken the personality. However, the roots of yoga lie in the practices of Tantra. The different practices of yoga such as hatha yoga, raja yoga, kriya yoga, kundalini yoga, all aim at awakening the human consciousness and releasing the blocked energy from inside. This is the theory of kriya and kundalini yoga: opening the chakras, energy centres, and raising the kundalini from mooladhara to sahasrara, thus creating a transformation in the field of consciousness.

This is the tantric approach to human evolution, because Tantra recognises that within every individual there is an immense source of potential energy, creativity, and strength. This energy potential exists in the realm of prana and chitta. *Prana* is the vital force and *chitta* is the mental or conscious force. These two areas have to be tapped. As human beings, we do not utilise the full capacity of our body, mind and consciousness. Even modern science says that in our present stage of evolution, we only use about ten percent of our brain and the remaining ninety percent is in a state of dormancy.

If we look at the concepts of modern psychology, we will find that thirty three percent of the mind has been classified as conscious, thirty three percent as subconscious, and thirty

221

three percent as unconscious. The superconscious, which is beyond the unconscious, remains speculative, because psychologists have not been able to identify its exact function. So, in this respect, our understanding of the mind and consciousness is limited, which clearly shows that we are unable to use the mental faculties fully. Tantra, with the help of yoga, provides a way to gain a complete understanding of our life, and to direct our activities towards an area where creativity and positivity can be expressed fully.

Would you say that those poorna sannyasins in the West, who live in the world, are living a tantric existence? What is the difference between a tantric lifestyle and karma sannyasa?

There are different approaches to Tantra. This question refers to *vamachara*, the left hand path, which is only one of the many different aspects of Tantra. For example, *siddhantachara* is a system of Tantra in which psychic meditation is the main theme. In this path, one has to remain totally isolated from the world for a period of time, and just work in depth with one's personality, in order to recognise and know the psyche. In siddhantachara, specific guidelines and techniques are given for achieving this.

Another aspect of Tantra is *vedantachara*. This system also involves a lifestyle which is isolated from the social environment. Here effort is made through the defined practices of kundalini yoga and through specific practices of meditation, to awaken the kundalini and to raise the level of consciousness through the force of will. Then comes the path of *yogachara*, which is the specific area where yoga has evolved from the Tantras. Then comes *dakshinachara*, the right-hand path of Tantra, which involves a balanced lifestyle, in which an effort is made to realise the aspect of wisdom, underlying the superficial level of consciousness.

Then comes *upasana*, which is worship of the inner self, and *karmakanda*, which is not the karma of action, but the implementation of this experience in a broader context. There are definite practices up to this point. Vamachara, the left hand path of Tantra, which is the fifth system, represents the aspect of interaction with the society and the family, leading a household life with a spiritual attitude. This is the most misunderstood as well as the most desired aspect of Tantra. In vamachara, there is acceptance of human relationships, of the natural and spontaneous expression of the instincts with a definite direction or aim, which helps to further the evolution of consciousness.

Mahanirvana Tantra and *Kularnava Tantra* are texts which emphasise the vamachara aspect, and they point out that there is another dimension to the actions that are performed externally. Take, for example, the drinking of wine. If drinking of wine could help us attain enlightenment, then every drunkard would be an enlightened being. If the consumption of meat, fish or grains, leads to enlightenment, then everyone would be enlightened. It is not the external act which is important, but what the act symbolises on the psychic dimension. The vamachara aspect of Tantra talks about consuming fish, and it is very specific, two fish only. What are the two fish? They symbolise inhalation and exhalation, which refers to the practice of pranayama. Vamachara talks about consuming meat, which we think of in terms of beef and pork, but here meat symbolises annamaya kosha, the dimension of matter. Controlling this dimension is represented by the consumption of meat.

According to vamachara, one's external actions, whether one is involved in relationships or practises brahmacharya, whether one is vegetarian or non-vegetarian, whether one drinks or does not, are not important. What is important is the attitude which enables us to free ourselves from the bondages of the annamaya and manomaya dimension. This is the actual teaching of vamamarga.

The sannyasins who are living in a household environment should cultivate an awareness and recognition of that lifestyle and also the aspect of harmony within it. As long as the awareness is there, you are definitely living the sannyasa way of life. If that vision is lost, and just the idea remains that "I am a sannyasin", then it is only a mental process,

223

intellectual gymnastics, by which you can remain happy throughout life. Saying that you are a sannyasin does not really make any difference. However, if you are able to implement some of the rules which help to maintain that vision, then you will be the winner, no one else.

So, it is your judgement and application of the knowledge which you have gained, which can finally decide whether you are a sannyasin or not. Initiations do not decide. They are only given to you with the hope that you will complete the journey. Sannyasa is the only system of education where the degree is given before you even start your studies. It is with that sincere hope that you are being given the degree, as an inspiration, but you have to complete the journey. It is a trust that the guru has placed in you. You talk about placing your trust in the guru. What about the trust that the guru has placed in you?

Could you explain the difference between classical and traditional yoga?

In ancient times it was believed that those people who wished to lead a spiritual life had to renounce, to live away from the society, concentrate more on their individual sadhana, contemplation and meditation, and live life according to the laws of nature. This kind of belief gave rise to the traditional concept of yoga which was to live away from the society and work hard on yourself. In fact, this belief is still prevalent today in the East as well as in the West. We believe that while living in the society, we can practise something simple and easy according to our needs, like asana, pranayama, relaxation and maybe some concentration. However, if we want to work on ourselves at a deeper level, in order to discover our inner nature, then we have to get away from the social environment and live in seclusion. We require a different kind of lifestyle in which hatha yoga, raja yoga, bhakti yoga or jnana yoga can be perfected.

Classical yoga does not require us to change our lifestyle. Perhaps this is because there are no places left in the world where we can go and be alone. Cities are growing day by day and maybe a time will come when the whole world will be just one big city. So, the main theme of classical yoga is that no matter what kind of lifestyle we lead, no matter where we live, we can still attain peace of mind. We can still express creativity which is not superficial, but which is coming from the depths of our being. We can practise the different yogas, no matter how secret or esoteric they may be, while leading a normal lifestyle, but with a different aspiration, a different mentality, a different attitude towards ourselves and our interactions in life.

This is why classical yoga gives more emphasis to the component of self-awareness, being a witness to yourself and to the things that you think, feel and do. Patanjali has emphasised this very strongly, "Be a witness to the thoughts, to the mental modifications, to the altered states of mind." In this way, you can develop inner discipline, so that your mental structure becomes balanced and harmonious, which is conducive to your inner growth. So, this is the main difference between traditional and classical yoga.

I have trouble visualising in meditation. Is this a block or some sort of personality defect? Are there any practices that would enable me to visualise in chidakasha? I cannot even visualise a candle flame.

Visualisation is a practice of dharana, holding the mind fixed on a particular image or symbol. If you are having difficulty with that, I suggest that you work with the pratyahara practices like antar mouna and ajapa japa, as the first step. Antar mouna helps to still the activity of thoughts, feelings and desires, so that you can realise the state of the mind. Ajapa japa will enable you to focus your concentration on something which is physical: the movement of the breath, awareness of the mantra combined with the breath. Go deeper into that aspect of focusing yourself on yourself. Practise this for a couple of months, without trying to visualise the symbol. Just try to focus on something which is very physical.

When you feel that physically, you have become more stable and one-pointed, then try the symbol visualisation.

225

Begin with the practice of trataka. Try to see the after image of the candle flame in chidakasha, which should be retained in your memory in the form of a photograph. Practise this for another month or so. In the fourth month, stop all these practices and try to focus on the symbol, which you create yourself. Generally, as the mind becomes more stable and fixed, the symbol becomes clear. Initially, visualisation is a process of simple imagination. However, as the mind becomes focused, you will gradually see the outline of the object, and with the intensity of concentration, you will see the actual image. So, give yourself four months to go through this process: two months of antar mouna and ajapa japa, then one month of trataka, and in the fourth month, focus on the symbol which is self-created.

What is the best way for me to progress in the practice of meditation—by the use of karma, bhakti or jnana yoga?

Different personality types have been defined and different yoga practices are suggested for them, such as, the practices of jnana yoga for the intellectual personality. Ramana Maharishi is a good example of a jnana yogi. In America, I came across a person who claimed he was a jnana yogi. Over the breakfast table he said to me, "Swamiji, every morning when I get up, I ask myself, 'Who am I and what am I doing here?' Then I go about my daily business." I was taken aback by his statement, because this kind of inquiry is not an intellectual analysis. If you read about the life of Ramana Maharishi, you will see that he used to live that enquiry continuously, not only at breakfast time, but twenty four hours a day. This inquiring attitude of his made him intensely aware of his inner being, and in this way he came to know his real nature. So, even in jnana yoga, there has to be a process of experience, in a living form, not just an intellectual process, and then it becomes a form of meditation.

For the dynamic personality, the practice of karma yoga is suggested. Karma yoga is not just hard work, but observation of the natural actions and reactions that are being performed and experienced by the human personality, and

226

harmonising the two. Harmonising the karma aspect in life with the attitude of yoga, to uplift the human nature, is karma yoga. Here also, this understanding becomes a meditative process.

For the emotional personality, bhakti yoga is very important. Bhakti does not mean singing the heart out in kirtan. There are nine different forms of bhakti. The first is *satsang*, 'to imbibe the truth', 'to realise the truth'. The second is listening to transcendental stories which can provide inspiration and act as a catalyst for us to come out of our shell. In this way, bhakti yoga has nine different forms. The last form is *sayujya*, 'identification with the spirit'. If one follows these different stages of bhakti, then one realises the inner nature through the aspect of identification with the spirit, in the last stage. Through purification of the heart and harmonisation of the emotions, one can come to that experience of unity within.

For the psychic personality, the practices of raja yoga have been described. The meditative process in raja yoga involves many practices, such as trataka, antar mouna and ajapa japa, which we have been initially exposed to as the first chapter of the yogic literature. There are also many other techniques which have not yet come to light. The important part of meditation is not the state of dhyana, but the state of pratyahara. I am convinced that pratyahara is the most important of the meditative stages. The word *pratyahara* has two meanings. The first is the literal translation of pratya-ahara, 'feeding the self'. With what? We have been feeding the self with junk from McDonalds. Now we have to feed the self with positive, creative and constructive input, which is conducive to the attainment of one-pointedness in the field of consciousness.

The second meaning of pratyahara is 'focusing the perception of the faculties of action and cognition on one point, whereby tranquillity is experienced'. The state of pratyahara is described as similar to a turtle withdrawing all of its limbs inside the shell, which is an accurate description. The turtle has six limbs: two arms, two legs, a head

and a tail. In pratyahara also, we withdraw the six anten-
nas, which are fully extended in our life; five are the senses
and one is the mind. In the stage of pratyahara, we need to
perfect the state of withdrawal. In the stage of dharana, we
need to perfect the state of holding the mind at one point.
This is not easy; it is difficult.

Dharana cannot take place until pratyahara is perfected.
Dharana is a continuity of that one-pointed state. Dhyana is
an extension of that continuity, where that one-pointedness
goes beyond the momentary fluctuations of the senses and
mind, and becomes a permanent state. Therefore, pratyahara
is the most important technique or group of techniques that
need to be perfected first. So, for any type of personality,
whether one is a jnana, karma or a bhakti yogi, one needs to
perfect pratyahara. Even when one is practising karma yoga,
there has to be full awareness of the extension of the senses
in the outer dimension and the effect of this on the inner
dimension. That is also a state of pratyahara.

We are aware of antar mouna as a technique of pratyahara.
There is also a technique called antar darshan, which is a stage
ahead of antar mouna. There is another technique called
hamsa dhyana, the swan meditation, which is a further stage
of pratyahara. We are in the process of bringing out the next
chapter of the pratyahara techniques. We have already brought
out the dharana practices, which is the second chapter, but
not the third chapter of dharana. When you are able to
practise these techniques as naturally, spontaneously and
easily as you practise antar mouna or ajapa japa, you will
derive a lot of benefit, because they are the next stage.

**What is the difference between visualising an image, and
visualising the colours and lights that arise in chidakasha?
In my practice, the colour blue always seems to be stable.
What does this signify?**

The different colours and lights that you may see in
chidakasha are related to the physical and the mental senses,
the senses of cognition and action. It is very much a physical, cerebral manifestation. The different colours that shoot

228

across chidakasha, even when we close our eyes at night, represent the sensory activity in the mind. Blue is the colour of akasha tattwa. If you can maintain that, and within the blue colour create a symbol of your own choosing, an image of your own creation, then you can superimpose on the natural state of chidakasha a direction for your mind to move in. So, this will be a further focusing of your attention.

I have problems bringing up emotions, which was especially evident in the practice of hridayakasha dharana we did yesterday. Would you suggest that this meditation should be done more frequently?

You should not expect miraculous results from the first practice. You will have to continue with it for an extended period of time. Only then will we be able to remove the emotional blockage.

We all tend to block our emotions and feelings. We are not able to release or direct our emotions properly. Emotion represents a different aspect of our life all together which is not linear. Intellect is linear; emotions are not. Most of the time, we are trying to understand and analyse our emotions intellectually, and this is a mistake. Emotions are the natural expression of the raw energies which dominate our consciousness. Yoga says that the mind, the consciousness, is governed by two different forces. One is the controlled force or energy which manifests through *buddhi*, rationality, understanding and knowledge. The other is the uncontrolled force which manifests through the channel of *bhavana*, feeling and emotion.

These are the two distinct expressions of consciousness. If we try to understand, analyse, control and direct the emotions through the intellect, problems are going to arise. We are not going to understand those bhavanas, deep-rooted feelings, and we are going to create more disharmony within ourselves at the vibrational level. Yoga says that one must isolate the emotional experiences and states from the rational. After isolation, there has to be recognition of the emotional state in its true form. Then emotion can be transformed

229

from a binding force into a liberating force. Hridayakasha dharana aims at bringing about this change in the emotions.

Whenever we try to combine intellect with emotion, the emotion becomes a force that binds the mind to a state of conditioning. This state of conditioning is experienced in the form of love and hate, peace and disturbance, satisfaction and dissatisfaction, pleasure and pain, which are internal feelings. These different expressions of emotion represent conditioning of the mind. So, eventually we must know and understand our emotions from an emotional, not an intellectual viewpoint, then we will have a better understanding of our own nature. We have never been trained to recognise the emotion as one field of perception and the intellect as another, but this is what must happen in the practice of yoga. A recognition has to take place and we have to know the difference between the two. Hridayakasha dharana can help us to realise the deep-seated emotions within, but we have to be regular in the practice.

I have difficulty feeling emotion, apart from fear or anxiety, in everyday life. Can you suggest other methods of awakening or opening to the feeling of emotion?

We are not able to feel, to think or to act as human beings. There is never any action from our side; there is always reaction. There is never any genuine feeling from our side; there is always an influence of the external factors which colour our feelings and thoughts. You may agree with me or not, but the fact remains that we project only our ego, fears and desires in our behaviour. So, the feelings that come up, anger, fear, anxiety, are all a projection of our ego. They are a projection of an imbalance within our personality which has never allowed us to act freely. We are not human beings, rather we are animals. Animals react instinctively, and we react intellectually. Animals do not project their egos and their shortcomings, but we do.

So, if we become aware of something that is happening deep within ourselves, we do not know how to handle it. When a deep rooted emotion comes up, either it is coloured by the

230

ego, the selfish needs and aspirations, or we do not know how to handle it. This is an area where we need to educate ourselves. We have lived for too long in our head space and blocked other centres of perception. If we want to understand something, we use our intellect and go on analysing and criticising it. Even the feelings which come up are conditioned. They are not unconditioned; they are not pure. They are coloured by the traits of our personality.

So, yoga and meditation become a process of self-education, re-education, in which we have to again start from the basics. What is the approach adopted by the raja yoga system, the eightfold path of yoga? The practice of yama and niyama to make us aware of the interactions and expressions of our subtle personality and nature; the practice of asana and pranayama to educate us about the body; the practice of pratyahara and dharana to educate us about the mind. So, this has been the system adopted by yoga. It is not only a practice, physical or mental, after which we again fall back into the same old habits. It is a system of learning about the body and mind, behaviour and spirit.

We always live on the surface of emotions and feelings. What we experience and feel is something which has been conditioned by our mind: like and dislike, acceptance and rejection, pain and pleasure, desire and repulsion. These are all self-centred ideas in relation to ego. We desire something good and we feel repulsed by something bad; that is ego satisfaction. Yoga takes us one step beyond, by making us aware of the other aspects of our personality, which comprise the qualities of head, heart and hand. The personality is made up of qualities belonging to the head, meaning the intellect; the heart, meaning the feelings, and the hands, meaning the ability to act, to perform. Yoga and meditation give us a greater understanding of how to act and how to stop the process of continuous reaction.

The practices of chidakasha, hridayakasha and daharakasha dharana aim at opening up these different centres of perception. Hridayakasha dharana is not just experiencing the feelings of pleasure or pain, happiness or

231

sadness, coming up. It is recognising the nature of emotion which arises from deep within, and this process takes time. You have to commit yourself to this process with conviction, faith and belief, that you want to harmonise, balance and discipline your personality. Only when you are able to commit yourself in this way will you begin to actually progress in the yogic path. Otherwise, whatever comes up from deep inside will be monitored by the conditioned mind. Even the most valid experience generated from deep inside will be analysed by the mind which is conditioned by the ego and selfish motives, therefore, the true experience will never come. So, you should work with the mind first, and try to develop a different level of perception, of understanding, then you can go into the emotions.

During the practice of hridayakasha dharana, I was able to still myself and concentrate on the heart chakra, but I found it impossible to be aware of darkness or light in the heart area. I could feel slight emotion coming and going, but I could not experience the requested emotion or colour. Where should I go from here?

We have always been more aware of the head centre than anything else in life. Even in the practices of meditation we have done in the past which deal with the chidakasha experience, we have closed our eyes and focused our attention in the region of the forehead. We have become accustomed to experiencing everything in the chidakasha area. If we have to visualise the symbol, we see it in chidakasha. Until now all our meditation practices have led us to see what happens in chidakasha. In the next stage of meditation, we have to move from the head space to the heart space. The same practices and visualisations have to be done in the anahata region. It will take time to get used to this switch over, but that is a necessary step.

Chidakasha, hridayakasha and daharakasha are the three spaces within the body where concentration has to take place. Each represents a dimension of experience in human life; chidakasha: the head space, covering the region of vishuddhi, ajna, bindu and sahasrara; hridayakasha: the heart space, covering the regions of anahata and vishuddhi, and dahar-akasha: the lower space, covering the regions of mooladhara, swadhisthana and manipura. Yoga has described these three areas as dormant, semi-active and awakened centres of consciousness. Chidakasha represents the awakened dimension of consciousness. By working in this dimension we do not become enlightened, but it is an area which we can identify with more easily. We identify more with our head, especially in the western cultures, whereas in the eastern traditions, we identify more with our heart.

So, there is also a cultural factor involved. What we teach in the West is different to what we teach in India, because of the different temperaments, the different cultural inputs and many other factors. However, this is what we have to remember, regarding meditation in the different centres. First we should begin to work with the area which we identify with most. Here, it is the head space, the chidakasha. After knowing the area of chidakasha, we move into the subtle aspects of our personality and that is hridayakasha. After working in hridayakasha for sometime, we again have to change and work in daharakasha. That way a homogeneous growth can take place within us. Know the head space and then move to the heart space. That has to be the direction of our sadhana.

Being an extremist, when I finally decide to do some sadhana, I go into it full on. I seem to attract karma very quickly at this time, which unbalances me. The more intensely I do sadhana, the more difficult life seems to become. What do you suggest?

Intense sadhana increases the sensitivity and you become more receptive to the influences that are around you. That sensitivity makes you uncomfortable. It is quite natural. When you encounter such situations, you should practise a short yoga nidra for fifteen minutes or so, after the completion of your sadhana. In the yoga nidra practice remove whatever influence you might have picked up in subtle ways, by creating an aura of strength around you. In this way, you can support and strengthen your own psychic personality, by giving it more power. You can awaken the prana and become less influenced by the environment. If you find it difficult to create an aura around you, then simply focus on manipura during the yoga nidra. Generally, prana is experienced in manipura in the form of a gradual, radiating heat. Fill up your entire being with that heat, and use it as a force to protect your inner being. It is a form of psychic defence from the negative things that attach themselves to you in this sensitive frame of mind.

Should Gayatri mantra be practised as a part of karma sannyasa sadhana?

If you want to combine Gayatri, Om and Mahamrityunjaya mantra, do so for one month. In the next month, leave Gayatri, Om and Mahamrityunjaya, and practise the karma sannyasa meditation. In the third month, again do Gayatri, Om and Mahamrityunjaya, and in the fourth month leave that and go into the karma sannyasa meditation[1].

Can one do a short sadhana for twenty to thirty minutes, or does one need to do a full hour with meditation?

Generally, I suggest that everyone should practise asana and pranayama in the morning and not meditation. If you practise meditation early in the morning, it withdraws the mind. Depending on their sensitivity, many people who practise early morning meditation, experience some difficulty in relating to their work and family. So, in the morning, practise ten to fifteen minutes of dynamic asana, five minutes of dynamic pranayama, and five minutes of centring yourself to feel relaxed and one-pointed. Meditation is to be done at night, as far as possible.

If we are fairly disciplined in our practice, should we continue with the sadhana that we have been doing or should we leave it and start the postal sadhana?

If you are satisfied with your practice, you can continue it. I would suggest, however, that you give the new sadhana a try.

---

[1] See page 134 for details of the karma sannyasa sadhana.

234

Should one give up the kriyas for the postal sadhana?

Yes, because the kriyas will be incorporated into these sadhanas in a slightly different way to what we have been used to. We have been taught a group of asanas and pranayamas, and we have been taught kriyas. Possibly, because of lack of understanding, we were not able to properly integrate the different techniques that we have learned. Some people, who have learned kriya yoga, think it is the last practice and they do not need asana and pranayama. So, they practise kriya only, but after some time stagnation takes place. If we can combine whatever we have learned, then our sadhana will be more complete and we can become better human beings. We tend to pick up one thing and say, "This is the arm of yoga, this is the leg of yoga, this is the heart of yoga," but we have never practised the complete form of yoga. Paramahamsaji has shown us all the components, and now the time has come to put them together and make a proper human being out of the sadhaka.

When should the personal mantra be practised?

You can practise the personal mantra in the morning after you have completed asana and pranayama, when you are trying to centre and stabilise yourself.

In spite of practising postures and meditation, there are times when anxiety becomes almost uncontrollable and I cannot relax. What do you recommend that I do in these circumstances?

Anxiety, tension or stress can be experienced at various levels at the same time. The four areas where anxiety and stress are usually experienced are: muscular, nervous, cerebral and emotional. First, you have to identify which level the anxiety is being experienced at. If it is nervous, cerebral, or emotional anxiety, then you need to adopt different approaches, and if you feel anxiety at all these levels, then a different approach is needed again.

If the body and the emotions are affected by stressful conditions, then it is advisable to practise some simple postures, such as tadasana, tiryaka tadasana, kati chakrasana, pawanmuktasana; pranayamas, such as nadi shodhana and brahmari, and yoga nidra for relaxation. If it is emotional anxiety, then two practices are quite helpful: trataka, candle flame gazing, and antar mouna, performed sequentially, first trataka then antar mouna. You will have to keep in mind that you are not going to get rid of your anxiety in one practice session. It will take continued effort to release and harmonise the blocked energies that are in conflict with each other. You have to continue your practices until you are able to reach a relaxed state of being.

I suffer from tightness in the jaw and compression of the head on the neck, also the neck twists sideways when I meditate. What can I do to help this?

There is an imbalance in the energies governing the head centres, and this imbalance is resulting in the tightening up of the mid-brain region and neck. Tension or tightness can be an insignificant thing, but the neck and head are very sensitive regions. Many nerves and blood vessels pass through the neck, which is a small, confined area of the body, and enter the brain. In order to release stress from the neck and head region, it is advised to practise daily the head and neck movements which are described in the pawanmuktasana series. When the tightness is released from the muscles and nerves with the practice of head and neck movements, one must perform neti, nasal irrigation, followed by bhastrika pranayama, bellows breathing. That will help you to deal with the problem and you will feel much lighter in the head.

Please give your opinion on paranoid schizophrenia. Some people are permanently institutionalised, while others are let out. Can this mad, out of control state also be classified as a state of mind?

According to yogic belief, the mind has its centres of gravity which it is attracted to spontaneously and naturally

236

in the normal state, but it can come out of those centres also. In some cases, when the mind becomes sensitive, it tends to identify with a particular event, situation, emotion, feeling etc., and become obsessed with that input. When the obsession becomes so acute that the mind is not able to project its natural state, then what results is known as imbalance or madness, and it is given different labels, depending on the intensity.

In respect to yogic therapy, we have developed some awareness in this area. However, with the use of drugs outside, suppression is caused. What can be done about this problem?

The drugs that are generally used are stimulants which create momentary hyperactivity in the brain so that the concentration or the obsession is diverted to another area. When the effect of the drug wears off, one again reverts to the same area of obsession. In the USA, we did some work with people living in mental institutions and halfway homes where patients go for treatment. We used to give yoga therapy to catatonic patients and to other groups also. We asked the doctors to give them their normal medication first, so that they would become a bit more receptive and understand the interaction that was happening with the therapist.

After medication, we used to start with pranayama. Asana they could not do. We would hold their noses and do the practice with them, so that they would inhale through the left and exhale through the right. Then we would ask them to copy. It used to be like the game, see the mirror image, which you play with children. Over a period of time, they became used to the practices and we found that they would be waiting for us to come. This meant that a certain expectation, a certain improvement had started within them. When we came, they would give us a nice smile of recognition as if some friend had come. We continued this for three months, then we taught the therapists of the institute, so that they could continue the work. In three months time, the catatonic patients showed thirty percent improvement.

237

At the same time, we used to work with other patients suffering from schizophrenia, neurosis, deep emotional problems, childhood trauma and shock. We always began with pranayama and after a month we would gradually introduce asana in the form of a game. By teaching pranayama first, we were able to regulate their nervous system and activate their brain. After that, with the practice of asana, we could start working on their physical body. So, in the first month we taught only pranayama; in the second month, asana and pranayama, and in the third month, bandha and shatkarma, neti and kunjal. In some cases, we even taught shankhaprakshalana, so they would be forced to run to the dunny at least eight to ten times in the day. That purging process had an activating and grounding effect, and made them aware of the necessities and realities of life. The third month was always the most fulfilling. Along with neti, kunjal, and in some cases laghoo shankhaprakshalana, we also introduced bandhas, because bandhas act on the three main energy centres: mooladhara, manipura and vishuddhi.

These three energy centres are the three areas of blockage in our body which you can feel at any time. When there is tension in the head, then you can feel the tightening of the neck muscles, closing off or blocking the mid-brain region. Whenever you feel tense, if you observe your body, you will always find that your stomach is tight. If you relax your stomach, the tension in this region, between manipura and anahata, generally goes away. People who have emotional problems always contract their stomach muscles tightly. The practice of uddiyana bandha or agnisar kriya, rapid contractions of the abdominal muscles, helps to release these blocked up emotional energies. If someone has gone through childhood trauma or abuse, then moola bandha is very effective for releasing that tension from inside.

If you work with people who are mentally disturbed, then definitely use the activating, stimulating pranayamas, such as kapalbhati, frontal breathing, and bhastrika, bellows breathing. In asana practice, apart from the general things you may teach them, three postures are very important:

238

(i) tadasana, palm tree pose; (ii) ardha matsyendrasana, half spinal twist, and (iii) dynamic paschimottanasana, forward stretch from the lying position. These three asanas are very helpful, because they work on these three regions where blockages occur. Gradually introduce the practices, allowing the effects of each practice to be felt, allowing the changes to be seen, before you bring in a new practice. Of course, you should start with the practices of pawanmuktasana to ground those who have lost contact with their bodies and make them more aware.

I have taken jignasu diksha, having been inspired by Paramahamsaji's teachings for a long time. At present I am involved in a water pollution research project with the University of Western Sydney as a microbiologist. Could I have some more information on the Yoga University as I see this as a way of merging my spiritual path with any professional skills I may have?

The Yoga University will have three faculties: Yoga Philosophy, Yoga Psychology and Applied Yogic Science, to begin with. We are keeping the option and the possibilities open to have more faculties later on. The Applied Yogic Science faculty is possibly the area where the practical aspect of water pollution or microbiology would fit in. This faculty will have three further divisions or branches of study. One will be research, initially into the practices of yoga, observing and monitoring the physiological changes that occur with the techniques of asana, pranayama, mudra, bandha, shatkriya etc. This will also include research into diet, for example, the effect of water, minerals and all the substances that we eat and drink, on the human system.

Another division of the Applied Yogic Science faculty will be therapy research. In this department, a multidimensional therapeutic approach will be adopted. Research will take place in the controlled environment of the laboratory. There will also be fieldwork, when we go out into different environments to see what can be done to improve the living conditions. Here the concept of health and hygiene will play a vital

239

role along with the yoga practices. If you are interested in assisting with that work, you will be most welcome.

This university will be managed professionally like other universities. Different skills will go a long way in furthering the knowledge, especially in and around the local community, so it will also be benefited. Some skills can be incorporated in other universities as well. In this university, we are planning to give post graduate degrees—MA, MSc, PhD etc., and we are looking forward to a positive interaction with people who are willing to contribute in different fields.

Can one have two gurus?

The initial spiritual connection has to be made with an external agent, and that agent is the guru. Once the connection has been made, you cannot disconnect it, no matter how hard you try. Guru is not something which can be adopted and thrown away in the different stages of life. This is the difference between the guru/disciple relationship and the normal husband/wife relationship. In the husband/wife relationship, we can go through the process of divorce, changing one partner for another, and this process of external change can continue until the end of our lives.

This kind of external relationship provides emotional security and stability, whereas the guru/disciple relationship does not. In fact, that is a great hangup for people who go to the guru with the idea of intellectual and emotional satisfaction, security and enjoyment. Being in the presence of a guru or having a guru is generally understood as a way of getting high in life. I do not agree with that concept at all. If you have that idea, forget it. Guru can have an external form but, no matter who he may be, he kindles a different kind of awareness and light in the deepest part of the human psyche, and that connection can never be broken.

A child stays in the mother's womb for nine months and there is a deep, psychic link between the mother and the child. After the child has taken birth and grown up, that link still remains in the deeper level of his personality; it is not broken. The relationship is there even though they may not

240

see each other for many years. That relationship goes far beyond the normal feelings and emotions. That is how the guru/disciple relationship is also. You can never hang out with the guru. You can hang yourself, but you can never hang out with the guru.

The external guru is the catalyst for an internal transformation, for an inner awareness and that is something you can never ignore in life. Try to understand the concept of guru, not from the intellect, but from the heart. Do not confuse the heart with your emotional sense of satisfaction and enjoyment, but consider it to be much deeper and cleaner than the normal feelings and emotions. In this respect, the outer guru and the inner guru are one and the same. Upon realisation of the inner guru, the outer guru manifests within. So, although the guru may have two natures, external and internal, ultimately they are one and the same.

What is the difference between a devotee and a disciple?

A devotee works from the heart whereas a disciple works in a different way by tuning himself or herself with the energy of the guru. This is the basic difference. The devotee is more of a bhakta. The emotional link, the faith and devotion are more active. In the life of a disciple, the inner link with the guru is on the psychic plane, and that becomes more active.

What is the purpose of initiation?

Initiation is a new beginning. In the Bhagavad Gita, Krishna says that people take birth two times in their life. The first birth is in the world of nature, the birth of the body. The second birth is in the world of spirit, the birth through initiation. The Sanskrit word for initiation is *diksha*, which means 'to have a vision', 'to be able to see'. Diksha is of different types, because it is a process of growth on the inner dimension. The ultimate aim of this initiation process is to experience the underlying unity, but before we can come to that state of perception, we have to go through a process of preparation. It is like passing through different classes in a school.

The first initiation for a spiritual aspirant is mantra diksha which is becoming aware of the vibratory aspect of our nature. This is class one in spiritual life, where we harmonise the vibratory field by tuning the mind with the mantra. That is one form of diksha, initiation, and as you progress, other forms of diksha also take place. The last form of diksha is *shaktipath* or transfer of energy. I do not mean the form of shaktipath which is given in public. When shaktipath is done correctly, the disciple can be enlightened in a second. This process of enlightenment is actually fusion of the mind and energy of guru and disciple.

So, the beginning is mantra diksha and the culmination is shaktipath. Shaktipath is not that simple, because once you receive it, you cease to be what you were. All the barriers are removed. Imagine an earthen pot that is submerged in water. There is water inside and all around it. The water inside and outside of the pot is the same. The pot is completely submerged in the water, but still there is the form, shape or identity of the pot. If the pot is broken, the water inside becomes one with the water outside, and the shape of the pot is destroyed. That is what happens in shaktipath. After receiving this form of initiation, we do not remain as we were. We become part of that cosmic, enlightening energy and we experience a new form of perception. It is perception of the spirit, of the inner self, and providing this dimension of understanding, which is the aim of diksha.

What is meant by surrender to the guru? Does it mean that one does not question anything the guru says or does?

Surrender is generally understood as letting go. The story comes to my mind of a disciple who went to the guru and said, "I want to surrender everything to you." The guru asked, "What do you want to surrender?" The disciple said, "I want to surrender my body, mind and spirit." The guru said, "Fine. I accept. Now, go back to your home, lead a normal life, and remember that you have surrendered your body, mind and spirit to me." The disciple returned to his home town where he owned a large orange orchard. When the season came for the fruits to be picked, the guru sent a messenger to the disciple asking him to send a bag full of oranges for the ashram. The disciple sent back a reply to the guru, "I have surrendered my body, mind and spirit to you, but not the oranges."

So, the question arises as to what surrender actually is. Surrender is not just blind obedience. It is the process of letting go of the barriers that we create around our ego, and not holding on to our ego. I once asked Paramahamsaji, "Why do many disciples feel that the guru exploits them?" He said, "As long as the disciple retains some part of his ego, this kind of thought will arise. But, when the disciple lets go of his ego totally and becomes natural and spontaneous, then no matter what the guru may be, the disciple will become a part of him." He gave the example of Milarepa.

Marpa, the Guru, really gave Milarepa a hard time. He made him construct seven houses out of stone on top of a mountain. "Construct a house," he would say. Then when the house was done, he would become angry, "No, I do not want it here. Remove it all, stone by stone, and construct it again in another place." Consider if you were in Milarepa's shoes. You would have said, "This guru is crazy", and you would have felt exploited or used. Did Milarepa feel this way? According to history he did not, because he was in tune with the energy and not with the personality of the guru.

When we create a distinction between the personality and the energy of the guru, then surrender becomes difficult. But if we understand the energy of the guru, then surrender is a natural process. It is identification with the guru on a higher plane, and not only with the guru, but with the cosmic energy and also with God, and that is the real surrender. Our concept of surrender is intellectual and, therefore, we are not able to understand it.

The recent video of Paramahamsaji in which he speaks about surrender is a real eye-opener. Could you please elucidate on this theme?

The theme of surrender is very apt, because at one point or the other, we have all thought about what it means and how it applies to us. The underlying qualities of honesty and flexibility are important components of surrender. If we consider these two aspects, then surrender is not so frightening after all. There should be no fear of losing absolute and total self-control. There seems to be a need to educate ourselves in this respect.

First is honesty. We need to know if we are truly honest or not, and honest to what? Because many times we are honest to our own ambitions, to our own selfish ideas. So, even honesty has to be viewed in a proper perspective. There must be a process of inquiry, in coming to recognise our honesty. More than an external factor, honesty is an internal experience. We cannot be honest to something, we have to be honest to ourselves. That honesty, that state of being honest to ourselves, should bring us to terms with ourselves. Without honesty, coming to terms with ourselves is very difficult.

We tend to hide from our own mental creations, images, impressions and samskaras. By hiding from our own creations, we are not being open internally. After all, honesty is a process of opening up, of recognising and assimilating that, and converting it into a living experience. In this regard, Paramahamsaji has said that even today, he cannot intellectually understand what surrender is; even today, he cannot do it. But he feels within himself that a link is made, a link is there, due to honesty in his own life, towards his commitment, towards his goal and direction, towards his guru and towards God.

The other component which we mentioned was flexibility. There is a saying that one should be humble and flexible, like a blade of grass. Trees which stand tall and upright and do not sway with the wind, many times are broken. A tree which can move with the wind survives the onslaught and remains standing. Flexibility is also a quality of life through which we learn to flow with the current and not struggle against it. Many times we have to make an effort to stop this struggle. We have to stop the ongoing, inner process of struggling to gain a solid support, and learn how to sway with the force that controls the environment.

The tree cannot control the flow of the wind, but the wind can control the swaying of the tree. If the wind blows to the right, the tree will bend to the right; if the wind blows to the left, the tree will bend to the left. So, there is an environmental factor which is more powerful than the personal factor. In our lives, when we try to stand up against the environmental factor, then clashes of ego, frustration and depression occur. Flexibility and humility are necessary to counteract this manifestation of ego. Flexibility is the training which awakens the quality of humility. If we work on these two levels initially in order to understand and to refine our interactions with other fellow beings, with God and with guru, then surrender is spontaneous and automatic, and it is neither a joyous nor a painful process.

Paramahamsaji has also mentioned two forms of surrender: one is the surrender of a bhakta and the other of a non-bhakta. The word *bhakta* means a believer, a person who believes in fate, in God, in guru, in personal effort, or whatever. But that link of being connected to something or someone is there. That is the bhakta link, the link of a devotee who is connected to something either personal or impersonal, physical or spiritual. The other type of surrender is of the non-bhakta, who is not connected to anything and is simply observing and allowing things to manifest in the course of time. In the surrender of a bhakta, there is more spontaneity and less inquiry, whereas in the surrender of a non-bhakta, there is more inquiry and less spontaneity. Ultimately, however, both come to the same realisation, that being a good conductor, purifying oneself, making an effort to maintain a link, is the way to go.

Would you comment on lineage and successorship in the guru/disciple relationship?

Discipleship is not proven by the quantity of love or surrender that a disciple has for his guru, but by coming in tune with the energy of the guru. That is what real discipleship is all about, because even in love and surrender we make mistakes. According to our concept, love is when two people

245

look at each other and become starry-eyed. That kind of love changes into hate when the two suddenly decide to look in different directions with their backs to each other. Whereas in the ideal relationship between a guru and a disciple, love is looking in the same direction, not towards each other or away from each other.

The same idea applies in relation to surrender. When love and surrender are augmented by the qualities of honesty and humility, then a connection takes place and the quality of one's receptivity changes. For example, there might be twenty different plugs hooked into one switchboard, and they are all 5 amp plugs. But it is also possible to change that 5 amps into 10, 15 or 20 amps, by changing the size of the plug, so that it can receive more power. This does not mean that the other plugs are insignificant and have no connection. It simply means that a disciple has that option to become a high voltage plug. This is actually what surrender is all about ultimately.

If guru says to us, "You be this", and that is acceptable to our rational mind and to our self-image and self-concept, then we accept it. However, if guru tells us to change, and this change conflicts with our self-image and self-concept, then there is a reaction to the instruction of the guru. This reaction means that surrender and love are not complete. We are still looking in another direction, and are now thinking of turning away. We are not looking in the same direction. This is all a play of ego which is manifesting as 'me', the important one, and guru who helps me to change according to my need.

The other mentality is one of humility: I am insignificant; change me as you deem fit. Those disciples who allow the guru to direct their course and surrender totally to his will, to the divine will, to God's will, have a different kind of experience and interaction with God and guru. There is the example of St. Theresa, which is a well-documented case. In times of meditation, ecstasy or samadhi, the signs of the stigmata would appear on her hands and feet. Such things can happen if the link is there with either an embodied soul or an impersonal energy which does not have a body, which is cosmic in nature.

Swami Satyananda, who lived with Swami Sivananda, experienced that kind of deep connection with him. This connection was even recognised by his guru brothers; it was not something which they did not recognise. They recognised and accepted it, because it was a reality. It was not just someone's mental concept or fantasy. A scientist can recognise the achievement of another scientist, but the layman cannot.

In this respect, I also feel blessed. I personally do not know if I have surrendered or made a link. I only hear Paramahamsaji say to others, "You know, I have given everything to Niranjan, and I do not have anything of my own now." The first time he said this, I wondered, "What does he mean by that? What has he given me? His power? If he has given me his power, then I cannot feel it anywhere. Has he given me his knowledge? If he has, I cannot experience that knowledge. Has he given me this? Has he given me that?" Whatever I asked myself, the answer was, "I cannot experience it." There was no sense of pride that, "He is saying he has given it all to me and now I am all-powerful and ready to roll." No, rather it made me even more thoughtful because he was saying, "I have given everything to him," and I know, "I do not have anything."

That is still my position, even today, I do not know what he has given me. But he has said it so many times that now I am thinking maybe there is some kind of a link by which he is channelling his energy and I am not aware of it. He is aware of it, because he is doing it from his side. I am not doing it from my side. So, just as Paramahamsaji said he feels that he has made it, I can say to you today that I feel I have made it.

Paramahamsaji has spoken about various experiences he had with Swami Sivananda in the guru/disciple relationship. He said that Swami Sivananda tried to perform ego-dectomy on him. Are there any such experiences in your life with Paramahamsaji that you can relate to us?

Well, I am sure he has performed such operations on me, because at different times I have felt the bumps and scars on my head. However, there is no conscious recollection of him performing such an operation. That could be because of my deep relationship with him. In this relationship, I see him in different roles. When I try to think about the kind of relationship I have with Paramahamsaji, I always come to the same conclusion. On the physical level, he is my guru and I am his disciple. On the mental level, he is my most intimate friend, and on the spiritual level, he and I are one. I do not think there is anything more to say about this. From early childhood, I used to be the 'ashram admittance committee' all rolled into one. As a rule, anybody who wanted to join the ashram had to pass through the test and get Niranjan's sanction and approval. This used to be very difficult process for most people, because in my childhood, I used to be a devil in the disguise of a sannyasi. I would do every kind of trick to annoy people: bother them, abuse them, frighten them, tear off their dhotis. I made them very angry and when they came to get me, I would go and hide behind Paramahamsaji.

I was a very destructive child, but Paramahamsaji never said to me, "Do not do this; do not do that." I used to pride myself on being the ashram electrical engineer. A new clock would come in and within half an hour I would be trying to see what it was inside the clock which made it tick. When I would try to put it back together again, there always used to be a few screws too many. Radios, cameras, tape recorders, all received the same kind of treatment, and Paramahamsaji never even once said to me, "You have done something wrong." But he worked on me in his own way, with his chisel and hammer. I am sure that in order to come to the level of expression which I have today, he must have worked very hard.

Did you work very hard?

Not at all, I enjoyed my life as it unfolded. One month after I had completed my tenth year, Paramahamsaji called me to Calcutta from Munger and said, "Your passport and ticket are ready. Now you have to leave India." I asked, "What will I do?" He replied simply, "I am sending you out to gain experience, to learn whatever you can. You have total freedom to choose your life. You can study, if you want. You do not have to come back to India, you do not have to be a sannyasi, if you do not want to. In the course of time, you can get a job. If you want a different lifestyle, you can lead it. I am giving you total freedom." He took me with him to Europe and left me in Belfast. From that time on, until 1983, I lived outside of India most of the time, coming back for a maximum of nine months at one time.

There were periods in my life when I did not meet Paramahamsaji for seven or eight years, but I never felt for one day that he was distant from me. Looking back now, I realise that I never felt I was away from him or that I was not able to see him. I felt that he was continually showering his affection, love and blessings on me internally, so what was there to complain about? Nothing. In fact, this feeling used to be so strong that once when he asked me, "Would you like to come back to India?" I replied, "No, I do not want to come back, because when I am away from you, I feel you near me, constantly guiding me. However, if you call me back, there is no power on earth which can stop me from coming to you." He called me a short time later, and I returned to India after his call.

So, I feel very privileged and blessed to have had a very different kind of relationship with Paramahamsaji. In this relationship, I have always felt him with me, even in my mistakes. I never felt guilty about anything or that I was committing a sin, because I knew that he knew it, and he knew that I knew that he knew it. It was that kind of a relationship.

How do you perceive other people? We hear of those who can read minds, see the aura or the active chakras. Is that what you do? Or do you, Paramahamsa, flow into people, unite with them, feel what they feel and think, and so know which chakra in the universal sushumna they have manifested through?

I put myself in your shoes. I do not have the ability to feel anybody's chakras; I cannot feel my own. Nor do I have the ability to read anybody's thoughts; I cannot read my own. I am just a yoga aspirant. However, I can stand in someone else's shoes and think and act as he does. In that way, I gain some insight into the personality that I am dealing with. Of course, I practise C.S. yoga, common sense yoga.

Are the projects that are under way in India in conjunction with or separate to the work of Sivananda Math? Also, do you envisage establishing a branch of the Sivananda Math in Australia?

I have not yet mentioned Sivananda Math. All the projects that you have heard of belong to Bihar School of Yoga. BSY has three letters in it. 'B' stands for Bihar School of Yoga, 'S' stands for Sivananda Math, and 'Y' stands for Yoga Research Foundation. So far, we have only dealt with the projects of 'B' I will tell you about the work of Sivananda Math in brief.

Sivananda Math was originally established in 1987, the birth centenary year of Swami Sivananda. It is dedicated to his ideals of seva. Paramahamsaji has said many times that our approach to seva should not be limited to our own structured institution, but should be extended to the society which has supported our growth since the time we took birth. This service to the society takes a different form. The projects of Sivananda Math have been structured to help the underprivileged sections of the Indian society. There are 16,548 ethnic groups in India, belonging to different work and caste environments. Many do not have the same facilities of social growth that the upper class people enjoy. Only ten percent of the population forms the upper class in India, forty percent are the middle class and fifty percent are the deprived class.

So what services do we render to the underprivileged section? We provide them with scholarships for their education. An average of four hundred students receive scholarships every year, and it is a continual process. We also provide relief at the time of natural calamities, such as famine, fire, earthquake and flood, which occur frequently in the state of Bihar. We go out to the affected villages with mule loads of food, clothes, and medicines, and help the people in these times of need. We also undertake projects

250

requested by the district or county administration. In 1989, when there was a shortage of potable water in Munger, forty handpumps were fitted in the town by the swamis with helpers from the villages. We also constructed a private bus stand for the Munger town.

Now Sivananda Math is working in the Deoghar region, where Paramahamsaji stays at present. Sivananda Math has opened a charitable hospital there, and doctors serve the local people whenever their turn comes. An average of two hundred patients are given free treatment every day. Depending on the dosage of medicine, the patients are also provided with food, especially if they are taking antibiotics. In order to manage the heat in the system created by antibiotics, food is sent from the ashram to those patients.

Currently, we are in the process of providing shelter for the village people. The overall aim is for each family to have proper shelter, for the eldest member of the family to have permanent employment, and for the younger members of the family to receive proper education. Last year, after the Convention, during the winter months from November to February, we went into the remote villages with truckloads of blankets and clothes, which were donated by the devotees. During this time, five thousand blankets and ten thousand pieces of warm clothing were distributed.

The distribution is very systematic. First we make a list of the residents of each village, the number of males, females and children in each family and their ages. Then bundles are made up, according to the needs of each family. When Paramahamsaji completes a round of his sadhana, then, as an act of *daan* or charity, we load the trucks up (we are slowly building a fleet of trucks) and go into the villages where each family is given their bundle. This is being done without any motive or financial gain; it is just an act of charity. It may sound like social service, but I feel it is not. The external act may be one of social service, but there is a definite purpose behind it.

When I first heard of Paramahamsaji receiving the mandate or instruction to provide his neighbours with similar

251

facilities to his own, I could not understand what was happening. Later, it dawned on me that there is a spiritual process behind this. In order to open one's heart and mind, it is necessary to have affection, love, compassion and devotion. Paramahamsaji has defined this in beautiful ways at different times. Imagine that two people are involved in an accident. One is a stranger and one is a close friend or relative of yours. For whom will your heart reach out in that moment of pain?

First, it will reach for the person with whom you are close. You will feel more for that person, especially if he or she happens to be your own kith and kin or offspring. In spiritual life it is necessary to overcome this limitation, and to develop a universal feeling which is the same for all. This universal feeling is one of affection, love, compassion and devotion. By developing these four aspects of feeling, then raising the mind beyond the conditioned love, affection, devotion and compassion, one can eventually transcend the human nature.

There are two forms of love: one emanates from the head and the other from the heart. Conditioned love, which is rational, intellectual, selfish and motivated, comes from the head. Unconditioned love, which comes from the deepest recesses of the heart, is pure and untainted. Many times, we tend to confuse conditioned love with pure love, because of our own limited nature and because we are not aware of our deep emotional blockages.

For the development of unconditional love, training is required. Just as one trains in yoga or in any other skill in life, in the same way, training is required to learn how to express this unconditioned, untainted aspect of affection, love, compassion and devotion, which is universal. Walking through the streets gooey-eyed, hugging people and saying, "I'm in love with everyone", is not real love. Just by feeling good vibes or by any other expressions of the conditioned nature, one cannot experience that real quality of affection, love, compassion and devotion.

Paramahamsaji is giving us an opportunity to experience that universal feeling, by creating an atmosphere, an

252

environment, where we are forced to think differently, without any selfish motive for profit or gain, and this is the work of Sivananda Math. This area of work is definitely going to grow. It is just a beginning. If you want to receive this kind of training and then implement it in any part of the world, in your own community, then you are welcome to come. You should try to have that exposure for a month, at least once in your life. Go to Deoghar, where Paramahamsaji stays at present, and connect there. Feel what is being done, what is happening around him, naturally and spontaneously, because he is definitely not making any effort to do it. He is just leading the higher stage of sannyasa life.

After a long time, Paramahamsaji has given an invitation for people to visit him from 18th November to 17th December 1994. During this time, he will be meeting everyone. So, it is a good opportunity to go and see what is happening. Stay there, walk around, be in Paramahamsaji's presence. See what work is being done by Sivananda Math. Receive inspiration from the presence of Paramahamsaji, then come back and carry on with your life. It is as simple as that, and you are all invited.

About establishing a Math in Australia, Swami Sivamurti has established a Satyananda Math in Greece, which is working on the same principles as Sivananda Math. If there is a similar desire or inclination in Australia, I am sure that something can be started for the community here, with the help of everyone. It would be another step in our individual and community spiritual commitment.

Could we hear about this invitation from Paramahamsa Satyananda?

There is an invitation from Paramahamsaji for all of you to come to Deoghar. This invitation is very important because, after leaving the ashram and the establishment, Paramahamsaji cut himself off totally saying, "I do not wish to see anyone. I am not a guru or a teacher and I have no disciples any more." When this information came to us all, we felt isolated, deserted and neglected. All these feelings and ideas

253

surfaced although, in fact, there was no reason to feel like this. What was actually happening from Paramahamsaji's point of view was that he had never considered himself to be a guru or a teacher in the first place, rather we made him into the image that suited us.

For many of us, Paramahamsaji became a guru, a teacher or an inspirer. He took on different roles according to our projections, and that is how we related to him in our own ways. We never allowed him to be himself. When he wanted to be himself, we reacted strongly and many people reacted negatively. That was our shortcoming, not his, because our own ideas and projections were being shattered. Paramahamsaji always considered himself as a disciple, a sadhaka, a spiritual aspirant. There are many aspects of his nature which can totally alter our consciousness, if we care to look deeply. His mind is always open for us to look into; it is not a closed mind.

At the time of his departure, Paramahamsaji said, "I did not take sannyasa to establish a mission or to become a guru. I took sannyasa to know myself. In order to pave the path for my growth and evolution, I had to exhaust my samskaras and karmas. I asked Swami Sivanandaji what I should do in order to exhaust my samskaras and karmas, and he gave me the mission to propagate yoga. I did that until I had completely exhausted every impression, samskara, karma, and even their shadow images, from my life. Finally the realisation dawned on me that I was free from my karmas and samskaras and that now I would be able to go further in my own spiritual journey, as an aspirant, as a sadhaka."

Now, compare this mentality with others that you may have come across. In Paramahamsaji, we find clarity of direction. If we are able to follow his example, then we will also attain clarity of direction, rather than getting caught up in our ego and emotional trips. In fact, this is what he has taught all these years through the practices of yoga: attain clarity of mind. Have we attained this clarity of mind? No. We have not been able to follow his guidance and direction; it is as simple as that. Despite our association with him for so many years, for

254

decades, we have not followed a single instruction of his for our inner growth and development.

Another source of inspiration is Paramahamsaji's acceptance of life and of difficulties and problems which would normally shake even the strongest of people. He has never fought against the current of life; he has always flowed with it. We fight and struggle with the current; we have not learnt to flow with it. In order to swim across a river that is flowing very strongly, it is necessary to swim with the current. This is the teaching of yoga, flowing with the current, which Paramahamsaji has done, and which we, as his disciples, have not been able to do. We are struggling now, and when I return to Australia after one year, we will still be struggling. Every year, when I return, I will find that we are all still struggling. We miss the simple lessons in life, because we do not consider them important.

In order to re-establish himself in the lifestyle of a sadhaka, it was necessary for Paramahamsaji to isolate himself from everything with which he identified. We were talking of ego identification, ahamkara. Paramahamsaji definitely has no ego. He is egoless, but for the sake of our understanding, let us say that he has dropped his identification with the past, and he has gone to another state of being, another state of life. His clarity of mind is just incredible. So, now, after establishing himself in this lifestyle, he has given us this opportunity by inviting everyone to his place in Deoghar. There he lives in solitude and isolation, without interacting with people, continuously performing higher sadhana. He has invited us all to go there and reconnect with him on the true spiritual dimension and not as a speculative, spiritual idea.

This invitation is open to all, and you should not miss this opportunity. If you do not go, and still you worry about what your relationship with Paramahamsaji is, and what it is going to be, then that is your problem. He is opening his doors and it is up to you to enter, receive the inspiration and inner guidance, and stabilise your spiritual life. Learn to experience life as it should be experienced, not only in terms of luxury, comfort, security and satisfaction, but also see how the fire of tapas, austerity, can touch a person's life and transform it.

This year for one month, from 18th November to 17th December, Paramahamsaji's doors are going to be open. This is a great opportunity because it will be an eye opener for all of you. I have come across many gurus but I have come across only one real sadhaka, and that sadhaka, that aspirant, is Paramahamsaji. I have come across many for whom the means has become the end, but I have never come across a person who has maintained that clear vision throughout the life. When you speak to Paramahamsaji, his ideas will come to you.

Initially, I could not understand why he was leaving. At the time of his departure, I asked him, "What will happen to you, after leaving everything behind?" In a beautiful way, he replied, "Let me be free from the lassos which you people throw on me. Let me just roam with the name of Shiva on my lips. It is my wish that when I die nobody should know that I have died. I am just a wave amongst thousands of waves in the ocean. When a wave reaches the shore it simply disappears. The same wave does not appear twice. The wave which rose and was recognised as me is now finished.

I am a sannyasin. I do not want my disciples standing around me at the time of my death with tears in their eyes. That is not the teaching that I have given. I do not want doctors beside my bed, stuffing pipes through my nostrils and stomach. I want to live a free life, to experience total freedom, both externally and internally, keeping the knowledge that 'I am a sannyasin' alive in me."

You should try to live like that sannyasin who has taught us many things, but whose teachings we have never looked at very closely. You should take inspiration from that sannyasin who always said, "No matter how many times you fall, always get up smiling and keep walking." Do not just say, "It is beautiful". Feel it in your heart, and when you feel that beauty in you, then I will consider my coming to Australia was a success.

Glossary

Acharya
Spiritual guide or teacher; preceptor.
agni
Fire; representing heat or fire of metabolism.
Aham Brahmasmi
Vedic mantra, 'I am Brahman'.
ahamkara
Ego; awareness of the existence of 'I'; centre of individual mental, emotional, psychic and physical functioning.
ahara
Craving; wanting fulfilment.
ahimsa
Non-violence, non-injury.
ajapa japa
Meditation practice involving spontaneous repetition and awareness of the mantra that is made naturally with the ingoing and outgoing breath.
ajna
Sixth pranic centre or chakra, situated at the top of the spinal cord at the medulla oblongata; seat of intuition, higher knowledge, 'third eye', centre of command, monitoring centre.
ajnani
Unknowledgable person.
akasha
Ether; first of the material elements or conditions of matter.

257

Akhara
>Traditionally, a place for training in arms; the place where the Acharyas of the sannyasa tradition stay.

Alakh Bara
>'Invisible boundary', invisible locality; the place where Paramahamsa sannyasins live in seclusion.

anahata
>Fourth psychic and pranic centre, or chakra, situated in the spine behind the region of the heart and cardiac plexus; emotional centre.

anandamaya kosha
>Sheath or body of bliss; beatitude.

annamaya kosha
>Sheath or body of matter.

antar darshan
>'Vision of the inner self'; higher meditative practice.

antar mouna
>'Inner silence'; meditative technique.

apana
>Sub-prana which is located in the lower abdominal region, responsible for elimination and reproduction.

aparigraha
>Non-covetousness, non-acquisition, non-greed.

artha
>Wealth; need for material security.

asana
>Steady and comfortable meditative pose; physical posture in which one is at ease and in harmony with oneself.

ashram
>'Place of work'; spiritually based community where people live and participate in a yogic lifestyle.

asteya
>Honesty.

atmabhava
>Awareness and experience of the Self.

avadhoota
>Final stage of sannyasa when a sannyasin has attained total transcendence of the body.

Avatar

Incarnated soul of divinity.

bahudak

'Supported by many'; stage of sannyasa.

bandha

Posture in which organs and muscles are contracted and controlled, creating a psychomuscular energy lock which redirects the flow of energy or prana in the body and locks it into a specific area.

Bhagavad Gita

Lord Krishna's teachings to his disciple, Arjuna, delivered at the commencement of the battle of Kurukshetra during the great Mahabharata war.

bhakta

Believer; devotee.

bhakti

Pure, intense, inner devotion or love; channelling of the intellect, emotions and self towards a higher purpose.

bhakti yoga

Yogic path of devotion.

Bharat

'Land engulfed in light'; name of India in vedic times.

bhava

State of being, according to Tantra.

bhavana

Feeling, emotion; ability to perceive subtle vibration.

bhaya

Fear or insecurity.

bhogi

Person caught in sensual gratification.

bhuta

Element, tattwa; one of the five elements.

bija mantra

'Seed' mantra; condensed, potent form of mantra.

bindu

Psychic centre at the back of the head.

bodha

Experiential knowledge.

259

Brahma
Divine spirit; God as Creator.
brahma granthi
Perineal knot; psychic block.
brahmacharya
State of living in constant awareness of Brahman; redirection of sexual energy towards spiritual or meditative experience.
Brahman
'Ever expanding, limitless consciousness'; transcendental or supreme consciousness, according to Vedanta; monistic concept of absolute reality.
Buddha
'Enlightened one'; enlightened sage who was born and lived in India approximately 2,500 years ago, after whom Buddhism originated.
buddhi
Intellect; discrimination; aspect of mind closest to pure consciousness; higher intelligence concerned with real wisdom; from 'bodh', to know.
buddhya
Performed by buddhi.
chakra
'Wheel' or vortex of energy; pranic, psychic centre in the subtle body responsible for specific physiological and psychic functions.
chetana
Consciousness; unmanifest aspect of consciousness and energy.
chidakasha
Space of consciousness experienced in the head region.
chidakasha dharana
Technique of meditation involving awareness of chidakasha.
chitta
Individual consciousness, including subconscious and unconscious layers of mind; functions are memory, thinking, concentration, attention and enquiry.

daan

'Gifting'; an act of charity.

daharakasha

Lower or deep space, encompassing mooladhara, swadhisthana and manipura chakras.

daharakasha dharana

Concentration on the symbols of chakras and tattwas within the lower space.

dakshinachara

Right-hand path of Tantra involving a balanced lifestyle, where effort is made to realise the aspect of wisdom underlying the superficiality of consciousness.

darshana

To glimpse; to see; to have an inner vision or blessing of the divine power.

deva

'Illumined one'; divine being.

dharana

Holding or binding of the mind to one point; concentration.

dharma

Natural role we have to play in life; duty and obligations; that which is established and firm; expression of natural sattwic qualities.

dhoti

Single piece of unstitched cloth wrapped around the lower part of the body. Top dhoti used for covering the upper body also placed over head and shoulders during meditation practice; traditionally geru coloured for sannyasins.

dhyana

Meditation; absorption in the object of meditation.

diksha

Initiation.

divya bhava

Divine state, according to Tantra.

drashta

Seer, observer; awareness.

Gayatri mantra

Shakti mantra of 24 syllables.

granthi

Psychic knot.

guna

Quality or attribute of the mind or nature; three in number: tamas, rajas and sattwa.

guru

Teacher; preceptor; one who can dispel darkness, ignorance and illusion from the mind and enlighten the consciousness of a devotee/disciple.

hamsa

'Swan'; stage of sannyasa.

hamsa dhyana

Technique of pratyahara meditation which develops the awareness of the personality.

hatha yoga

System of yoga consisting of practices for physical and mental purification by means of shatkarma, asana, pranayama, mudra and bandha.

havan

Fire ceremony which cleanses the environment of negative influences.

hridayakasha

Psychic space of the heart centre.

hridayakasha dharana

Meditative technique involving concentration on the heart space.

ida nadi

Major pranic channel which conducts the passive, mental force or manas shakti.

indriya

Sense or sense organ; see also karmendriya and jnanendriya.

ishta devata

Form or vision of divinity; personal deity, personal symbol of the supreme.

Ishwara

Undecaying principle; eternal principle; that which never changes.

Ishwara pranidhana

Dedication to the supreme being in thought, word and action.

jagrit

Conscious mind.

jalandhara bandha

'Throat lock'; the chin rests forward upon the upper sternum, arresting the flow of breath through the throat.

jhola

Shoulder bag.

jignasu sannyasa

Aspirant, spiritual seeker; preliminary stage of sannyasa.

jiva

Individual identity.

jnana

Intuitive knowledge, cognition, wisdom.

jnana kanda

Vedic theory of knowledge.

jnana yoga

Yoga of knowledge and wisdom attained through spontaneous self-analysis and investigation of abstract or speculative ideas.

jnanendriyas

Five organs of sense perception and knowledge: ears, nose, eyes, tongue and skin.

jnani

One who practises jnana yoga.

jyotir lingam

Enlightened shrine of Shiva; there are twelve such shrines in India.

kaal sanyam

Time management.

kaivalya

Self-realisation, samadhi, nirvana.

263

kama

Emotional need or fulfillment.

karma

Action in the manifest and unmanifest dimension; law of cause and effect.

karma kanda

Vedic theory of ritual.

karma sannyasa

Second stage of initiation into sannyasa for householders.

karma sannyasi(n)

One who evolves by developing inner qualities of renunciation, surrender and detachment whilst performing worldly duties.

karma yoga

Yoga of action; action performed with meditative awareness; yoga of dynamic meditation; yogic path of selfless service.

karma yogi

One who performs karma yoga without attachment to the results of the action.

karmendriyas

Five organs of action: hands, feet, tongue, excretory and reproductive organs.

kirtan

Devotional songs or chanting of mantras with musical accompaniment.

kosha

'Sheath' or 'body'; realm of experience and existence.

kriya

Action; motion.

kriya yoga

Practices of kundalini yoga.

kundalini

Vital force or latent energy residing in mooladhara chakra, often referred to as the serpent power.

kunjal

One of the shatkarmas for cleansing the stomach by the voluntary vomiting of warm, salty water.

kutichak
  Hut dweller; stage of sannyasa.
madhya
  Tantric reference to wine.
Mahamritunjaya mantra
  Universal Shiva mantra.
mahat
  Greater, total mind, including manas, buddhi, chitta and ahamkara.
maithuna
  Tantric sexual union.
mala
  'Garland'; string of 108 beads made from tulsi wood, sandalwood, rudraksha seed, coral, crystal or other precious stones, used to count the number of mantras repeated during japa or mantra sadhana.
manas
  Rational aspect of mind which creates thought/counter thought.
mandala
  Diagram within a circumference symbolising the deeper aspects of man's psyche.
manipura
  'City of jewels', third psychic and pranic centre or chakra, located behind the navel in the spinal column, corresponding to the solar plexus in the physical body.
manomaya kosha
  Mental sheath or body.
mansa
  Tantric reference to meat.
mantra
  Subtle sound or combination of sound vibrations used for liberating consciousness from the limitations of mundane awareness.
math
  'Monastery'.
matsya
  'Fish'.

maya

'Illusion'; partial understanding; wrong notions about self-identity.

moksha

Liberation from the cycles of birth, death and rebirth; inner freedom.

moolabandha

Psychic lock; contraction of the perineum in males, or the base of the cervix in females.

mooladhara

First psychic and pranic centre or chakra, situated in the perineal floor in males and at the base of the cervix in females; connected to the coccygeal plexus.

mouna

Silence.

mudra

Psycho-neural gesture or attitude which alters and redirects pranic energy within the mind and body; also means grain.

mukti

Release, liberation, transcendence of the consciousness from the chain of birth and death, and from the illusion of maya.

muni

'Silent one'; an ascetic.

nada

Psychic or internal sound.

nadi shodhana

Purification of the nadis.

nashwara

Decaying principle; that which is subject to change.

neti

One of the shatkarmas for cleansing the nasal passages with warm salty water. Stimulates the olfactory bulb above the frontal sinuses which aids in the awakening of ajna chakra.

nidra

Deep sleep.

nigraha
Control.

nirakara
Formless; unmanifest.

nirvana
Self-realisation, samadhi, kaivalya.

niyama
Five observances of conduct or character; second step of raja yoga.

Om
Universal mantra considered to be the origin of all other mantras; cosmic vibration of the universe; same as Aum.

Om Namah Shivaya
Shiva mantra, 'I salute Shiva'.

paramahamsa
'Supreme swan'; having completed their work, paramahamsa sannyasins live in the Alakh Bara and devote themselves totally to sadhana, thus approaching the final goal of moksha or self-liberation.

Patanjali
Ancient rishi who codified the meditative states into the system of raja yoga; author of the *Yoga Sutras*.

pashu bhava
Instinctive state, according to Tantra.

pati
Master.

pawanmuktasana
Group of asanas which release air, wind or gas from the body.

peetha
Abode; place; seat.

pingala nadi
Major pranic channel which conducts the dynamic force of prana shakti.

poorna sannyasa
Third stage of initiation into sannyasa; complete renunciation.

prajna

Wisdom; aspect of knowing where one becomes the knower, the witness.

Prakriti

Manifest and unmanifest nature; cosmic energy.

pramana

Knowledge based on direct experience.

prana

Vital energy; inherent vital force permeating the whole of creation, existing in both the macrocosmos and the microcosmos; sub-prana situated in the chest region, controlling the lungs and heart.

pranamaya kosha

Energy sheath or body.

pranayama

Yogic technique of breathing, breath control and breath retention which expands the range of vital or pranic energy.

pratyahara

Withdrawal of the mind from the senses.

Purusha

Pure consciousness, totality of consciousness.

purusharthas

Four areas of human endeavour to be fulfilled; artha, kama, dharma and moksha.

raga

Attraction.

raja yoga

Yoga of awakening the psychic awareness and faculties through meditation; eightfold path classified by Sage Patanjali in his *Yoga Sutras*.

rajas

One of the three gunas; the nature, attribute or quality representing dynamism; state of activity and creativity combined with full ego involvement.

rishi

Seer of truth; realised sage; one who contemplates or meditates on the Self.

rudra granthi

Psychic knot or block between ajna and sahasrara chakras.

sadhaka

Spiritual aspirant.

sadhana

Spiritual practice done regularly for attainment of inner experience and self-realisation.

sahasrara

Abode of superconsciousness; 'thousand petalled lotus'; highest chakra or psychic centre which symbolises the threshold between the psychic and spiritual realms, located at the crown of the head.

sakara

With form; manifest.

sakshi

Eternal witness.

samadhi

Culmination of meditation; state of unity with the object of meditation and the universal consciousness.

samana

One of the five sub-pranas, situated between the navel and the diaphragm, which controls the digestive process.

samarpan

Balanced dedication; *sama*, 'equipoised, harmonised', *arpan*, 'to offer'.

Samkhya

One of the six systems or darshana of vedic philosophy; spiritual science dealing with the twenty four attributes of human nature.

samsara

Illusory world; unending cycle of birth and death.

samskara

Unconscious memories; past mental impressions which set up impulses and trains of thought.

sankalpa

Resolve; willpower, determination or conviction.

sannyasa

Renunciation; dedication.

269

sannyasin
Renunciate; one who has detached himself from worldly affairs and strives to attain self-realisation.

santosha
Contentment.

santulan
Balance, harmony, equilibrium.

Saraswati
Goddess of learning.

satsang
Gathering of spiritually minded people, in which the ideals and principles of truth are discussed; association with the wise.

sattwa
One of the three gunas; pure, unadulterated quality; state of luminosity and harmony.

satya
Truth, reality.

sayujya
Identification with the spirit.

seva
Service performed with body, mind and spirit.

Shakti
Feminine principle; inner, creative energy; represents manifest consciousness.

shaktipath
Transmission of power or energy from guru to disciple; form of initiation in kundalini yoga.

Shankaracharya
Enlightened sage who expounded and spread the Advaita philosophy throughout India and founded the Dashnami order of sannyasa; spiritual heads of the modern sannyasa traditions from this lineage.

shankhaprakshalana
Shatkarma that uses saline water to clean the small and large intestines.

shantih
Peace.

shatkarma

Six purification techniques of hatha yoga consisting of neti, dhauti, nauli, basti, trataka, kapalbhati.

shaucha

Purity, cleanliness.

Shiva

'Auspicious one'; Lord of the yogis; male principle; represents cosmic consciousness.

shoonya

Void, vacuum, nothingness.

siddha

Adept or perfected person; one who is able to control the elements and nature.

siddhantachara

System of Tantra where psychic meditation in total isolation from the world and environment is the main theme.

siddhi

Psychic power, perfection, accomplishment.

sloka

Verse.

smriti

Memory; one of the five vrittis.

sukta

Vedic hymn.

sutra

'Thread' of thought which outlines the ancient spiritual texts.

swadhisthana

'One's own abode', seat of one's collective unconscious; second chakra, psychic or pranic centre located at the base of the spinal column, directly behind the pubic bone; associated with the sacral plexus; governs the urogenital system.

swadhyaya

Self-study, self-knowledge, self-awareness.

swami

'Master of the self'.

271

swapna
Dream state.
swara yoga
Science of the breathing cycle.
tamas
One of the three gunas; state of inertia, dullness or ignorance.
tanmatra
Subtle nature, quality or essence of the elements; five senses: smell, taste, sight, touch and sound.
Tantra
Ancient universal science, philosophy and culture which deals with the transcendence of human nature from the present mundane level of evolution and understanding to transcendental knowledge, experience and awareness; the process of expansion of mind and liberation of energy.
tapas
Austerity; process of burning impurities.
tattwa
Essential element; true or real state.
teertha
Sacred place.
tejas
Second dimension of consciousness; subconsciousness; dream state; brilliance, golden light or flame.
trataka
One of the shatkarmas; a dharana technique of gazing steadily at one point to focus the mind.
tripundra
Three horizontal lines drawn on the forehead with sacred ash.
turiya
Fourth dimension of consciousness; superconsciousness; simultaneous awareness of all states of consciousness; state of liberation.
turiyateeta
'Beyond the fetters of nature'; stage of sannyasa.

tyag
Path of renunciation.

udana
One of the five sub-pranas, situated in the extremities of the body: arms, legs and head, which controls the motor functions and sensory organs.

uddiyana bandha
Abdominal retraction lock; drawing of the abdomen and stomach towards the backbone after exhaling.

Upanishads
'To sit close by and listen'; ancient vedic texts, conveyed by sages, rishis or seers containing their experiences and teachings on the ultimate reality.

upasana kanda
Vedic theory of worship.

vacha
Interaction or karma in the manifest world.

vairagya
Non-attachment.

vaishwanara
First stage of expanding consciousness as defined by Vedanta; *vishwa*, 'manifest dimension', *nara*, 'change in manifest dimension'; consciousness which is undergoing constant change.

vamachara
'Left hand path' of Tantra; the aspect of interaction with society, family; leading a normal lifestyle with a spiritual attitude.

Vedanta
'End of perceivable knowledge'; one of the six darshanas or systems of the vedic philosophy, which deals with the transcendental and manifest nature of consciousness.

vedantachara
Aspect of Tantra in which the lifestyle is isolated from the normal social environment and kundalini yoga and specific meditation techniques are practised by the aspirant.

Vedas
Ancient scriptural texts of Sanatan or the eternal dharma; revealed texts expressing the knowledge of the whole universe; the four Vedas are: Rig, Yajur, Sama, Atharva.

veera bhava
Warrior state, according to Tantra.

vichar sanyam
Thought management.

vidya
Knowledge, particularly of spiritual truth or non-mundane reality.

vijnana
Intuitive ability of mind; higher understanding.

vijnanamaya kosha
Higher mental sheath or body.

vikalpa
Unfounded belief; imagination; doubt.

viparyaya
Wrong knowledge; misconception.

vishnu granthi
Psychic knot or block between manipura, anahata and vishuddhi chakras, representing the bondage of emotional attachment.

vishuddhi
Fifth chakra, psychic or pranic centre located in the spine behind the throat, connected with the cervical plexus, tonsils and thyroid gland; centre of purification.

viveka
Discrimination; right knowledge or understanding.

vritti
Circular pattern of consciousness; mental modification described in Patanjali's *Yoga Sutras*.

vyana
One of the five sub-pranas; reserve of pranic energy, pervading the whole body.

yajna
Complete ritual of the fire ceremony performed for external and internal purification.

yama

Five restraints or rules of conduct; first step of raja yoga.

yantra

Geometrical symbol used to develop concentration and meditation.

Yoga

System of thought and practices leading to a state of union between two opposite poles, i.e., individual and universal awareness.

yoga nidra

Technique of psychic sleep which induces deep relaxation.

Yoga Sutras

Ancient authorative text on raja yoga by Patanjali.

yogachara

Yoga which has evolved from the Tantras.

yogi

Adept in yoga.

INTERNATIONAL YOGA FELLOWSHIP MOVEMENT

A charitable and philosophical movement founded by Paramahamsa Satyananda at Rajnandgaon in 1956 to disseminate the yogic tradition throughout the world.

Medium of conveying the teachings of Paramahamsa Satyananda through the affiliate centres around the world.

Paramahamsa Niranjanananda is the first Paramacharya of the International Yoga Fellowship Movement.

Provides guidance, systematised yoga training programme and sets teaching standards for all the affiliated yoga teachers, centres and ashrams.

A Yoga Charter to consolidate and unify the humanitarian efforts of all sannyasin disciples, yoga teachers, spiritual seekers and well-wishers was introduced during the World Yoga Convention in 1993.

Affiliation to this Yoga Charter enables the person to become a messenger of goodwill and peace to the world, through active involvement in various far-reaching yoga related projects.

BIHAR SCHOOL OF YOGA (BSY)

A charitable and educational institution founded by Paramahamsa Satyananda at Munger in 1963 to impart yogic training to all nationalities.

Paramahamsa Niranjanananda is the Chief Patron of BSY.

Focal point for a mass return to the ancient science of yoga.

The original school, Sivanandashram, is the centre for the Munger locality.

Ganga Darshan, the new school, established in 1981, is situated on a historical hill with a panoramic view of the Ganges.

Yoga Health Management, Teacher Training, Sadhana, Kriya Yoga and other specialised courses are held throughout the year. Renowned for its sannyasa training and the initiation of female and foreign sannyasins.

Provides trained sannyasins and teachers for conducting yoga conventions, seminars and lectures tours around the world.

Has a well-staffed research library and scientific research centre.

SIVANANDA MATH

A social and charitable institution founded by Paramahamsa Satyananda at Munger in 1984 in memory of Swami Sivananda Saraswati of Rishikesh.

Head Office now situated at Rikhia in Deoghar district, Bihar.

Paramahamsa Niranjanananda is the Chief Patron.

Aims to facilitate growth of the weaker and underprivileged sections of the society, especially the rural communities.

Activities include: distribution of free scholarships, clothing, farm animals and food; the digging of tube-wells and construction of houses for the needy; assistance to farmers in ploughing and watering their fields.

A small dispensary has been established for the provision of medicine, and veterinary services are also provided.

Tribhuvan Office, a three storey complex to deal with Sivananda Math's activities, will also house the satellite dish system for providing global information to the villagers.

All services are provided free and universally to everyone regardless of caste and creed.

YOGA RESEARCH FOUNDATION

A scientific, research-oriented institution founded by Paramahamsa Satyananda at Munger in 1984.

Paramahamsa Niranjanananda is the Chief Patron of the institute.

Aims to provide an accurate assessment of yoga practices within a scientific framework, and to establish yoga as an essential science for the development of mankind.

Conducted a symposium of over 100 medical professionals from India and abroad with a view to consolidating interest and work in yoga research and health investigation at Munger in 1988 and 1989.

At present conducting international research on the effects of yoga on respiratory disorders involving 10,000 subjects worldwide.

Future plans include literary, scriptural, medical and scientific investigations into other little-known aspects of yoga for physical health, mental wellbeing and spiritual upliftment.

SRI PANCHDASHNAM PARAMAHAMSA ALAKH BARA

Sri Panchdashnam Paramahamsa Alakh Bara was established in 1990 by Paramahamsa Satyananda at Rikhia, Deoghar, Bihar. It is a charitable, educational and non-profit making institution.

Upholds and propagates the highest tradition of sannyasa, namely vairagya (dispassion), tyaga (renunciation) and tapasya (austerity). Propounds the tapovan style of living adopted by the rishis and munis of the vedic era and is intended only for sannyasins, renunciates, ascetics, tapasvis and paramahamsas.

Alakh Bara does not conduct any activities such as yoga teaching or preaching of any religion or religious concepts.

The guidelines set down for the Alakh Bara are based on the classical vedic tradition of sadhana, tapasya and swadhyaya or atma chintan.

Paramahamsa Satyananda, who now resides permanently at the Alakh Bara, performs the Panchagni Vidya and other vedic sadhanas, thus paving the way for future paramahamsas to uphold their tradition.

BIHAR YOGA BHARATI (BYB)

The Bihar Yoga Bharati Institute was founded by Paramahamsa Niranjanananda in 1994 as an educational and charitable institution for advanced studies in yogic sciences.

It is the culmination of the vision of Swami Sivananda Saraswati and Paramahamsa Satyananda.

BYB is the first institute in the world of its kind to impart comprehensive yogic education with provisions to grant higher degrees in yogic studies such as MA, MSc, MPhil, DLit, and PhD to the students.

It offers a complete scientific, yogic education and training according to the need of the present times, through the Faculties of Yoga Philosophy, Yoga Psychology and Applied Yogic Science.

Residential courses of three months to two years are conducted in a Gurukula environment, so that along with yoga education, the spirit of seva (selfless service), samarpan (dedication) and karuna (compassion) for humankind is also imbibed by the students.

SWAMI SIVANANDA SARASWATI

Swami Sivananda was born at Patta-
madai, Tamil Nadu, in 1887. After
serving as a medical doctor in Malaya,
he renounced his practice, went to
Rishikesh and was initiated into
Dashnami Sannyasa in 1924 by Swami
Vishwananda Saraswati. He toured
extensively throughout India, inspir-
ing people to practise yoga and lead
a divine life. He founded the Divine
Life Society at Rishikesh in 1936, the
Sivananda Ayurvedic Pharmacy in
1945, the Yoga Vedanta Forest

Academy in 1948 and the Sivananda Eye Hospital in 1957.
During his lifetime he guided thousands of disciples and
aspirants all over the world and authored over 200 books.

SWAMI SATYANANDA SARASWATI

Swami Satyananda was born at
Almora, Uttar Pradesh, in 1923. In
1943 he met Swami Sivananda in
Rishikesh and adopted the Dashnami
Sannyasa way of life. In 1955 he left
his guru's ashram to live as a wandering mendicant and later founded the
International Yoga Fellowship in 1963
and the Bihar School of Yoga in 1964.
Over the next 20 years he toured inter-
nationally and authored over 80
books. In 1987 he founded Sivananda
Math, a charitable institution for rural
development, and the Yoga Research Foundation. In 1988
he renounced his mission, adopting kshetra sannyasa, and
now lives as a paramahamsa sannyasin.

SWAMI NIRANJANANANDA SARASWATI

Swami Niranjanananda was born at Rajnandgaon, Madhya Pradesh in 1960. At the age of 4 he joined the Bihar School of Yoga and was initiated into Dashnami Sannyasa at the age of 10. From 1971 he travelled overseas and toured many countries for the next 11 years. In 1983 he was recalled to India and appointed President of Bihar School of Yoga. During the following 11 years he guided the development of Ganga Darshan, Sivananda Math and the Yoga Research Foundation. In 1990 he was initiated as a Paramahamsa and in 1993 anointed Preceptor in succession to Swami Satyananda. Bihar Yoga Bharati was founded under his direction in 1994. He has authored over 20 books and guides national and international yoga programs.

Contents

PART ONE

PART TWO

PART THREE

PART FOUR

Questions & Answers – List of Topics